MINDF  S

AND THE ART OF

CHANGE BY CHOICE

RADICAL LEADERSHIP FOR MANAGING CHANGE

PHILIP COX-HYND

Foreword by Paul Lindley – founder and chairman of Ella's Kitchen

"Philip took great care with engagement; the consequent changes set us up for continuing our company's exceptional growth in a better-managed and more focused way."

Mindfulness and the Art of Change by Choice

Second Edition Published in 2017 by

Panoma Press Ltd
48 St Vincent Drive, St Albans, Herts, AL1 5SJ, UK
info@panomapress.com
www.panomapress.com

Book design and layout by Neil Coe.

Printed on acid-free paper from managed forests.

ISBN 978-1-784520-96-0

The right of Philip Cox-Hynd to be identified as the author of this work has been asserted in accordance with sections 77 and 78 of the Copyright, Designs and Patents Act 1988.

A CIP catalogue record for this book is available from the British Library.

This book is available online and in bookstores.

Dedication

The gestation of this book has been over many years and as with the first edition, this second edition is published in a year of great and volatile change. I dedicate it to Chalice and Harley, standard bearers of the new change generation.

Acknowledgements

Many thanks to Mindy, for your structure, process and support, all of which helped give birth to this book.

Huge thanks to Wendy for all your wonderful encouragement, and for being the conduit for all my words, via your fingers, onto the page.

And very many thanks to my dear friend Gray for invaluable help with your detailed challenging of some of the ideas within this book. You have taught me that to have ideas challenged is to make then clearer and stronger.

Contents

Foreword by Paul Lindley, founder and chairman of Ella's Kitchen.

Leadership, as General – and later President – Dwight D Eisenhower once remarked is the art of getting others to do what you want them to do because they want to do it. It requires a great deal of diverse skills, strategies and tactics; some undoubtedly are functional and discipline led, but most are emotional and people led. Our strongest leaders engender inspiration, respect, trust and vision being qualities that differentiate them from managers and those that are leaders in name only. It's all about understanding where you are going and why others may want to join you on that journey. In short, it's about understanding what makes people tick – including ourselves.

I have a view that business isn't really about money and that drive to maximise shareholder value, it's about people and the aligned interests people have to optimise all stakeholders' value. I believe that if you understand what really motivates each key stakeholder in a business, you have a chance of creating an exceptional business. If you don't, you won't. I think truly inspiring leaders know that we all, as human beings, are motivated by achieving both internal and external rewards, and although the external rewards like financial bonus, job title and office location may be important, the really important rewards are those that satisfy our needs to be recognised, to be connected and to be valued. Maslow expressed it in his famous hierarchy of needs pyramid which I've seen interpreted in the business context as the need to earn a living, be loved, learn and leave a legacy, for ourselves and for our companies. Building strategies to overtly incorporate the internal drivers of behaviour and motivation are what our extraordinary leaders do, and really is what the theme of this book reveals as we uncover the layers of behaviours and mind-sets needed to lead in the face of accelerating and unpredictable change.

I think about it as though business doesn't really exist. It's just a collection of people, aligned in mission, perhaps connected by formal contracts, all desiring internal as well as external reward and recognition. It's the potential of tapping into the human-ness of business that excites me, and it's what I have tried to do, constantly and consistently, in building the business I founded, the organic baby food brand Ella's Kitchen to become the UK's number one baby food brand and be sold in over 40 countries around the world. Ella's Kitchen is built on a strong foundation of values, leading to values-led decisions, values-led hiring of employees, values-led product development and a wholly values-led approach to making profit with a greater purpose than simply making money itself.

Our mission – to improve children's lives by developing healthier relationships with food – and our activities to show how this is always actioned – is what motivates the team, our suppliers, customers, consumers and shareholders. We seek a human-eye lens to our challenges, we promote empathy, communication and relationship building with our Ella's lexicon of language, with our mindfulness classes, and our constant drive to develop a culture where people talk and listen to each other as often as possible. In short we try and understand what drives ourselves and our colleagues and how our teamwork can build on the common drivers. I'm often asked how Ella's became a $100M company within 7 years and be recognised as a great British entrepreneurial success story and the answer lies not only in the fantastic products we innovated and sell at the right price to the right people at the right time, but equally importantly it's the trust we have earned from all our stakeholders that our mission is sacrosanct, and this credibility in turn motivates each stakeholder to meet the challenges of change and grow our business impact with energy and true belief.

Philip really understands the key constituents to managing change successfully, and demonstrated this whilst working with us at Ella's over a four year period, guiding us through the growth-led changes we constantly faced.

Philip sets out in this book the methodology he used with us at Ella's and writes in an engaging and logical way, providing a roadmap, to encourage us to understand ourselves, to understand our colleagues, to meet our challenges and to manageably effect change. I hope that like me, as you read through the book, you'll find as much out about yourself as you do in how to manage change and inspire others. And if you do, this journey will help you be a better leader. Keep smiling!

Paul Lindley, September 2016

Introduction

Managing change successfully is a mix of art and science. Some have even described it as alchemy, or a dark art!

Often the key difference between change feeling at worst a threatening experience, at best an exciting one, is the degree of choice involved, and this book is about how to ensure everyone in a company or organisation feels they have a choice in any change.

Perceiving choice in difficult change situations can be challenging. Change can feel stressful because it tends to feel like an overload of things to *do* and little time to just **be**. Indeed, one of the biggest challenges in life is to balance 'doing' with 'being'. Success is predicated on how much activity anyone can do, and change compounds the amount of things to do. Most people realise, doing too much will lead to stress. Doing less may sound like it's the obvious remedy, and yet this isn't always practical as a busy life is not only spent managing the day-to-day as best as possible but also spent thinking about and learning from the past and contemplating if not worrying about the future.

Mindfulness is becoming a widely accepted tool to combat stress and can be especially useful when it comes to approaching change as choosing your experiences as they happen is at the core of what mindfulness is all about.

A mindful approach to change leads to what I call 'change by choice'

Although I introduce mindfulness as a vital new skill for leaders of change, it is only *new* in as much as it has not until relatively recently been introduced to the workplace. Reassuringly, it has been tried and tested! In fact, mindfulness is derived from the essence of the centuries-old Buddhist meditation called Vipassana. Vipassana is a mental discipline aimed at training the mind to stay in the present and respond to the present based on the now, rather than comparing the present to a past that has gone for ever or to a future that hasn't happened yet. This is a discipline that takes years to hone, and something I have been practicing since 2003.

Being 'mindful' is not a definitive destination; it is a state of being that is acquired through practice as one would train to run or to get fit. I wouldn't go to the gym for a month, increase my fitness and then say, "Great, I am fit now, no more gym for me!" A nice thought, but not realistic. The same with the discipline of being more in the now, being more mindful.

The importance of mindfulness

The ability of our minds to shape our reality, either in a positive way or in a negative way, is very strong. At times of change, our mind is quick to see loss and to view the change as negative. As a manager of change it is our role to counter this tendency, and one powerful tool at our disposal is mindfulness training.

When the very early Buddhist teachers developed courses to teach mindfulness in the form of Vipassana, the root of mindfulness, the courses were a minimum of ten consecutive days long, with no talking, no eye contact and no writing nor reading; ten days of meditative practice ten hours a day, focused on honing new habits of the mind to stay more in the now.

These ten-day courses are still taught all over the world.[1] They are free, as is the Buddhist tradition. I attended my first UK ten-day course in 2003 after putting it off for eight years. It sounded far too daunting!

Building what I learned into a useful part of my everyday life turned out to be a 'slow burner' for me in that I did not manage to meditate regularly after that course. So as with the gym analogy, my new-found mental 'fitness' fell away.

I ended up doing two more ten-day courses and only then, in January 2011, I finally found the resolve to meditate most days, if only for a minimum of 20 minutes per day. Years earlier, my sceptical mind had heard the recommendation of meditating for up to two one-hour sessions per day and had responded with the thought, "You must be joking, where will I find two hours a day?!"

> "My sceptical mind kicked in again with, "You won't do even ONE hour a day!"

1   For more information on the learning of Vipassana meditation, the route of mindfulness: www.dipa.dhamma.org

However, I knew I was on to something and so by 2011 I wanted to start practising regularly again to get the benefits of calmness I'd achieved on the courses. My sceptical mind kicked in again with, "You won't do even ONE hour a day!" Then my better nature retorted with, "OK, I'll make a bet with you: I'll do a minimum of 20 minutes a day every day for a year just to see what the effects will be. I can always find at least 20 minutes!" I remember a stunned silence from my sceptical mind. It was dumbstruck!!

So it was that I started to integrate mindfulness into my life on account of investing at least 20 minutes each day, sometimes longer. I missed only six or seven days that year. As a result my rise to frustration slowed down. Also my sleep improved and I needed less of it, thus freeing up time every day. The calmness I'd felt after the ten-day courses, started to be with me on a day-by-day basis.

Since 2011, I have attended a ten-day course most years as a kind of boot camp for the mind, a chance to submerse myself in the practising of mindfulness as a ten-day top-up for the year to come.

In 2011 I also started to teach mindfulness as part of the change work I deliver in client organisations. Being more mindful, more conscious on a moment-to-moment basis has revolutionised my life and my work.

Mindfulness and the basic principles of this book

Although mindfulness is **not** something I intend to explore in great depth in this book as a stand-alone subject, I **will** be referring to the basic principles of mindfulness as they relate to bringing about change, **and in particular to change that is created out of choice rather than coercion.**

At the heart of mindfulness lies the notion that I can either react in a knee-jerk fashion to my emotions, thoughts and experiences if my expectations are not fulfilled in some way, or I can find a **choice** in every experience I have and, through this choice, give myself a chance to **respond** in a thoughtful and considered fashion.

With this notion of a more mindful approach to life, an increased ability to respond, a response-ability[2], I will be exploring the major issues and pitfalls that you may come across when trying to bring about and manage change in your workplace... and, for that matter, in your private life too. In doing so, I will show why choice is such an important ingredient of successful change.

A context for two levels of mindfulness

In this book I will explore the notion of mindfulness on two distinct levels.

Firstly the level described so far in the introduction: a discipline that evokes a greater awareness of how you are 'being' in relation to the now, to what is real moment by moment, and thereby leads to a calm equilibrium.

The second usage is more colloquial: a parent may say to a child, "Be mindful of the traffic when you cross the road." It's being more conscious of what you do, more deliberate, choice-led, aware, more *mindful.* Although most would aspire to this state, I have found that when this aspiration is sought in conjunction with the first more profound form of mindfulness, then transformative experiences are far more likely to take place and on a deeper level within individuals, and even more so when groups of such mindful individuals are working together.

---

2   Later in this book I develop the idea that the ability of a corporate body to respond in a mindful way determines the degree to which its members will be willing to take responsibility for making change happen.

Part One of this book contains a series of chapters under the broad heading of **The Psychology of Mindful Change.** Understanding the way you and others around you respond to change, both positively and negatively, is important if you are to overcome resistance to change through mindful choice. Blocks to change are often strongest, yet unacknowledged, in the very people who say they want to deliver change!

Part Two builds on the psychology of mindfulness and change, and details **The Practicalities of Bringing about Change** in a more mindful or choice-led and sustained manner. It reveals what the instigator of change needs to do and shows how to involve others so that **choice** feels like an important and *genuine* part of the change process.

An appreciation of the **psychology and practicalities** of change by choice should help the results of mindful change be both deep rooted and long lasting.

I've chosen to write the book in a conversational style. It contains a sprinkling of true-life stories, analogies and case histories. Through this approach I've attempted to explain mindful change in a way that, hopefully, you will be able to relate to, be it change in the workplace or in your personal life – the psychology and the practicalities generally hold true for both.

The book has been written from the experiences that colleagues and I have had, working first in personal development then, since the early 1990s, on corporate culture development. Throughout I've tended to rely on common sense, rather than on complex academic theories.

The methods we use are informed by real life experience. If an idea tends to work with companies or individuals, the material stays; if it doesn't seem to work, we move on.

So there is no particular methodology that we slavishly adhere to. However, through the experience we've gained there have emerged three key principles regarding the psychology of mindful change and five golden rules relating to the practicalities.

These two sets of guidelines together form the basis for guiding mindful change by choice, from your first idea of how you might want things to be different, through to the results you manage to achieve.

PART ONE

THE PSYCHOLOGY
OF MINDFUL CHANGE

CHAPTER 1

A context for 'choice'

The phrase *change by choice* points to something that we human beings desire: if change has to happen at all, let it be by choice.

Throughout this book and particularly in Part One, I explain the **psychology of mindful change**: how and why we tend to *embrace* change, or *resist* it. The key to these two options or responses is likely, at some level, to be the degree of **choice** that individuals experience when it comes to change.

In the second part of the book, when we explore the **practicalities of change**, we will see how they are all underpinned by a sense of mindful **choice**, which can be created at several stages of the change process.

Both 'change' and 'choice' are curious in the way we respond to them. Change is something we all know is a constant and yet at times we would love aspects of our lives to stay the same, particularly when the change on offer threatens to be uncomfortable.

Choice also contains an inherent conflict. On the surface, choice may sound simple: I choose to do something, I choose to have something or I choose not to. Yet there are times in life when something changes in a way I don't like and yet to resist the change can make things worse. And besides, changing it is beyond my power. For example, my daughter gets engaged to someone I think is wrong for her. If I resist the change, if I come out against the engagement, I risk straining my relationship with my daughter. I seem to be in a no-win situation. Yet within this seemingly hopeless situation I have various choices, if only I can become mindful of them. I could choose to get to know her fiancé better to discover his, to me, hidden virtues. I could choose to trust my daughter to find out herself the things I notice in her fiancé. I could view their impending marriage as something she will learn – and perhaps exit – from. And so on.

In some instances, therefore, it is desirable and possible to expand my realm of choice, so that in apparent no-choice situations I am able to be mindful of my attachments or cravings for the outcome I say I want, and still *find* a choice that *is* available to me, rather than feeling 'done to' by feeling forced to accept a change I did not want.

Finding a choice where one isn't obvious

Human beings are a mix of reactive animal[3], (a legacy of our distant ancestors), evolved reflective consciousness, and a store of memories. The reactive part is simple: I feel an emotion that I don't like and my instant instinctive reaction will be to blame the person or the thing that caused the emotion. Put simply, if someone kicked me, my split-second reflex reaction might be to want to kick them back!

Shortly after the reactive emotion has died down, my reflective consciousness might kick in. We all have the ability to reflect on our thoughts, emotions and actions and choose whether to give vent to our initial reactive instincts or to follow a more measured response: this is mindfulness in action.

In the heat of the moment, emotions kick in very quickly and it's quite an enlightened person who is able to overcome their initial reactivity. However, I suggest that overcoming initial reactions isn't a realistic goal. The more achievable ideal is to be able to increase self-awareness to the degree that purely reactive behaviour can be spotted, be it a few seconds, a minute, an hour, a day or even a week after the event and, at that point, *respond* by making things right or clearing up the emotional damage that a knee-jerk reaction can cause. This is the discipline of mindfulness and it takes a while to develop. It is a new habit to cultivate: observe what is going on within, and either refrain from acting out of our reactions, or if we do, then once the mindful realisation has occurred that we've been reactive, then *respond*, exercise a mindful choice. Of course we

---

3   Called the lizard brain (by Seth Godin in *Linchpin*) or the chimp (by Professor Steve Peters in *The Chimp Paradox*).

can just react if we want to: we can blame, have an argument; on some, often 'unconscious level', these are also choices.

Blame or response - is there a choice?

It was many years ago that I first came across a real life example of this choice between a knee-jerk reaction and a more considered response.

When I was being trained to become a facilitator for a fairly confrontational personal development seminar, I was under the tutelage of a very powerful and remarkable woman. Being around her was both illuminating and daunting.

One day we were walking through London and she was pressing me for my understanding on some deep philosophical issues. She pushed me for answers and challenged my responses and then she threw in deeper points for me to contemplate and offered ideas that were unsettling.

This conversation was challenging enough, yet it was compounded by the practicalities of walking along busy streets, wending our way to a venue we had to get to while under quite a tight time pressure. She knew the way. I simply followed.

At some point in our deep conversation and without any warning, she crossed the road and I dutifully followed, still trying to maintain the thread of our debate.

Philosophy or fish and chips!

When we got to the other side of the road, without stopping her brisk walk, she bent down, in full conversational flow, and picked up a ball of greasy chip papers. I remember thinking, 'This is weird', but didn't comment as I didn't want to lose the thread of what we were talking about. We continued walking and talking for a few hundred metres until, without comment, she threw the chip papers into a waste bin on the pavement and crossed back to the other side of the road.

At this point my concentration finally broke and I stopped walking. I asked, "I'm sorry, what did you just do?" and pointed at the waste bin across the street.

She smiled a smile that seemed to acknowledge my confusion, yet warned me of a reply that she suspected I probably wouldn't grasp.

She continued, "As we were walking I noticed the chip papers then I noticed the voice inside my head, the tiresome commentator that we all have. It made a snide smug comment about the 'bloody litter lout'. I noticed my reaction and quickly realised I had several choices. I could succumb to living with litter and a feeling of embitterment, or I could write to the council, or I could pick them up. On this day, I decided to pick them up." I was stunned and didn't quite know what to say and before I could respond she simply replied, "You see in every situation we do have a choice beyond a simple reaction. It's recognising what these are and deciding what to choose." This is mindfulness or mindful choice in action.

We continued our debate, but I found it hard to concentrate as I was surprised that anybody would have bothered to exercise choice where most would simply not even have noticed the chip paper, let alone elect to exercise a positive response. However this incident not only highlighted this woman's ability to make choices in her life, from the banal to the big, but it reminded me that there are always choices that, if spotted and exercised, put us in the driving seat, rather than leave us blaming others and feeling disempowered.

The choice in every no-choice situation - taken to another level

Many years after the chip paper incident and having done my best to spot my reactions and exercise choices, even when they weren't obvious, I came across a true story that left me speechless.

I was staying in a hotel where I was about to take a leadership development seminar for a group of senior directors of an electronics company.

As I was getting ready in my hotel bedroom to go down to the workshop room, a news story on the television caught my eye. A woman in New York emerged on the steps of a courthouse, having won a case on appeal.

The newscaster explained that this woman and her lawyers had secured a successful charge of rape against her attacker, through the appeal court. These words seemed strangely at odds with the radiant face of the woman who had been the victim.

Before getting involved in corporate change, I'd spent many years in the field of personal development, leading seminars that were open to all. As a spin-off from this work I had coached individuals on a one-to-one basis, some of whom had been victims of abuse including rape. In most cases the rape victim was suffering from emotional damage or even a kind of haunting – understandable from such a trauma. Yet a brief look at this woman on the television told me that any sense of victimhood appeared to be absent. So I listened intently to the background story.

Where on earth is the mindful choice in this?

Several months before, the woman, who lived in a fairly affluent part of New York City, came home after work, entered her apartment, locked the doors and sat down to relax. Suddenly she was startled by a man who jumped out of a cupboard brandishing a knife, spouting these threats: he was going to rob her, rape her and kill her!

Now few of us, thankfully, will ever be in that position and as a man I will not pretend to understand the full impact of that kind of situation. Yet as I was hearing the background story in my hotel room, I had just been working on notes for the workshop I was about to take and my notes were covering the subject of finding choice in difficult situations. So as I heard this woman's story, I remember thinking, "My goodness, what choices could anyone possibly make in this hopeless and completely no-choice situation?"

It was at this point that the story really started to grip me as it was explained that the woman had the presence of mind to say to her attacker, "You can take anything you want from the apartment, as long as you don't harm me." 'Wow', I thought, 'that was a choice that she found within this no-choice setting, but it wasn't enough.'

The attacker said, "No." 'So then what?', I thought. Remarkably, the woman came back with a further choice that she was prepared to make. She offered this to her attacker, "If you take whatever you want from the

> "You can take anything you want from the apartment, as long as you don't harm me."

apartment and if you must have me, then use a condom and don't hurt me, then so be it."

This time the attacker accepted. He did rob her, he did rape her using the condom she provided, but he didn't harm her physically and he left. Eventually the attacker was caught and in the first trial the judge threw out the prosecution on the grounds of consent. The woman then had the strength of character to fight the judgment and take it to appeal and it was the successful outcome of this action that I was witnessing on the television.

Creating empowerment by recognising a choice

It dawned on me that the smile and radiance of the woman wasn't due to her *wanting* to have been raped – nobody would *want* that – but, by identifying and exercising some mindful choice within what appeared, on the face of it, to be a completely no-choice situation, she had retained her power and ultimately her dignity.

Since watching this story I have strived to find a mindful choice in every no-choice situation. I must admit that I have not always succeeded but when I have it reminds me of the secret to dealing with change that I don't want: find choices that put me back in the driving seat.

The notion of mindful choice at this fundamental level underpins the approach to change explored throughout the rest of this book.

CHAPTER 2

The psychology of change: Three KEY principles

Picture the scene: an hysterical woman running, shouting over her shoulder to a burly man pursuing her, "You'll never catch me, you'll never catch me… if you don't run any faster you'll never catch me!"

This old joke is one I remember as a lad, listening with my family to *Round the Horn* at lunchtime on Sundays.

Like many jokes, it starts off by conveying something you think is one way and then the twist, in this case through language, shifts the context and delivers the humour. Of course as a lad I hadn't worked this out, it just struck me as funny.

The twist in the joke is that the seemingly unwanted advances to the woman apparently running away are actually being sought.

Underlying this story is something we are all aware of: the attentions of the man are unacceptable when unsolicited; yet those same attentions are acceptable when sought by the woman. Attentions invited are preferable to attentions forced upon us.

And so it is with change. When change is *invited*, OR, when change is an unarguable 'given' that can be *accepted,* then on some level it becomes change that is *chosen, change that is more mindful*. Whereas anything that feels as if it is forced or imposed on us tends to generate resistance and, in time, resentment.

"What models do you use?"

Many years ago I was being interviewed by a management journalist about a change project we had just completed. I was a bit daunted by the process initially as he kept referring to theoretical models used by consultancies, models to explain this management process or that organisational style expressed in some kind of complex jargon. In contrast, my work has been amassed through a range of eclectic sources and shaped through the experience of many corporate projects over the years, and so I hadn't particularly found the need for theoretical models.

However, after a pause and a deep breath I found these words coming out of my mouth, "About the only model we use is based on the observation of how human beings seem to best respond to change. It's based on a three-stage process of **awareness, responsibility** then **accountability** – in that order. We have found that this tends to lead to **real and mindful buy-in, true engagement**."

This interview was a seminal moment as I realised later that the journalist had helped tease something out of me that I knew, yet up until that point hadn't realised I knew. As I started to develop the notion, it's something that many have seen to be true for them as it's just drawn from observation of how we human beings tend to respond to change by a mindful choice.

So what are behind these three fairly long and, in some cases, over-used words? And why do they tend to imply a sense of choice in this order, but a feeling of being 'done to' if the order is reversed?

In many ways it is easier to grasp how these three stages work in the human psyche by looking at the three words or stages in reverse order:

I am unlikely to offer myself to be **accountable** or to be measured in some way, for something I have not yet bought in to or that I am prepared to own or to be **responsible** for, and in turn I am unlikely to feel responsible for something I do not understand or have little **awareness** of, or it's relevance to me and my life.

And yet in many situations, change is often 'forced' upon people this way around, or at least that is the impact.

The key to limiting resistance to change lies with the starting point, with **awareness**.

There are two broad types of awareness in this context. There are rules, laws, a 'what's so' in any situation that cannot be easily changed. Whether the what's so is embraced or resisted will be seminal to how this kind of situation plays out. I call this the '**what's so**' scenario of awareness.

Then there are many situations where there may be a whole range of alternatives or changes for the better available, if people just pause, reflect, and consider. I call this the '**what if**' scenario of awareness.

As with many things, these ideas are best explained by way of an analogy.

Driving the point home: a 'what's so' scenario

Imagine you are driving your car at 36mph along a 30mph section of road. You may be conscious that you are speeding or you may not; however if you were to be flagged down by a policeman with a speed gun you might not like it and you might want to argue a little. However most people at that point would have had their AWARENESS raised to something that they are sub-consciously mindful of at least, that in this case, the speed limit is 30mph and doing 36mph for whatever excuse is against that law. This is a '**what's so**' that to most is pointless arguing with.

Once a period of reaction and trying out excuses has passed, most of us will tend to drift into the second phase of the cycle, to take a more mindful approach, a sense of **responsibility** or ownership for the action. Once you are prepared to take ownership, this enables you to be **accountable** so that when the request for the fine to be paid pops through your letterbox, you are prepared to settle the account and pay it.

Notice there is no mention of 'it was my fault' or joyous willingness. That would be unrealistic, unless you are a Zen master! Not many people always stick to the absolute letter of the law and yet, when we don't, only a few of us are prepared to have a sustained argument with the law if we know that, bottom line, we've broken it.

However, as I mentioned earlier, the *physiological power* of this three-stage process

> "The *physiological power* of this three-stage process is only really understood when experienced in a different order."

is only really understood when experienced in a different order. Back to the driving analogy.

You've paid your fine and the following week you are driving fastidiously at 28mph along this 30mph section of road, probably feeling pleased with yourself that you're not going to get caught out *this* time. However, the same policeman with his speed gun flags you down. I don't know about you, but if this happened to me my reaction might be somewhat volatile. Imagine the reaction if after protesting your innocence the policeman replied, "Well it's a very dangerous section of road, so the speed limit was reduced from 30mph to 25mph last weekend; we just haven't got all the signs up yet." My initial reaction would be best left unprinted!

Regardless of the legal notion that ignorance is no defence in the eyes of the law, my instinct would probably be to fight this one and it would all be based on the principle that I was *not* made AWARE of the change. Therefore I'm damned if I'm prepared to be held RESPONSIBLE for something I haven't bought into. So I will probably be prepared to fight, being held ACCOUNTABLE for the consequences of something I don't accept, even though it's the law of the land. Any notion of choice has also been extinguished, replaced by a sense of imposition.

A crash course in a new 'what's so' reality

If the reasons for change are a given like a law, or are very obvious and generally accepted as a 'what's so', then the awareness, responsibility, accountability sequence is easier to manage as long as the vast majority have accepted the nature of the 'given'. When the 2008 financial crash happened, most people became very aware of the global situation via relentless media coverage. So much so that many accepted pay freezes or even pay reductions in a way that would not normally be the case if the underlying 'what's so' had not been bought in to.

Doctors demand a second opinion! A 'what if' scenario

How these three components of change by choice make for a successful change intervention in a 'what if' scenario, is in many ways very similar to the 'what's so' scenario, save for a critical sense of emphasis on the *awareness* of change. Rather than using an analogy this time, it can help to observe what goes wrong in a real example especially when a change intervention is mismanaged. We could not do better than examine one very public intervention that failed.

While writing the second edition of this book, junior doctors were objecting to the prospect of a new contract in England. The government had described the current arrangements as 'out-dated' and 'unfair', pointing out they were introduced in the 1990s. Ministers drew up plans to change the contract in 2012 to one that would provide greater provision for a truly '7-day NHS'. However talks broke down in 2014. As a result, the government said it would *impose* the new contract in England, and the British Medical Association responded by initiating the industrial action process.

I think we can agree that this ranks as a failed intervention, even though it has since been resolved. However the failure equates to the time it will take to restore trust, which is likely to take many years.

Where did it go wrong?

The government had **awareness** of a good case for action, namely that your prospects of a good outcome if you were admitted to a hospital at the weekend were not as great as if you were admitted on a weekday. So the vision was 'equality of outcome whatever your day of admission'.

Their proposed action, their solution, was to adjust rosters so that more junior doctors would be on duty at the weekends.

So all three components were in place, surely?

No. The junior doctors were definitely accepting of the 7-day NHS vision, the *what*. But they simply disagreed with the *how* and therefore baulked at the changes in working practices and income the government's proposed action would foist upon them. In simple terms, there was no joint **awareness** co-created as to how the vision of a more 7-day NHS could be brought about; not enough of the multifarious 'what ifs' or ways to achieve the vision were fully explored with minds sufficiently open to hear each other.

The press fixated on the argument about rosters and pay rates and one would be forgiven for believing that that was the sticking point. Solve that and all would be well. But the point of contention came earlier. The doctors maintained that the government had misunderstood the report they were relying on as proof of worse outcomes for weekend admissions. In their view, and in the view of the report's authors, such a conclusion was unjustified.

So, in other words, the change initiative fell at the first awareness hurdle. There was no consensus on *how* to deliver the vision. The government needed to go back and get a second opinion.

Without joint awareness of the problem, it was not possible for all parties to own or take **responsibility** for the way forward. The government trying to force **accountability** via an imposed contract would never work, not if the government wanted hearts and minds to comply, not just a contractual obligation demanding bodies do what was expected.

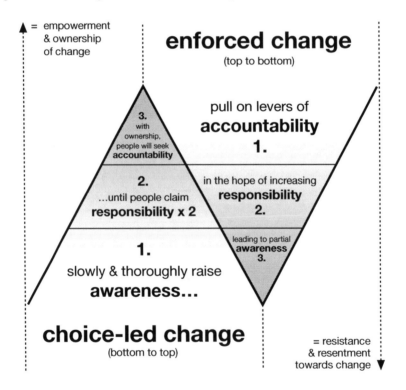

THE 3 KEY PRINCIPLES OF
change by choice

Like the second half of the driving analogy, the government had slipped into the three-stage process in **reverse**; attempting to force **accountability** via an imposed contract, in the hope it would make the junior doctors own or **respond** to new ways of working, and in turn hope they would 'wake up' to the same **awareness** as the government for why they wanted to achieve the outcome that both sides wanted in principle.

The intervention was doomed from the start because the range of how to achieve the joint outcome, the full range of 'what ifs' were not explored together, not co-created. (More on the practicalities of how to do this in Part Two of this book).

Get these three components right, and you are more likely to get real buy-in, profound and lasting engagement.

To summarise, if you want to bring about change that sticks, ensure that you:

1. Establish 'what's so' or 'farm'/co-create a company-wide 'what if' **awareness** to proposed change. This starts a mindful approach.

2. Feedback this awareness in such a way that a critical mass takes **responsibility** for implementing the change out of a sense of choice, and recognises they have the authority to do so.[4]

3. Make sure every step is owned by a specific individual who has accepted **accountability** for it being met.

This sequence creates *real* mindful buy-in, change that some would pay for or literally buy.

The repercussions of ignoring the three components of change by choice are stark, especially when exposed to public view as this was. They are sometimes more difficult to spot in a more secluded business setting, when the symptoms of not having firm foundations for change may be less obvious.

---

4   Whereas authority is most often viewed as if granted from on high, I am talking about the authority that comes from acting, of one's own accord, as a change champion, an ambassador for the desired future state, an authority that comes from being seen to be aligned with everyone's dreams and aspirations.

An important case history

So far in this chapter the three key principles have been explained through analogy and example. From this point to the end of this chapter, the importance of these three principles is explored via one case study. We also start to look at the importance of 'change in the round', not just a change to this or that aspect in isolation.

This case study is important because it covers both 'change in the round' and 'the three principles'. It is also catalytic to the development of the mindful 'change by choice' process, so it goes into more depth than other case studies within the book.

Management consultancies attempt to win new clients based on new thinking and cutting-edge theoretical models. One such model of change that became something of a fad in the 1990s was Business Process Reengineering.

The basic idea was developed initially from a re-worked model of production used in manufacturing. At its core was the notion of taking the varying processes of a company and their departments which, in most companies were vertical, and turning these vertical structures into a more seemless horizontal flow of connecting processes. This meant redesigning processes to ensure that departmental disciplines are more complementary to each other; that all departments work hand in glove and flow horizontally across the business from 'raw material' to finished product and happy customer.

Reengineering the mindset

The firm that invented the concept and coined the name had done very well out of selling and delivering a series of process reengineering projects. It was the American company CSC Index. In fact the number one best seller *Reengineering the Corporation* was written by the management consultant Mike Hammer with the then CSC Index chairman Jim Champy. The book explored the notion that vertical departmental silos should be deconstructed and integrated in a more output-friendly set of horizontal processes. This idea sounded enticing.

There are examples within companies where one department doesn't work very well with another department, where cross-discipline understanding is poor and collaboration is weak. This is where the underlying interdependence within all aspects of a company is somehow ignored, as people lose sight of the big picture and focus instead on their own small patch.

"You've come through to the wrong department; putting you thr...."

As a customer it can be very frustrating to be on the receiving end of this. How did it feel the last time you telephoned a company and explained your story, only to be told you'd got the wrong department and, without explanation, you were put through to somebody else and you had to explain the whole story again? You're left with the impression that the organisation is no more than a succession of cul-de-sacs.

The drive in organisations toward a more customer-focused or output-driven approach was initially fuelled by the process-reengineering model. So what happened to process reengineering? Well in truth there are aspects of it that are superb common sense and are still good to implement, but the reason why 'process reengineering' as a concept lost favour and contributed to the demise of CSC Index is worth exploring. The clue lay in the way CSC Index worked with the client companies to reengineer processes. The short answer was that the three key principles were unwittingly ignored.

CSC Index organised what they called 'process labs': large rooms, sometimes off-site, which were populated by the brightest, the cream of the company's thinkers, hand picked to ensure they were representative of the different levels and disciplines. The consultants coached them over a period of months. They started with a blank sheet of paper. They would talk and think through the ideal processes that together would produce the most efficient route for delivering the company's product, whilst ensuring the most positive outcome for the customer.

These labs would become an exciting hotbed of new thought; the word 'process' was broken down to simply mean a set of connected actions; a bit like a relay baton being handed over in a race, only this time between departments and between disciplines. Not a bad definition. They were encouraged to value each stage of the process, to understand

> "You're left with the impression that the organisation is no more than a succession of cul-de-sacs."

what each department or discipline had to contribute. This blue-sky thinking produced a set of processes that were slick, interlinked and more efficient. For all that, there appeared to be a flaw.

"So what do you do?"

In the mid 1990s I found myself at a friend's dinner party one Friday evening, rather tired from a full-on week, trying to adjust my brain to a social evening and the beginning of the weekend. I was motioned to the seat next to a man I hadn't met before, of similar age, who happened to look very similar to how I felt!

After a bit of an awkward silence between us and, probably spurred on by the ever-increasing level of easy social interaction between the other guests, we turned to each other and I asked, "So what do you do?" He took a big breath as if preparing himself for a confessional answer and replied, "Ah well, I'm a... a... [pause] consultant." I smiled and with a sense of relief replied, "Me too."

Even at that stage of my career that particular 'c' word was one I'd become uncomfortable with. Yet to this day I've not found a replacement word that doesn't sound pretentious to my ear. Calling myself a specialist, an expert or a trouble-shooter always sounded awkward. Anyway, as we talked further it became apparent that he harboured his own discomfort in calling himself a consultant, as he, like me, considered himself a 'doer' and not a theorist.

It transpired that his area of expertise was very different from mine and he was fascinated when I talked about the cultural side of managing change. He worked in IT for CSC Index, this being the first time I'd heard of them. He knew that the firm needed to evolve its own way of thinking and out of that evening there developed a working relationship between my company and the senior consultants within CSC Index London.

At that time initiatives to implement the teachings of *Reengineering the Corporation* had begun to hit up against the bulwarks of entrenched management power. As chairman of the consultancy entrusted to oversee such initiatives, Jim Champy, resolved to write a sequel, *Reengineering Management*. The problem was that 'collegiate leadership', the subject matter of the second book, was proving difficult for the CSC Index consultants to 'live out'. Being a consultant in a firm is often a *competitive* way of life, not necessarily a collegiate one!

A life-changing telephone call

After a couple of months from starting to work with these guys I received a telephone call late one evening from the managing director of CSC Index London. After we'd exchanged pleasantries he said, "We've just won a large contract with Pfizer Pharmaceutical. The brief is simple: we need to help them get their drugs to market more quickly, so less of the patent life of each drug is lost in development and more of the 20-year licence is used selling it."

My initial thought was 'How interesting' and 'What's led you to call me with this news at 7pm?' His reason for the call started to become clearer as he explained this, "The problem is we've spent a few weeks with the company and realised that it's not just about reengineering processes or the accompanying IT systems: there's a major job to be done in changing attitudes and the culture of how they operate."

I agreed to meet him, still not completely clear how we might be able to help and yet the meeting that took place turned out to be momentous – for Pfizer, for my career and for the direction of our thinking towards 'change by choice'.

It's not what you do, but the way that you do it

The truth was that CSC Index weren't clear how to bring about the cultural change that they were starting to realise was necessary. It was the way people thought, their attitude and mindset that were the key to changing what they did. This uncomfortable realisation was compounded for CSC Index by the fact that, around that same time, some of their other process-reengineering projects were starting to go sour. This was mainly due to their clients' staff perceiving the reengineering of processes as an imposition and resenting it. They felt these new ways of doing things were being parachuted in, without there being any *awareness* of a *case* for action let alone any **buy-in** to the action *proposed*. CSC Index was fearful that the Pfizer project might go the same way.

The crux of the meeting that followed was the request for my company to be an associate company to CSC Index on the Pfizer project. Our goal was to bring about such managerial and cultural changes as were necessary in order for the processes and system changes to be effective. There was a further twist: the lead CSC Index consultant who lived in Boston USA, who was going to drive the project, would be based in Groton, Connecticut where the drug development team that Pfizer had given him to work with was based.

Pfizer then changed this initial decision as they wanted to minimise risk. They asked us to 'experiment' on a drug development team that was working on a slightly less important angina drug, a drug that nevertheless had interesting side effects. This team was based at Pfizer's plant in Sandwich, Kent.

Teaching some 'stiff' lessons about change

So having accepted the role of 'culture change expert' within the team of consultants, I found myself attending a three-day conference on the south coast of England to learn about this new angina drug. On my second day there, I found out that the head consultant wasn't prepared to live and work in the UK for the 18-month life of the contract so, by default, I was to be the lead consultant.

I spent those three days furiously writing notes, trying to understand how the pharmaceutical industry worked. The conference decided that they would recommend to the Pfizer Board that they should commit the company to the huge cost of the phase-three trials of this failed angina drug, as its side effects might have a small, but worthwhile market. The code name of the compound was UK96480; the trade name later selected was Sildenafil and, further down the line, the name chosen to market it under was Viagra!

It would probably be somewhat priggish not to mention some of the stories relating to this product! Many of them convey an important change lesson to be learned. Others were just plain funny. For instance, I have been privy to Viagra jokes like 'don't leave them under your pillow as they will give you a stiff neck'. Probably a comment made at the end of the conference was the funniest, the laughter springing from who said it as much as from what was said.

But first some context about how this drug enforced a range of changes on an organisation that may have been planning change, but not this.

The original compound had been trialled in phase-one studies (in the lab and on animals) to test the effectiveness of the indication, namely that it could reduce the effects of angina. The results were poor, but not poor enough to scrap it, so phase-two trials were designed and carried out. These were small-scale trials on people. Again the results for helping with angina were still quite poor but some of the men, who had been unable to get an erection, found themselves 'rising to the occasion' if there was a nurse they fancied in attendance! (The point about the nurse needing to be one that the man found attractive indicated that it was not an aphrodisiac, which increases libido or sexual desire, but only worked in conjunction with what would normally turn these men on.)

The conference I attended had been organised to gather all the Pfizer research and development scientists together from all over the world. They were there to debate the evidence and to see if there was a consensus for recommending phase-three large-scale trials in people to the board. Any phase-three trial is a very expensive and lengthy process.

Unforeseen change of branding and change of direction

It became apparent that this pre-phase-three conference was like no other, for several reasons. Firstly, even if phase three could prove that the compound was safe and effective in helping 'erectile dysfunction', as the condition is called, was there a market for it? And if so is it a market a respectable pharmaceutical company should be involved with? This had important ramifications for Pfizer. Did the company *want* to change its brand by developing a drug in this area? Did the scientists, who had a real passion for helping mankind, want to be associated with this kind of drug? This issue was emerging as a significant change in tone if not in substance, and so it was becoming critical to obtain a strong degree of buy-in to the proposed action

By the time of the conference, the British tabloids had managed to get hold of the story of the phase-two discoveries. This led to several knock-on effects. One was that the general information desk at Pfizer was suddenly bombarded with the world's press telephoning, along with many 'pervy' blokes, saying all kinds of sexually-orientated things down the line! The problem was this information desk was populated by several part-time women, all in their middle years, who were only used to a trickle of calls about the latest diabetes drug or vaccination being developed. Calls about experiments to arouse men were not something these women were used to. This called for another unplanned change. A large crew of unshakable media-savvy telephone answerers had to be drafted in. One of many unforeseen impositions on Pfizer's existing culture.

Is there a market for this?

As for the market need, I remember several letters being read out at the conference from men as far apart as Indonesia, Italy and India. They had all got to hear about the phase-two trials and were pleading to be considered for the phase-three trials, as their marriages would be 'in ruins' if they were not helped to be able to father children. Interestingly, there was no process in place at this stage of development between R&D and the marketing department, so no one in marketing was asked to find out if such a potential market existed. Another change that would need to be addressed.

Although there was anecdotal evidence from men who were desperate enough to father children that they spoke out, there was no reliable data on erectile dysfunction and therefore no idea of the extent of the market for a treatment. This was mainly due to men's embarrassment in admitting to something that up until then was not thought to be curable by medicines outside of the herbal and alternative variety.

The thought that most of those who went on to use Viagra would do so as a lifestyle drug was something completely outside of the Pfizer mindset. That entailed a change in Pfizer's view of itself that wasn't so much resisted as never considered. Pfizer employed serious-minded scientists who worked on mainstream research and who hitherto could not have imagined themselves developing something so frivolous as a lifestyle drug. Who would have predicted it would gross the company $1m per day a few years after its launch!

It was against this rather straight-faced backdrop that, at the end of the third day of the conference, the compound development director, David Cox, stood in front of his 70 or 80 fellow scientists to sum up the conclusions of the three days. He finished his summary by announcing the decision to recommend to the board that they should move to phase three.

Then, in his tweed jacket and open-toed sandals over socks, he announced that a mission statement would be needed to bring everyone together in the common cause that lay ahead of them. As he was saying they needed a mission statement, he was unbuttoning his shirt! This produced some giggles. He had a white T-shirt on underneath and, with flawless timing, he undid the last button, quickly drew back

> "Our mission is to boldly go, where no man has come before!"

both sides of his opened shirt and in a deep, Patrick Stewart-type voice, read out the words on his vest, "Our mission is to boldly go, where no man has come before!"

A failure to read the prescription

The two years that followed, working on the Viagra project, were fascinating, exciting and very demanding. I learned a tremendous amount about how mainstream consultancies worked, of process reengineering and of systems design and implementation. My role in all of this was to ensure that there was a blended approach to change-in-the-round, not just a blinkered obsession with one aspect, such as processes or systems or culture.

One thing became very clear to me fairly early on as the project proper got under way. The reason that process reengineering seemed to have had such shortcomings wasn't to do with the process reengineering concept being flawed, it was to do with the way the new processes were developed and implemented.

Nobody seemed to spot that if you take the cream of an organisation, stick them in a room for three months, get them to design the best integrated processes they can think of, that there may be a problem when you try to introduce these flashy new processes to a workforce they hadn't seen for 90 days. There seemed to be a blind spot among those who had been seconded to the process labs and the consultants fired up with their brave new world. Why wasn't a more all-involving approach taken by CSC Index as championed by their own chairman, Jim Champy, in *Reengineering the Corporation*? You must make a compelling argument for change, he said. That's the wedge for getting people unstuck. Then you must ensure everyone understands what the company needs to become, the vision. That's the magnet.

Ironically the answer to the question was to do with the prescribed three-stage approach NOT being followed. In simple terms, the people who had designed these flash new processes had bought into the case for action and vision in a way that those not present hadn't, i.e. the people back in the plant who found themselves being tasked with doing things differently, without having been *consulted,* without having been part of the thought process.

'Not invented here': a real stumbling block to change

If those not party to the reengineering deliberations had been involved, they may have come up with similar conclusions; but 'not invented here' is a visceral reaction - a syndrome frequently encountered by CSC Index in its client work. Where staff haven't had the need for change raised *enough* in people's **awareness**, the more new processes are pushed, the more people refuse to be **responsible** for making the changes work. In a few extreme cases when people were held **accountable** for implementation failures and threatened with dismissal they, quite understandably, were prepared to fight.

In short, no *real* buy-in. No sense of mindful choice.

The breakthrough with the Viagra project was when my fellow consultants came to agree that winning the hearts and minds of the broader Viagra team we were working with was important, and that enabling the *team members* to understand the case for action and put forward ideas for what needed to change was a critical *first* step. This all had to happen *before* we could start to look at process, systems and structure.

Pfizer senior managers compounded this initial resistance, as they were reluctant to afford the extra time needed to build up this **buy-in** to the case for action and the proposed changes as, to them, the answers were obvious. However, the extra months invested in getting the rest of the Pfizer V-team on board and, importantly, prepared to come forward with their *own* ideas as to what needed to change, proved far more productive in the long run.

This team alignment was especially important as the Viagra project hit up against some **unforeseen change**. Unexpected change is unsettling and can't be planned for, or buy-in to remedial action sought so easily, so the fact that the team understood the case for action, had helped *choose* the proposed action and had signed up to play their part in implementing it, was crucial to moving forward with one mind in the face of unexpected eventualities.

Certainly a lot easier than me and a band of consultants with a few senior managers trying to push change upon them from the top down.

Mindful choice-led change

One of the consequences of this more mindful choice-led change was a desire, even requests from team members, to have their progress measured, to offer themselves to be held **accountable!** The achievement of this degree of commitment created a momentum for change that grew in strength over time and only needed guidance, rather than a constant push.

The success of the team that trail-blazed an integrated approach to doing things inspired others within the Pfizer organisation. The change process we fashioned not only ended up getting Viagra to market months ahead of schedule, but also formed the blueprint for how to get drugs to market more quickly for other drug development teams within Pfizer.

In summary

Next time you want to change something, be it at home, your local pub or at work, be mindful of those affected, and help them to understand and warm to the initial idea, i.e. raise or create awareness AND a degree of ownership or responsibility for the idea *before* you start *implementing* the idea or holding them accountable. Otherwise to them the change idea may feel like a 'done deal'.

*We have covered the importance of generating **awareness** of the action needed, of having a critical mass embrace **responsibility** for carrying out the action and of having specific individuals accept **accountability** for success, in that order, and of doing so throughout an organisation. We have seen how this mindful approach is more likely to equal **profound buy-in** to change and its implementation. It is implementation that is the subject of Part Two: the practicalities of bringing about mindful change.*

But first let's look at the two main types of change: prescriptive and organic.

CHAPTER 3

Two main types of change: prescriptive and organic

"…So what would you say has been the soundtrack to your life?"

I heard this coming out of the radio in my car as I drove one Saturday morning – 'an intriguing question' I thought. I can't remember now what the famous personality's answer was, but I did reflect on what the answer may have been for me.

Beatles' hits were certainly the most memorable soundtracks I grew up to, and part of me never wanted it to end. So when they finally announced their parting, this lad who was then 14 felt sad and despaired that things would never be the same again.

I remember, in the months that followed, going to my youth club and a friend saying, "You've got to hear George Harrison's solo album. It's on three discs and it's brilliant!" In truth I can't recall listening to all the tracks but the image of a long-haired George Harrison sitting in a garden chair with his legs splayed, in black Wellington boots up to his knees, looking straight at the camera, is an enduring image. This image was made even more powerful to me by the title placed above his head *All Things Must Pass*.

Getting on for 40 years later, like many people, I have dealt with my fair share of change: things coming and going in my life. Some I bemoaned the loss of, others I couldn't wait to see the back of! In that respect there's a bitter-sweetness to the phrase 'All things must pass', a duality. It can be both a cause for regret and a cause for rejoicing.

There are so many experiences in life that are exciting, challenging, enjoyable and fun that it would be great if they never changed, never passed. Conversely, there are so many experiences that we would like to move on from, change far quicker than would happen naturally, or simply avoid altogether. It's at these times, such as an illness, redundancy or divorce that it's easy to forget the reality: *all* things *must* pass.

There are two ways change happens: naturally (our distant ancestors would ascribe it to acts of god) or by the hand of man. I'm going to use the terms 'organic' for natural and 'prescriptive' for man-made.

In this chapter, we will explore how to deal with **organic change**, the constant that is always with us. We will also look at how to plan a piece of **prescriptive change,** by which I mean a determined effort to create the change we want rather than rely on chance, the flow of life… or business, to bring us the change we want.

The key to happiness: lose attachment to cravings and aversions

One of the central tenets of the Buddhist philosophy is the notion that there is a 'universal law of impermanence': *all things must pass* put in another way. It is the human 'addiction' to craving certain experiences and avoiding others that is at the root of all unhappiness. Therefore craving and aversion are the addictions to cleanse from the mind. This is at the very heart of acquiring the mindfulness discipline.

Now I don't know about you, but when I first heard the idea of unhappiness resulting from attachments and cravings I didn't much like it, mainly as I realised it felt like it might be true. Most of my own discomfort was to do with the fear of losing the stuff I wanted to keep and concern about holding on to feelings and experiences I didn't want to lose. Many people tussle with this dilemma, which is probably part of the human condition. Again it brings into question the notion of choice and how to be mindful in the way we could choose things we don't like, or how to find a mindful choice in a no-choice situation.

I once read somewhere that the human species is a contradiction compared to most other species on this planet of ours. On the one hand if we look around at the range of things we can eat, climates we can survive in, cultures and ways of living our lives that to each group of people appear to be 'normal', it's easy to conclude that we are the most adaptive species on the planet. And yet when you look at the conflicts, the tussles, the struggles - both individually and between groups and tribes and countries - we are, at the same time, the most contrary and resistant species on Earth!

Here are some examples, which seem a bit ridiculous as I write them down. If I look at the trees, they are not fighting the onset of autumn and the loss of their leaves, nor are they dreading the growing pains of spring as new buds burst. The sheep aren't arguing with the rain because they expected it to be sunny. I don't think there has been any recorded evidence of salmon having a good old moan when they have to swim up that bloody river just to mate, give birth and die! I know plenty of people, me included at times, who'd be complaining to the government if this were true for people.

Nothing in this universe of ours is static. We even know now that a lump of wood or a stone is made up of molecules and atoms, which, in turn, have particles constantly moving within them, with space in between. The universe is expanding, new stars are being born, older stars are dying, the seasons come and go, people live and die, *all things must pass*. Being mindful of this is the key. After years of Vipassana meditation, there are times when I swear I can feel the molecules moving in my body!

Organic, on-going change: danger or excitement?

When we stop to think about how change of any kind can feel, then the emotions of fear, discomfort, and worry can sit alongside feelings such as excitement, fun and satisfaction. Change can feel like an emotional 'double-edged sword'.

One of the things that separate us from most other animals (as far as we know) is our ability to reflect on ourselves; this is the essence of mindfulness. Now some pet lovers would dispute this, they would argue that some animals they know certainly feel things

"We are the most adaptive species on the planet. And yet we are the most contrary and resistant species on Earth!"

and may well have a sense of self. I'm personally happy to leave that question open.

What I do know from observation and from my own experience into mindfulness, meditation and exploration over the years is that we human beings try to make sense of our world through our thoughts and through our emotions. It is this mechanism that facilitates self-**awareness**.

From the previous chapter, we understand that awareness is the first step in a process that leads to ownership/**responsibility** and, in turn, willingness to be held **accountable**. Indeed, *self*-awareness (i.e. mindfulness of how we generate our thoughts, feelings, and opinions, and the ability to reflect on what just *really* happened) is the key to moving beyond reactiveness to change and seeing our *internal* reality as no more than a figment of our own creation. Increased self-awareness increases our ability to respond, our personal **response-ability**. **This is an aspect of mindfulness of particular relevance to how people view change.**

Fight, flight or attraction

Whenever we experience something, we have thoughts, and our body will produce adrenalin to induce one of three responses: fight, flight or attraction. What is interesting is that some things make me feel excited and other things make me feel wary and uncomfortable, often dependent on the context or my expectations. Attachments or cravings again.

A doctor friend once explained to me, the physiological signs of emotions are very similar whether I am feeling pleasant (positive) or unpleasant (negative) emotions. For example, if I was mountain biking and my body was wired up to a machine that could measure bodily signs – the shallowness, deepness and frequency of my breathing, my heart rate, my tension areas and my perspiration – the readings would show the symptoms of exhilaration. If on another occasion the same machine measured the same bodily responses whilst I was in a job interview, the readings are likely to be very similar, and yet in this scenario I may describe the feeling as one of apprehension. Similar body sensations, different interpretation. Practising mindfulness can help one discern the difference between a real physical threat (mountain biking), where the body's high state of preparedness is useful, and a threat to one's emotional equilibrium (job interview) where the body's state of being on-edge can be counter-productive, and even harmful to one's health.

Here's another example. I happen to like skiing and, if you do, I imagine that you may identify with this to a degree and if you've ever done any kind of physically challenging activity you may get a sense of what I'm about to explain. When I book a skiing holiday I get a rush of excitement, often months in advance. I picture the blue skies, the crisp snow, the exhilaration, the fun we'll have, and so on. If I really focus on how I'm likely to feel at the top of the first slope on the first day and I was wired up to the machine my doctor friend talked about, all of those body sensations would be registering quite strongly. Most people, me included, would probably describe those body sensations as a mix of excitement, fear, apprehension and anticipation. Indeed, out of context it can seem quite a crazy thing to do. In fact, if you're not a skier you are probably already having some of those thoughts! On some level, I have 'chosen' to hold skiing and all the pain and exhilaration associated with it as a predominantly positive activity, otherwise I wouldn't do it!

"Beam me up Scotty"

There was a comedy sketch once, involving the American comedian, Bob Newhart, where a group of aliens was debating whether to invade Earth. They were advanced enough to be able to morph into human form and be telepathically linked to one another. The mother ship set off, hovered in space and happened to beam down a fellow alien into the Alps one winter.

The alien landed, looked at the humans around him and the telepathic conversation went something like this:

Mothership: "So what's it like down there?"

Alien: "Well it's colder than the average temperature we calculated for this planet but within the range of tolerance for this species."

MS: "So what are they doing?"

Alien: "The humans are all wearing slightly weird clothes, part protection and part status symbol."

MS: "So how are they getting around?"

Alien: "Well they're in these strange boots that immobilise their ankles and they find walking very difficult."

MS: "Is this to stop them running away?"

Alien: "No it's so they can strap lengths of steel and plastic to their feet and go downwards on snow and ice."

MS: "Wow, our calculations show that this could be dangerous for humans. Have we beamed you into some kind of punishment centre?"

Alien: "No, it's not what they would call a prison, they are paying huge amounts of money for it and form large queues to keep doing this activity all day!"

MS: "So how do they avoid injury?"

Alien: "A certain amount of skill, it appears, but most seem to get bumps and bruises, some break things and occasionally somebody dies."

MS: "And they do this out of choice?"

Alien: "Yes, they can't get enough of it."

MS: "We've made a mistake, they're not worth invading. We'll beam you back now!"

A threat to one's body or to one's emotional wellbeing: which is worse?

In contrast, here's an analogy that most of us have some experience of. I was moving house once and everything seemed to be going smoothly. The mortgage was arranged, the money was in the right bank account, solicitors seemed to be doing the right things, and eventually contracts were exchanged.

As the completion date approached, I got a call from my mortgage company saying there'd been a clerical error and for various reasons the mortgage couldn't be advanced to coincide with the agreed completion date. Irritation and panic were just two of the emotions I remember feeling before I went into action mode. I talked to my solicitor to see if completion dates could be moved. He suggested the better option would be a bridging loan rather than rock the boat with a buyer who had already shown signs of being potentially difficult.

So I arranged to see my bank manager and felt calm as I arrived, as he had always seemed a nice enough person and I'd been with the bank and him for many years. I didn't think a lot of it when I was told, as I arrived, that my bank manager was on holiday and his boss, the area manager, would be seeing me instead.

Being kept waiting: a warning sign

It was only as my wait took me over the 10- then 15-minute mark past my appointment time that I started to feel uncomfortable. 'Why am I being kept waiting, I've got a life to lead as well, what's going on?' and similar such thoughts came into my mind. I then remembered that my bank manager had said on a couple of previous occasions that his boss could be quite awkward and always seemed to have a point to prove. My mind started to whirr with thoughts like 'Will he be awkward with me?' 'What if he says no?' 'What if I can't get a bridging loan?' 'What if the buyer gets difficult and sues me for breach of contract?' 'What if, what if, what if…?'

Then a bank teller called me through and, as I passed through the office door, I noticed the name of the area manager happened to be the same as my art teacher at school: the one who used to clip me round the ear for no reason, the one who was always awkward, who was always going for me. Then I saw the silhouette of the area manager against the sunny window and his profile reminded me of a boss for whom I had no respect, who I thought was weak. All of these thoughts were swirling round on top of a range of emotions.

If at that point my body had been wired up to the same machine as when I was skiing, then it would have registered a change in breathing, heart rate, muscle tension, sweat, and probably on a physical level I was showing almost identical changes in my physiology. The adrenalin was pumping but the emotions weren't that of apprehension and excitement as I faced the first ski run; all the emotions were ones I wouldn't have chosen: a bit of fear, mild concern, slight irritation, a bit anxious. I was **aware** of the feelings, but not able to **respond** positively in those initial reactive moments. Fear overridden by my ability to be mindful in that instant.

As it happened, it turned out not to be that awkward. The bank loan eventually happened, the house sale went through and life carried on. But if somebody had offered me the choice of feeling the body sensations of one or other of these two situations, I'd have gone for the skiing every time; yet I don't know anybody who has broken their leg, dislocated their shoulder or died going to see their bank manager!

Self-observation is the starting point

The problem with observing this stuff is that in the cold light of day as I write it down and you read it, these observations are obvious and kind of a big 'so what?' Yet it's the ability to mindfully observe this stuff that puts us in the driving seat or at the end of somebody else's leash. In Chapter 1, the first of the three key principles to successful change by choice is to raise **awareness**, to 'truly observe'.

Our ability to mindfully distinguish between the prospect of death or injury, on the one hand, and the likelihood of disturbance to our emotional equilibrium, on the other hand, is critical if we are to think straight and serenely ride the rollercoaster of life.

"I don't know anybody who has broken their leg, going to see their bank manager!"

In business, the notion of constant evolution or organic change can feel more challenging to make sense of sometimes. It's one thing to look at the natural world and see that everything ebbs and flows, the seasons come and go, species are expanding or contracting, everything is interdependent and evolving, there's a natural sense of order. It's more difficult to spot organic changes needed within a growing company, and also difficult to know the consequences of changes made sometimes.

Back to the natural world for a moment; there are also many examples particularly over the last 100 years, of man's intervention in the natural world that in some instances have had knock-on consequences that we didn't always foresee.

As our ability to influence nature such as the large-scale dam projects for example, or how man has influenced climate change, have shown us that we can't always foresee the sometimes-negative effects of man-made change in the natural world.

Straightening parts of certain rivers hasn't worked for reasons we couldn't foresee and nature ended up having the upper hand. Man-made climate change is the biggest example to date of unanticipated consequences from actions we have all unwittingly been a part of; actions that until relatively recently many did not realise or will not accept were contributing to such outcomes affecting our ability to live well on this planet.

Organism, organised, organisation: organic

So what's the point of using examples in the natural world and relating them to the human experience or the workplace? Well, we may recognise that 'an organisation' – be it a club, a charity, a company, a government department, or any collection of people coming together to achieve something – all have aspects we can recognise in living organisms.

In fact, it occurred to me a few years back the connection between 'organisation' and 'organism', implying a sense of order. And yet so many man-made organisations, when you go deeper below the surface, are disorganised or even dysfunctional and therefore not as effective or productive as they could be.

Organic changes often trigger or force people and organisations to react, before such changes can be objectively shaped or mindfully planned. **However, organic or constant on-going change is a part of life and training yourself to be flexible, agile, mindful to change and therefore more responsive, rather** than fixed and reactive, is often all that can be done to manage or adapt to change that is organic and not foreseen or planned.

If you look at companies considered successful, particularly those which have maintained a high level of success over a longish period of time, they are organisations that have been able to adapt, change, and grow, often in ways that at the time may have appeared strange, unconventional, and even plain daft. Who'd have thought that a worthy organisation such as Amnesty International, dealing in the relief of pain and suffering, could have been rescued when it was on the brink of falling apart, by a bunch of comics? As those who were running this organisation many years ago found out, the path to **prescriptive or planned change** is not always an obvious one.

No laughing matter?

I once met and got to know a fascinating man called Peter Lough, who was talking about phases of his life and how he had not mapped out a career plan but, like many, had found himself being swept along by the current of life in mainly fascinating ways. Through some of the convictions he held, he found himself many years ago working for an ailing Amnesty International. Its profile was moribund, its funds were depleted and after a short period of time it was obvious to Peter that things had to change – but how?

As he pondered this problem, Peter was helping to open the trickle of envelopes one day when he pulled out a cheque for £10 from a Mr J Cleese. Peter stopped and thought, "It can't be", then thought, "Why not?" Even famous people have consciences and Peter put the cheque in the pile.

As Peter pondered the weak state of his organisation he started to think of Mr J Cleese and whether the two could come together in some beneficial way. Eventually Peter had the courage to contact the cheque writer and it did indeed turn out to be one of the Monty Python founding members.

They talked over a period of time and Peter discovered that there were other friends of John Cleese who also had a conscience and would like to do something to help, so the idea of the first Secret Policeman's Ball started to take shape in Peter Lough's mind and, well, you know the outcome of that!

One aspect of the story that was fascinating to me was that Peter said that initially he had many critics for trying to link such a serious organisation with a gang of satirists and comedians: it was an inappropriate route to change a worthy organisation. And yet it was Peter's opinion that to have stayed the same would have hastened Amnesty's demise and other routes to change had not occurred to him, or others, up until that time.

See change from a different angle

The well-trodden route for company success has predominantly been an entrepreneur or group of business people getting together, trying some ideas and, if they become successful, growing and expanding their business. They may invite investment and eventually invite investors to buy shares in the enterprise. The relinquishment of ultimate control in floating their company is counterbalanced by the powerful cash injection of mass shareholder investment.

When Richard Branson entered the big-company-dominated, often state-owned, world of the airline business, the route of growth through flotation seemed the only real way to progress. For Branson, he wasn't quite prepared for the lack of personal control, and the constant pressure from the City to steer 'his' company in the direction they wanted. This was the trade-off for selling his company. So Branson broke the mould. He went against the received wisdom of other companies around him and sold his Virgin Records in order to buy back Virgin Atlantic. A risky strategy, a piece of **planned change** that was unconventional yet proved to be successful.

If you always do what you've always done...

These two examples of Amnesty and Virgin lead us into another aspect of change that needs to be understood. 'If you always do what you've always done you'll always get what you've always got'. There's a lot of truth in this old phrase and it's fine when 'what you've always got' happens to coincide with what you currently want.

And yet, it can be dangerous too.

There's another spin on a phrase that you may have heard, 'The definition of madness is to constantly keep doing the same actions whilst expecting a different outcome'. The trick, be it in your personal life, your business or your workplace, is be mindful of when it's time to change, listen to your body and intuition slightly ahead of being forced to. An obvious statement you might think, and yet an easy trap to fall into.

For example, in the early 1990s, Microsoft had become so successful and so world dominant that it was easy for the managers and leaders within the organisation to assume that what they had always been doing up until then was what they should continue to do, as it had brought them success thus far. So to continue doing what they'd always done made perfect sense. When we were asked to be involved with part of the organisation at that time, many at the top found it difficult to accept the perception of many customers and partners that the organisation was, at times, arrogant and inflexible.

It's often hard to come to terms with feedback that feels harsh and critical and yet when we're able to have the grace to examine feedback rather than succumb to a knee-jerk reaction of simply rejecting it, there are often grains of valuable truth within the apparently harsh words. Bill Gates had the vision and the foresight to help launch a culture-change programme called MS2, which was designed to cascade through the entire organisation and embrace accusations of arrogance and complacency to ensure that, where it might be true, it could be addressed.

There was a fear among some within Microsoft: they felt that to change anything in a highly successful organisation, wherein most felt attached and proud, was a crazy thing to attempt. 'If it ain't broke, don't fix it' was the attitude of many and yet Gates was astute enough to realise that, while it wasn't broke, he needed to act on the signs of an impending 'stress fracture' before it turned into an actual break. **Planned change** was called for, rather than just relying on the **organic** process of change by evolution.

The writing's on the wall

"he needed to act on the signs of an impending 'stress fracture' before it turned into an actual break."

Business is littered with organisations that didn't see the need for a **prescriptive or planned piece of change** and kept on doing what they'd always done and yet expected a different outcome. The history of the British car industry culminating in the creation of British Leyland is a poignant example.

Consolidation within an increasingly global car market may well have been the best route to go, but the structures and working practices did not change sufficiently to allow the consolidation to be effective. The stories of polarisation between the powerful unions and the disorganised management are legendary and yet there are many other factors that, in hindsight, should have been changed but weren't.

For example, the retention of well-loved brands within the BL empire such as Triumph and Rover seemed a sensible idea and could have worked, but there was a fundamental lack of coordination between these two when it came to developing new models.

For Rover the push for a new model resulted in the Rover 2000. The designer of the Mini, Alexander Issigonis, designed this new car and it was heralded as a brave break from the traditional, tank-like, slightly old-fashioned previous Rover styles. It was hoped the Rover 2000 would carry the Rover brand to a new, more modern customer base.

The mistake was that, at the same time, the designers at Triumph came out with the Triumph 2000, which was aimed at the same target market as the new Rover 2000. This error was compounded by the dealerships of both brands being encouraged, through the structures in place, to competitively 'fight' with each other for the same finite customer base.

In short, there was no overall vision from BL to coordinate the products into a single brand range. This, combined with the out-of-date working practices and the disorganised management structure, led to the organisation lumbering to its crumbling end. What's interesting is the chorus of people, from the workers to the press, from business people to the public, complaining that this could be allowed to happen, "It's the end of British industry. We've always been successful at making cars. It shouldn't have been allowed to happen." The truth is success isn't a right: if you always do what you've always done you *don't* always get what you've always got. Changes around you may require you doing some things differently, if only to avoid the tag of madness derived from doing the same things and expecting different outcomes.

Organic and prescriptive change

There are many examples of prescriptive or planned change in our work and non-work lives. On a personal level, planning a family, moving house, getting married, changing schools or jobs are examples of planned change that are choice-led. Anything that is done out of desire feels a lot more comfortable than when it's forced upon you. The 'opportunity' side of change in these instances is far more prominent than the 'danger/beware' aspect. The three principles are in place: (1) you're **aware** of the need to change, so (2) you own or are **responsible** for the process and (3) you are happy to be **accountable** for the outcome.

It's often seemed curious to me how friends I've known over the years manage to move house, get pregnant and, in respect of one of them, change jobs all at the same time. It's almost as if changing one aspect of your life has a knock-on effect that encourages the changing of additional aspects, regardless of all the associated stresses and strains. Logically it would be a lot more sensible to plan all of these changes separately, but that's rarely what we tend to do.

There's often a sense of throwing caution to the wind when it comes to such life-changing events. Even if a house move or a pregnancy is planned, we can't plan every eventuality within those particular journeys. So in the end it has to be a mixture of plan what you can and be flexible enough to respond to the unexpected along the way.

We all know that planning aspects of change within our personal life to achieve outcomes we want can sometimes be fraught with trauma and difficulty, so it's not surprising that when these changes are thrust upon us – an unplanned pregnancy, a forced house move, a change in job that wasn't our choice – resistance fuelled by fear and feeling out of control, can be an additional obstacle to a set of changing circumstances. Finding the mindful choices within the apparent no-choice situation is often hard.

Having the foresight to plan change

Equally, within business there are many aspects of change that *can* be foreseen and, therefore, to varying degrees, planned for. It could be a merger or acquisition, an expansion of the business due to success or contraction due to changing markets. It could also be due to diversification or simply to re-energise a flagging culture.

Some items on this list are more apparent and therefore can be planned ahead of time more easily than others. The simplest reasons for change are those that are triggered by a clear objective or goal, such as wanting to grow the company. The more specific the size of the growth, and the time by which you want to achieve it, the clearer the routes to fulfilling this goal may become. Classically this would either be growth through acquisition or growth by increasing market share. However even in these more obvious scenarios for change, it's not always easy to realise that these goals may mean having to review what you've done thus far. It's easy to assume that keeping on doing what your company has always done will be what you need to keep doing to take it on to the next stage.

For instance, the processes and systems of a medium-sized company may be working extremely well, but may not necessarily be appropriate for when the transition is attempted from medium- to large-scale business. It's quite scary or daunting to have the courage to tinker with ways of doing things that up until now have produced success. And yet changing things that you predict may need to be altered, ahead of the curve, can often make the difference between being proactive rather than reactive to circumstances.

This brings us on to a fundamental dilemma of the notion of change.

A few years back, a friend of mine gave me an article entitled *The Boiled Frog Syndrome*. It's a quite well-used analogy and you may be familiar with it. When I first heard it, being quite a visual person, the phrase immediately conjured up a rather disturbing image to do with cooking and substituting frogs for the way fresh lobster is traditionally cooked! However, as I read the article, an uncomfortable truth dawned on me through this analogy.

The need to change can creep up on you

Apparently if you were to place a frog in a pan of cold water and slowly bring it to the boil (not that you'd want to!) the frog is likely to stay in the water and eventually die from being boiled alive, as it can not detect the incremental changes in temperature and, therefore, doesn't change its behaviour in advance of its impending doom. However, if you were to coax a frog to jump into a pan of hot water, it would immediately jump out to save its skin.

There are so many times in life, either in our personal world or business world where the initial signs of discomfort that 'the water we are swimming in' is starting to heat up, may be subtle and ignored or rationalised away. Being mindful of these subtleties is key.

And yet if these subtle tell-tale signs that continuing to do what we've always done may not be producing the outcome we've always got, at what stage do we instigate action? In the cold light of day, it's easy to think that making some changes as 'the water becomes tepid' would be far more effective than waiting until the water has reached boiling point.

The year 2008 has gone down in history as a financial crisis year. There will be many people in the future who will look back on 2008 and say, "Why didn't we see it coming; do we never learn from past mistakes?" Again it brings us back to the human paradox: our ability to change as a species is pre-eminent and yet our resistance to the uncomfortable is so strong we would often rather avoid mild discomfort and bury our heads in the sand than change. Mindfulness meditation helps develop the ability to register discomfort and distinguish what needs to be acted upon, and what is to be simply observed and experienced.

The value of hindsight

Of course hindsight is a wonderful thing. Perhaps the factor that divides the victims from the victors in circumstances of change, are those who are able to understand context and timing. This at least will give someone who may be feeling a victim of change a chance to start the process of climbing on board with the changes proposed.

> There will be many people in the future who will look back on 2008 and say, "Why didn't we see it coming; do we never learn from past mistakes?"

So detecting tell-tale signs that something needs to change, *before* it becomes blindingly obvious and often therefore too late, is an important mindful response to hone. You're then left with the question, "What do I change and how?"

The term 'change management' is usually applied to business and yet a quick search on Google can reveal that it's a phrase that means many different things to different people. Some of the definitions are as follows: *the management of IT and systems within an organisation; managing change through process, particularly connecting processes between departments or divisions,* or *change management is the process of defining and implementing strategy.*

Of course any phrase can mean whatever you want it to. The danger is that all of those definitions are not wrong, but by themselves are potentially dangerous as no single phrase covers the whole picture.

Keeping a healthy balance

It has become far more acceptable now for the majority of people to talk about keeping healthy. Years ago, being really fit was the preserve of athletes and sports professionals. As a boy I can remember watching a marathon at the Olympics and it wasn't unusual to see runners stumble into the stadium at the end of the 26 miles in various stages of near collapse. Some athletes *did* collapse and were helped to the finish line or carried off.

Nowadays not only is that sight extremely rare for trained athletes, but to run a marathon has become a commonplace goal, open to most ordinary people. In fact, for many, running has become so normal that people go to extreme lengths to make it even more difficult. For example, the person who ran the London Marathon in a diving suit and took days to complete it; the people in their 80s and beyond who seem to defy the laws of nature and manage to run a distance that, legend has it, *killed* the original runner of the distance to the town of Marathon.

Now anyone attempting to train for any 'fun' run – be it a 5-kilometre, 10-kilometre or marathon distance – may well be bombarded with a plethora of advice. I grew up as an asthmatic and fortunately was given physiotherapy as a 14-year-old and taught how to breathe from my diaphragm to help me breathe my way out of an asthma attack, rather than just rely on sprays and pills. This was extremely empowering and enabled me, in my 20s, to start running, something I couldn't do much at all in my teens. I've gone on to run many marathons, some of them longer distances than the traditional 26 miles, and my preferred terrain has been hilly or mountainous country.

It's obvious to most: to run well takes a lot more than just... running!

When I first started running I was considered something of an oddball, even foolhardy. However, as the years have gone by, running for the ordinary person has become more and more acceptable. The sport has become defined by much more than simply putting on a pair of running shoes and getting out of the door.

For most of the keen legions of fun or charity runners, many aspects of their lives have undergone scrutiny if they want to achieve their goals without harming themselves too much!

It is now understood that being mindful of what you eat, when you eat and how much you eat has an important effect on the performance of a runner. The kind of training you do in addition to the running and what stretches are done before and after exercise are key factors as well. In addition, there's the importance of the right running shoes, keeping your body at the right temperature, building up stamina – in fact a whole range of activities that the runner is encouraged to undertake while training that are in addition to getting out and pounding the roads.

Not too many years ago, most of these additional activities were simply not recognised, or were frowned upon as being somehow 'soft options' or peripheral to the main activity of running. This is also true of most of the sports. Gone are the days when cricketers or footballers simply turned up and played cricket or football. It was once encouraged to drink and eat what you like, have a good time and turn up to play your sport!

As diet, training and, latterly, psychological understanding started to be introduced to many of the professional sports, there were many commentators and fans who seemed to suggest that in some way these people were 'cheating'; that doing things off the field to improve performance was in some way 'simply not cricket'! Yet now the holistic approach to mind, spirit and all aspects of the body is pretty much accepted as the way to maximise performance in any chosen sport.

Change outcomes are achieved by doing many varying things

This principle makes sense if you're looking at making planned or prescribed changes to something in your personal life or within business.

It is rarely the case that an objective will be met or a piece of desired change achieved without understanding that mindfully changing many of the less obvious aspects may well be as critical as applying change to the obvious.

So you may have spotted that something needs to change; that it needs to be planned: the less obvious as well as the apparent may need to have changes applied to them. However, this can all feel very daunting, trying to execute change on *yourself*.

At this point, it's worth noting that if you're in a senior position it can often feel somewhat lonely. This experience is usually compounded when you're the sponsor of a change programme. It is therefore important to find an objective and supportive partner in the change process, to mentor and coach as well as provide objective input to you personally and the process in general. If the change experts you use for the programme can't provide this key supportive role, then it is still important enough to be sought from a separate provider.

Own the changes. They can't be shipped out to someone else while you run the business

A few years ago, the change management company I helped to found was contacted by a large national organisation to see if we'd be interested in tendering for a change management project. Our initial enthusiasm slowly started to wane towards the end of our initial meeting. The meeting was with the managing director and the HR director. The MD had explained well, to my ears, the challenges his company was facing and some of the changes, predominantly to structure and culture, that he and his colleagues felt would probably need to be made in order to get the company to its next stage.

As I said, it was all going well until the MD, having concluded his scene-setting, turned to the HR director and said, "Well there you go, it's up to you to make the changes happen, I haven't got time to be involved and I don't want it to impact on the board and myself as we've got a business to run." This is one of the very few occasions when we declined a piece of business!

This was a classic example of having the **awareness** but trying to shift the **responsibility**, completely, on to someone else. This would have made any **accountability** strained and probably resisted. This was 'change by dictate', not even attempting to create a degree of 'change by choice'!

On another occasion, I recall being invited to a speculative meeting and was enthusiastically questioned by the CEO as to how to bring about the changes he and his colleagues wanted to achieve. It slowly became apparent that the questioning was less to do with understanding how we may be able to help them bring about change, but more to do with checking out how he'd already decided he was going to do the changes himself, stacked up *against* what we, as 'expert outsiders' might propose. When this realisation dawned I summoned the courage to check out my assumption.

His reply somewhat blatantly confirmed that he had no intention of involving outsiders in his change process, as it was pretty obvious to him what needed to be done and he couldn't see what would stop him and his colleagues bringing about the change on the workforce themselves. "I pay them to do what needs to be done, not to express too many opinions," was one of his closing remarks. I didn't maintain contact with him after that meeting.

'Physician, heal thyself'; objectivity is key to seeing and delivering planned change

We didn't really mind being quizzed for what knowledge we had to offer, it was more of a concern that, in my experience, they were probably about to make a mistake. It's not that we necessarily had any more knowledge in how to manage the change they were proposing; it's more that the difficulties of doing it on yourself are easy to overlook. This is partly to do with the 'cobblers children' syndrome or the notion of 'physician, heal thyself'.

"I pay them to do what needs to be done, not to express too many opinions"

In simple terms, it is very difficult to have the kind of objective overview needed to manage change in a holistic and sustainable way if you're trying to do it on your own organisation, or your own personal situation.

Mindfulness can be bolstered by objective external opinions sometimes. Having experience in the field of meditation or even mindfulness doesn't always place you well to be able to make the best use of that knowledge when it comes to applying it to yourself.

Most people realise this in the cold light of day, yet will often resist it when they are in the throes of managing their own change.

For example, there are times when I've toyed with decorating a room at home rather than bring in the decorators. Sometimes, especially earlier in life, DIY seemed the most affordable option and the less professional results seemed an acceptable trade-off. However, as life moves on and expectations rise, the expert result is something I feel I deserve. Yet I've tussled, as you may have done at times, with justifying the extra cost for something I believe I can do myself. The most difficult challenge, I've found, is to start the project, realise that my patience or skill at sanding and preparation isn't what I thought it was, given the high standard of result I want, yet the 'I've started so I'll finish' mentality, plus a dose of wanting to save face, makes the decision to call in the experts a more difficult one!

Now I'm well aware as I write that this particular point can easily come across as a thinly-veiled or even blatant advertisement for the benefits of hiring change management experts! So I'll come clean and acknowledge that there is some truth in this, but it's from the viewpoint that **expertise**, **objectivity** and a particular kind of **relationship** are key to bringing about sustainable change.

Expertise is fairly obvious: having good expert knowledge about what to change and how to change is important whether you are trying to change your health, trying to redesign your home or trying to change aspects of your business.

Objectivity is again fairly clear to most, in that we all know that an objective, unbiased and slightly distanced opinion from friends or experts can often be more astute than that of ourselves, when we're in the midst of the thing we're trying to change. In addition, it's so easy to overlook the possibility that trying to affect change in something we are closely involved in can, in most cases, demand a degree of change in ourselves. I will explore how leaders and instigators of change need to be prepared to do things differently *themselves* later on in the book. But suffice it to say for now that if a CEO or leader wants to bring about change, then the notion of them and their style remaining *exactly* the same is often a contradiction and them being able to spot what **planned change** may be needed in their *own* approach is almost impossible for them to self-identify. In this instance, their own mindfulness may benefit from other external views.

So finally what kind of **relationship** is it best to build with an objective expert? The ways in which I have become involved with various change management projects over the years have often been convoluted and unplanned.

Who keeps an eye on the 'change experts'?

In the minds of many, when they hear consultants talk about 'deliverables' it is often said as meaning a PowerPoint presentation or a report or a set of written recommendations.

Along with estate agents and traffic wardens, consultants, for many, have entered the lexicon as pariahs: people who charge you a fortune to borrow your watch to tell you the time.

So within this context of helping a company deliver a piece of planned change, the kind of relationship that is needed is one that is more to do with hands-on partnering rather than arm's-length consulting.

Expertise and **objectivity** may be accepted as important to bring about sustainable outcomes from a planned piece of change. In addition then, the people you employ to help you do this must be able and prepared to 'roll their sleeves up', guide, mentor, show, do the nitty-gritty of change alongside and with you, rather than mouthing PowerPoint instructions from the wings. This approach will produce the kind of **relationship** that is needed to sustain change results, a more mindful relationship.

Now, partnering and 'hands-on' are fine and dandy phrases but are also potentially unsettling as they denote a greater level of intimacy and trust. This conclusion is spot on and, as with any relationship that requires intimacy and trust, the relationship between a change management expert and an organisation (or a decorator and house owner, for that matter) at best needs to be built up slowly. It needs to have constant input both ways to ensure that a true sense of *partnering* the outcome can be achieved.

In summary, be it organic change or planned change, there are many things to consider, not least of which the fact that change, even mindful choice-led, can get 'messy'. It is not an armchair activity, it's a contact sport.

CHAPTER 4

Change is a contact sport

I popped round to see a friend the other Saturday and was greeted by her 14-year-old son. With a big grin on his face, he announced that his limp was to do with his bruised ankle and that I shouldn't be worried about the swelling on his head either, as the rugby match that morning, responsible for both injuries, was one they'd won, so it was all worth it!

Not being a rugby player myself, I greeted this news with a mixture of empathy for his enthusiasm, mixed with a stomach-churning discomfort to the thought, 'Why would you want to do that?' Then I spent some time reflecting on sports I have enjoyed including rock climbing, rowing and mountain marathons, which, to me, all seem 'normal'. The conclusion I came to was that rugby is as normal to those who take part as my crazy sports may appear to me!

Interestingly, those fascinated with sport, particularly those that have an element of contact and therefore physical danger, seem to split into two broad camps. There are those who play the sport or have played it and also enjoy watching it. They are able to empathise from personal experience with the tactics, the moves, the thrills and spills, the 'almosts', the injuries and the triumphs.

Contact sport enthusiasts with 'no contact'

There's also another category of enthusiast, no less committed, who may never have played or taken part in their favourite sport, but are equally committed to watching and following. It would be a brave person to suggest that this latter category of enthusiast was any less committed to the chosen sport.

I have many fond memories from when I was a boy of watching the wrestling on a Saturday afternoon with my father. Now my dad was of the generation that wouldn't believe that Jackie Pallo or Mick McManus were 'playing' at being good guys or bad guys. No, my dad believed that all he saw was real and that his frustration, for example, at the 'ref' for not intervening firmly enough, was justified.

What's also curious is that my father was a bit overweight and hadn't played any sport for many years and yet would claim to be a serious wrestling fan, even though the closest he came to experiencing the rigours of the sport was an increase to his blood pressure whilst watching it!

The human being's ability to experience something intellectually and emotionally without *actually* experiencing the thing that is generating the intellectual and emotional response is quite extraordinary. When friends tell me of a good film they've watched or book they've read, it's because the experience has generated some kind of emotional response, be it laughter or tears or the excitement of a thriller. Yet on reflection it's obvious that in most cases those stories didn't actually ever happen and, even if they did, the emotional response that we get from reading or watching their recreation can only ever be second-hand or at best empathetic, if the stories are similar to experiences we may have had ourselves.

This may well sound blindingly obvious, yet I suggest it's good for us to reflect and be mindful of this from time to time if we are to understand the difference between intellectually or even emotionally understanding change, as opposed to actually having to experience it in real time.

The only way to change is to do things differently

There are countless examples in all aspects of life where we attempt to do something with the expectation of what that endeavour will be like. How will it feel, how will the outcome affect us and what will our responses be to the results? The part of our survival mechanism that is designed to keep us safe constantly feeds us thoughts, in response to the never-ending stream of emotions generated by the adrenalin a body produces. This sequence is started by a response to what is going on around us, or simply thoughts.

As mentioned in the previous chapter, something happens out there; your senses experience it, your body produces adrenalin and, depending on whether your mind thinks that the situation is one you want or don't want, sends the signal for flight/fight and accompanying 'negative' emotion or the message 'pursue this' with the accompanying emotions of excitement/exhilaration. The degree to which you can develop a mindful approach to this process, will be the difference to being reactive, or responsive: victim or victor.

One example is moving house - something most of us have or will experience at some point in our life. Putting aside moving home for some reason out of our control, most of us *choose* to move house because we want to live in a different place, a bigger or a smaller home – in other words, it's mindful and choice-led.

Now most of us have heard about the emotional roller-coaster that house-moving can be from friends and stories that we've read, even if not experienced directly. Yet it's easy to overlook what these pitfalls might *actually* feel like in advance. To downplay them or to have 'selective amnesia' is preferential to help us focus on the desired objective.

Of course some do the opposite and the negative side of the 'what ifs' becomes all-consuming and sometimes overpowering to the point of some being unable to do anything: decisions frozen by fear. The bottom line is none of us know what doing something differently will feel like until we *actually* do it.

This is true of a sport we play every week, an experience like moving house or changing job that we may have done many times before, getting married, even getting divorced. None of us know what these experiences will actually hold until we go through them.

The danger is to allow the preconceptions of 'an easy ride' or 'this is bound to be fraught with danger' to influence setting off to do *anything*. Being mindful of how it is actually playing out in the moment is the discipline to practice.

You can't make an omelette without breaking some eggs

So far I've used examples to do with everyday life which you've probably experienced to some

> "The bottom line is none of us know what doing something differently will feel like until we *actually* do it."

degree. We know life is a 'contact sport' and that it has its ups and downs and yet, when it comes to bringing about change within a group of people, in business, at work, even in, say, a youth or sports club, the same principles apply. It's easy to forget that change in these circumstances is as much a contact sport as other activities.

The 'contact' in most cases may be just emotional yet, as we've discussed, emotional change in many instances can be more threatening than physical change. I have worked with many CEOs who would much rather go back on to the rugby pitch and endure swollen ankles and bruised heads than face the pitfalls of changing their board or restructuring their company!

In truth, most aspects of change, particularly corporate change, would probably do well to carry a health warning. The old expression, 'You can't make an omelette without breaking some eggs' is again a no-brainer, but when it comes to you being potentially one of the eggs that gets broken, many become more cautious.

One managing director, a couple of months into a change programme, started to be concerned. Although he understood the proposed changes and was certainly still committed to the outcomes, he was becoming less comfortable. He started to have the dawning realisation that the changes were starting to affect the overall feel of the culture of his company. This is something we'd discussed many times. I had pointed out to him the fact that culture should best be thought of as a word to describe *everything*: the 'how people feel' as well as 'what they do'. However, the reality of the changes and how they were manifesting themselves was, understandably, concerning as the reality unfolded.

A crunch point came when it became apparent that two directors weren't 'right'. One director wasn't prepared to change and might well threaten to resign. The other was being identified by many as part of the overall problem the changes were trying to fix, yet he was not prepared to accept this.

So the MD called me to a meeting and voiced his concerns that he might lose these two fellow board members and, surely, he maintained, wasn't the impending loss of these two colleagues an indication that the change process wasn't working?

There is never a definitive answer for every situation but in this case I maintained that the opposite was true. Eventually the MD could see that I may be right, sat with his own discomfort and, eventually, weeks later he accepted the resignation of the one and instigated the removal of the other. In turn, within only a few weeks, the MD realised that although his fears were natural, the decisions had been spot on.

This example shows how although an overall endeavour – in this case a change programme – was initially deemed as important for bringing about an objective, not all outcomes along the way are necessarily comfortable, as emotional 'contact' kicks in.

Absorbing the 'new' into muscle memory

Comedians and satirists are often astute at picking up on language or antics that, when exaggerated, strike a chord and make us laugh.

It wasn't so many years ago that the language of the wine taster came out of closeted obscurity for most, and through the likes of Jancis Robinson and Oz Clarke, descriptions for wine such as, 'I'm getting gum boots and horseradish' or 'mouldy blackberries with an after-tone of toffee' started to hit our screens.

This is an extreme example of trying to explain, in an intellectual way, something that can only ever be experienced directly. This whole book is another example!

The comedy came from the increasingly implausible range of adjectives being called upon to try and explain something that is ultimately unexplainable. The *only* way to 'get' a wine is to drink it! What's interesting, though, is that to the novice palette the ability to discern the subtlety of aroma and flavour that can generate such flowery and bizarre adjectives is a skill that can take a lifetime to acquire. As we all know, there is no shortcut; the only route is to drink and spit thousands of wines over many years.

When I first entered the world of change management many years ago, I did so through the route of personal development: making changes in people's attitude and behaviour as the primary route to organisational change. Experience has shown that this is still a key component, but by no means the only one (more of this later on in this book).

How to become a good cyclist?

In those early years, we took a stand at a management and training fair. On our stand we tried to get across the notion that our key selling point was our approach: to enable managers and leaders to think and *act* differently, rather than just learn theory. The challenge was how to convey this at the exhibition.

Somebody in our company had the idea of putting a blue velvet drape around the inside of the stand and placing just two items within the empty space. One was a big colour manual on the sport of competitive bike riding; this was suspended against the blue velvet backcloth and picked out by a sharp spotlight. The other item was a muddy mountain bike on a stand with a pair of worn-out cycle shorts draped across the crossbar. The only other item was the phrase written on a big board, 'Which one will get you to become a really good cyclist?'

This may sound crude and probably naïve as a marketing ploy, yet I remember it generated a lot of interest and many conversations. At its heart lay the proposition that few would disagree with, i.e. human beings may grasp doing something differently with their intellect, within the pages of a book, yet neither the book you're reading now nor any other will bring about sustained change in *behaviour* without practised repetition of actually *doing* certain things differently and getting to the point of being able to 'own' how it feels, comfort or discomfort. This is being mindful once more. These actions will need to be repeated on multiple occasions over a sustained period of time until the new becomes the norm.

All fingers and thumbs, starts to feel better

A friend showed me this simple exercise: place this book where you can read it without holding it, now clasp your hands together, interweaving your fingers and thumbs in whatever way you naturally find yourself doing it.

Note whether you have your left thumb on top or your right thumb on top. Have you ever pondered what this means? Well apparently this has been researched (amazing what people get paid to research): the consensus seems to be that this is nothing to do with right or left-brain dominance or genetic programming. When we sit and relax we tend to adopt what is called 'resting behaviours' with our hands, arms and legs. We cross our feet, we fold our arms and we clasp our hands. It's unconscious for the most part.

Now before I explain any more, unclasp your hands and now intertwine your fingers and thumbs in the *opposite* way, including your other thumb ending up on top. How does this feel?

I've done this with many people over the years. A very few experience no or little difference. Most experience a degree of discomfort from mild through to, in a couple of cases, feeling dizzy and, in one case, sick after keeping their hands in this position for several minutes. I've also heard people say, "This doesn't feel right, it isn't comfortable, this isn't me!" Why would this be?

Well, the understanding seems to be that when children first learn to explore, or copy from others, the various resting behaviours, they are likely to do so in random ways. As they continue to adopt these behaviours, they tend to cross their legs, fold their arms or, in this case, clasp their hands in the same way they did last time, until clasping their hands (in this case) becomes either, for them, with the left or right thumb on top. So the way you do it is purely done out of years of habit: you doing it one way, many more times than the other way round.

So, no deep psychological meaning, but still powerful in that the more the child repeats a behaviour, the more the neurons in the brain fire a signal along the synapses in between to create a groove, if the response has been repeated many, many times. For instance, if I change my name to David tomorrow, even if I only use David from now on for the next ten or fifteen years, if somebody shouted out in a crowd the name Philip in fifteen years time, it is almost certain that my habituated response would be to turn my head. Decades of neuronal pathway in my brain has insured that 'Philip' will get a response. It is in my muscle memory.

The interesting part is that if you've still got your hands clasped, the discomfort may have started to ease. Certainly if you were to sit with your hands clasped in the other way to your initial instinct for ten minutes, every day, for about 30 days, experts have discovered that you are likely to feel a degree of comfort with the new way of clasping your hands, without losing the comfort for your preferred way.

When the new becomes part of the new-norm

When I first came across this little 'party trick', I found it mildly curious but also thought it a bit of a 'so what?' It was only later that this thought dawned on me: if a human's resistance to such a small and innocuous change can be accompanied with thoughts of 'This isn't right', 'This isn't me', then it isn't so surprising that when we're asked to change much more significant behaviours, resistance can be frenzied and persistent. It's also important to grasp from this simple experiment that there are no short cuts to experiencing change as a new norm. The only way that works is constant practice and experiencing the new until it becomes ingrained in the muscle memory as part of the individual's new and natural ways of doing things. One of the disciplines in mindfulness meditation as taught in Vipassana, is to sit still for the hour or so you may be meditating and notice what pain or discomfort you may sense from time to time feels like. Crazy you may think, and I thought so too when I first started meditating. The curious thing I found was that discomfort or even mild pain simply disappeared in time without me moving. If I simply observed the body sensations and moved on to concentrate on another part of my body, then often when I returned my attention to the part of my body that was in pain, the pain had gone. This process can train the mind to transcend mild discomfort, rather than to always seek the comfortable options, which is not always the best approach to life.

This principle of repetition to achieve absorption into muscle memory is easy to accept in some scenarios and less so in others. For instance, if a friend announced they were going to get fit and then went on to explain that they were going to achieve this because they'd joined a gym, bought the gear and had attended a keep fit class once, we might scratch our heads and think 'That's not going to do it.' (I touched on this analogy in the introduction to the book). As much as you might complain, you know deep down that if you are serious about something like keeping fit, or becoming competent at any sport or hobby, it's only practice and repetition of the new, regardless of the accompanying discomfort, that will enable the results to be achieved.

> "The only way that works is constant practice and experiencing the new until it becomes ingrained in the muscle memory"

On different occasions over the years we've been called into various companies and organisations to help bring about a piece of planned change. In many cases our involvement has not been the first outside-led intervention. A degree of fatigue or cynicism from many within a company at the prospect of 'yet another change initiative' is often a predictable response.

Holistic change: covering all aspects, including those not obvious!

In most cases, this resistance isn't triggered by just another initiative; it's the fact that in most previous cases the initiatives were either too 'on the surface' with insufficient follow-through to make any real difference, or not holistic. In short, there was insufficient follow-through for the **new to become absorbed as the new normal.** There's no way round this, it's part of the way we human beings are made.

My 17-year-old daughter has just spent the last six months learning to drive. Watching and helping her through this experience has served as a powerful reminder of two aspects of this change absorption process.

The first one is seeing so graphically how *long* it takes a new driver to learn unfamiliar actions and responses. My daughter has grown up watching me drive and yet the amount of repetition needed for unfamiliar actions to become second nature, a part of her muscle memory, has been a good reminder of this learning process.

The second aspect of the absorption of change is to do with a desired outcome often being achieved through a series of small and sometimes disconnected actions, from the desired overall result. Again, learning to drive is a great example of this.

About four weeks after my daughter started having lessons, I found her tearful and despondent. When I enquired as to whether this upset was triggered by the driving lesson she had just had, she said, "No it's not the driving that's hard, I think I *know* how to drive. It's that he keeps telling me to find the biting point and to look in my mirror whilst I'm looking forward and switch the indicators on and off, all at the same time! I want to drive, not learn all these separate and confusing bits!"

'Technique frees the artistry'

This outburst reminded me of when I was 20 and in my second year at drama college. At this stage of my life I wanted to be an actor. Many of my friends and I were becoming increasingly frustrated that we were being given very little opportunity to act; it was only in the third year that acting seemed to take precedence. Most of the lessons in those first two years were to do with set building or movement classes, voice projection, dialect, stage management - all kinds of things that to us then seemed peripheral to the job of *acting*. So one day four or five rebellious fellow students led by yours truly decided to march into the principal's office and demand that we be taught more acting!

The principal was a very relaxed and elegant lady in her 70s, with a blue rinse and a polished, resonant voice after years of working in and around the theatre. Her response was measured and calm. She listened to my rambling complaints and when I had run out of things to say, she paused. Then came her reply, "My dear boy, all of these lessons will teach you techniques and disciplines as, unfortunately, I cannot teach you how to act."

Got her! A red-handed admission! With her reply I remembered a surge of indignant self-righteousness, as her words seemed like the admission of guilt we were looking for. However, before I could summon a smug answer, after another pause she continued, "While I cannot teach you how to act, I can teach you technique, for it is technique that frees your innate artistry."

I'm not sure how much of the profound I took away from this reply at the time, which left us speechless I think, but I do remember feeling somehow outgunned. Certainly it was not long afterwards that the real truth in what she had said started to dawn on me and, over the following years, I realised that it's one of the truest pieces of advice I've ever been given.

Becoming **aware** of all the techniques that I needed to practise led me to take greater **personal responsibility** for my level of proficiency. This meant that when I delivered a performance I was more comfortable being **accountable** for the reviews I received. Exercising the mindful *choices* of learning through muscle memory and the holistic approach of many 'small' disciplines combine to deliver a desired

> "While I cannot teach you how to act, I can teach you technique, for it is technique that frees your innate artistry."

outcome. This is true of any new activity or a change for the better. None of this can be achieved successfully by intellectual understanding alone; the **contact sport** of integrating change and learning through *doing* is the way success gets delivered.

Working out *what* needs to be changed, both personally and organisationally, to produce a different outcome is, in most cases, far more subtle than identifying the obvious. Breaking down actions into bite-sized chunks and understanding what needs to be changed that may not have a *direct* influence on the outcome is also key.

As all drivers recognise, driving – that fluid, second-nature experience – is only achieved after mastering the biting point, the width judgments, the multi-tasking; all, over time, become second nature and blend together to become the experience of 'driving a car'. In short, when you're looking at bringing about change, identify the outcome, yes, but be mindful not to think it can simply be brought about by a single linear route. It is a holistic approach of many things, accompanied by repeatedly doing things in the new way that together will deliver the result.

Avoiding overload. Don't do too much too soon or at the same time!

Many people go through periods when taking on lots of differing commitments, both in and outside of work, makes for a busy and rewarding life. There is a great deal of truth in the saying, 'If you want something doing, ask a busy person'.

Being involved in many activities can be very exhilarating as well as exacting for the individual. There comes a point for most people, however, when being involved in so many activities can start to feel too much. What started out as a series of choices may drift into a feeling of being overwhelmed and out of control. It is not always the quantity. For example a friend of mine had a demanding job, was a town councillor and played golf, as well as having a young family. A lot to juggle, but he seemed to manage, if not thrive on it all.

The difficulties came when the councillorship started to be more demanding, there was a re-structure at work that he was involved with implementing and one of his children started teething, resulting in less sleep for all. He would more than likely have been able to cope with one of those changes, but all three at once started to produce a sense of overload. In addition, his sense of increasing overwhelm crept up on him slowly (boiled frog syndrome again), and so his ability to make adjustments to other parts of his life didn't strike him as necessary until he was close to exhaustion.

This story, which you may well relate to, helps to remind us that the ability of individuals and companies of people to engage with change on numerous levels and, in some instances, all at the same time can, for some, be exhilarating and for others overwhelming, to the point of it being counter-productive. Mindfulness can help in being able to notice subtle changes in stress more quickly. Changing what you notice is a key first step, as it is impossible to change something you are not yet aware of.

Change things yes, but not at the expense of the daily business

One of the worst cases of 'change inertia' took place in a large company that we were called in to help rectify. To outside eyes, unattached to timescales and their outcomes, it was fairly obvious that what had been taken on was massive. The objectives for the change programme were laudable and probably very necessary, yet the directors driving the change had under-estimated what was involved regarding the knock-on effects on the day-to-day business and, importantly, the ebb and flow of the business cycle.

It was clear to us that as the new business stream the company had started gathered momentum, the speed of change had to slow down somewhat if the people trying to do both were not to grind to a halt. The simple truth was that there wasn't enough realism built into the original timescale for change.

Nobody had *really* 'stood still' enough to become mindful of what was really going on. So nobody really understood all of the little component bits that needed to be done differently in order for the overall objective to happen. There was nowhere near enough time allowed for new behaviours to be absorbed into muscle memory. The one thing people tend to do under pressure is to revert to what they know and so, if people are learning new ways of doing things, they need to be given more time, not less, if the new behaviours are to become as ingrained as the old ones. Better more time is found and spent integrating the new behaviours at the beginning of change, than time wasted later on when the change starts to fall apart due to poor integration of the new changes.

Some interventions will trigger unexpected consequences, which will take time to deal with. Some groups of people will understand the changes and what is required from them more easily than others. These groups or individuals can sometimes be surprising. There have been several occasions when initially, a senior manager or director has been a great advocate of change and yet, as the process unfolded, the individual became more resistant to what was required as it slowly started to impinge on his or her own personal style.

Keep updating your true position against what you predicted

The unnerving truth is that, in most examples of human endeavour, working out a detailed plan or map by which to carry out a route to change can only, at best, be a guide.

The reality of change is that it's often messy, impossible to predict in all its subtleties and can be made far more dangerous by blindly sticking to a map or plan, no matter how well thought through it might be. It's critical to keep updating the plan as it relates to the emerging reality, week by week, month by month.

It's a bit like sailing a yacht: you have to keep updating your position with where you *actually* are, as opposed to where you said or thought you should be. Like sailing, or countless other examples, change is a contact sport. Be mindful of that and do your best to mindfully *embrace* the emotional knocks and scrapes; 'feel the pain and do it anyway' as the saying goes, and you will do yourself a great service.

CHAPTER 5

Managing people takes time. Mindful change takes time

"Describe in detail how to prepare a slice of buttered toast." 'What a simplistic question, what on earth is the relevance of this to effective communication within business?' I wondered how much the company had paid the trainer to come up with silly exercises like this.

These were just some of the thoughts that flashed through my mind when the toast question was put to me many years ago on a business communication training course for senior managers. However, I managed to suspend my cynical disbelief enough to have a go at the answer, which, if my memory serves me right, I polished off in about two sentences. My impatience with the time it took to be given the next, and hopefully more meaningful exercise, was replaced with a degree of disbelief.

The trainer rejected my description as being insufficient. He went on to point out that the instructions specifically stated that I was to describe how to prepare a slice of buttered toast, *for somebody who had not made toast before.* This response just seemed to fuel my frustration and the interchange descended into an argumentative debate between the trainer and me about the relevance of such a silly exercise! "Who on earth doesn't know how to make toast, is the person I'm describing it for a bit stupid? I wouldn't have anyone working for me who hadn't got enough initiative to fill in the gaps. If somebody can't figure out how to make toast, I wouldn't employ them!" These were just some of my arguments to defend my reasoning.

'Isn't it obvious?'

As the debate continued over quite a long period of time, something rather uncomfortable started to dawn on me, which started to make me feel slightly crass and annoyingly humbled as I realised what the trainer was actually doing. Throughout the interchange he showed extraordinary patience and at each stage of me throwing the request he'd made back in his face, he calmly explained more and more context as to the purpose of the exercise.

He also pointed out that I had a huge range of assumptions about the fictitious person I was responding to. The overall conclusion that started to emerge was that my ability as a manager to get the best out of my people was fundamentally dependent on the time I was prepared to put in. Explaining what I wanted those that I was managing to deliver wasn't always a simple task.

Now I don't recall having to give a detailed explanation to anyone I've managed on how to make toast. However, there have been many examples in my working life where I have asked somebody who reported to me to do something that, to me, was simple and obvious and yet to them appeared to be complex and difficult.

This brings us to another aspect of managing change: you getting clear about what needs to be done differently is one thing. Getting this across to others around you so they can deliver what is *really* needed, without you taking over, is often a different matter! **Managing people takes time. This is even more true when it comes to managing people to bring about change.**

If a job's worth doing...

It is *so* easy, particularly at times of stress, to blame those you are managing, be it people at work or children at home, for being 'thick' or 'awkward'. The next step from this kind of assertion is to stumble into what is the last resort for many when it comes to delegation, "Well, I may as well do it myself!" In circumstances like these, I've

"If a job's worth doing, it's worth doing myself!"

found myself changing the age-old adage of, 'If a job's worth doing, it's worth doing properly' to 'If a job's worth doing, it's worth doing myself!'

What is at the root of this?

At the core of the answer lies the fact that, for many, doing stuff is far more exciting than planning or explaining how to do it. In these increasingly busy times, the art of delegation has fallen out of favour.

When I was a boy, I remember walking home from junior school to have lunch before walking back again, something that would be a mystery to most people nowadays. But it gets more bizarre than that. I also remember that my father, who was a production planning manager at a factory some 15-minutes drive away, also used to come home for lunch. How on earth did he have the time to come home for lunch? Now I'm not a nostalgic person and I'm certainly not interested in extolling the virtues of a time gone by. The reasons lie in recognising that there have been massive changes in the last 20 or 30 years to do with forms of communication such as email, mobile phones and, latterly, mobile communication generally. In addition, there have been increasing demands on what we expect to have in our lives, from holidays to consumer durables. It all has to be paid for; not just with money, but with *time*.

Not enough hours in the day

Overall, more people within a household expect to work and more people who work expect to put in far longer hours than ever before. On top of this, the internet and electronic devices have connected us to each other in ways that a previous generation could only have dreamed of. The one thing in all of this that has remained a constant is the number of hours in a day. It's also arguable that although our ability to multitask, stretch our intellectual and emotional capacity to greater and greater limits, and the fact that some devices can increase our use of previously unusable time (like 'working' whilst we travel), there is ultimately a limit to what we can actually do, especially do well, within any 24-hour period.

I recently finished a rather tortuous change management project with a company in a very competitive sector. It was tortuous because the CEO and most of the team, while in theory committed to the change programme they'd employed us to help bring about, were *so* time-poor that progress was almost unachievable. The situation got so bad that, at one point, during a snatched conversation with the CEO at 7pm on his way to another client dinner, just after he'd telephoned his children 'Goodnight' from the back of a taxi, I asked him a short series of questions: 'How many hours had he spent on average in the last week answering or writing e-mails? How many hours in meetings? How many hours on the telephone?' The total number of hours was alarming, even to him, as he had a total in excess of what he felt was reasonable.

This was before we looked at the hours travelling and before my final killer question, "How many hours have you spent mentoring your people or working on strategy?" The answer revealed that these two key components of his job, which were the lion's share of the KPIs for his role, were woefully neglected. He paused and with tiredness in his voice said, "I simply don't have enough time to fulfil my job description. In reality I barely have enough time to react to what this job throws *at* me."

The situation this CEO found himself in may well sound very familiar and it's very easy to argue that this kind of experience is unchangeable, that it's just a product of the age we are living in.

Faster, better?

However, if we just give in to the perception that life will continue to get ever faster and ever more complex and that we are bound to get ever more 'time-poor', then it doesn't take a rocket scientist to work out that at some point we will just be causing 'wheel spin' in our lives: masses of action with little beneficial output. Many people are already in this state. The answers aren't easy and to an extent they are obvious and yet, in some ways, they require us to swim across the current.

One of the key answers lies in reclaiming the ability to say 'No' to communication overload and unsustainable demands on our time. This of course brings up all kinds of understandable fears, but the alternative is the white-knuckle ride of ever-increasing speed, which must inevitably lead to our coming off the tracks.

Now I don't propose to debate the deeper philosophical question of where Western society is heading and whether the free market capitalistic model of bigger, faster, more profitable, ever expansive growth is ultimately sustainable or not. What is apparent is that many managers and directors have become so reactive and so 'time-poor' that their ability to do their jobs has dramatically decreased their efficiency. Being mindful in such settings is a tall order for many.

In simple terms, we have to say 'No' more, reclaim some time, in order to spend more time with ourselves, true downtime such as short bursts of meditation, and also reclaim the time it *really* takes to delegate to others: the time it *actually* takes to coach others so that we get more done via other people, rather than trying to do more than is achievable by ourselves. Unless this is done, more people will grind to a halt or fall apart. Many have lost sight of what it really means to manage people, an art at the centre of most successful companies.

More time now, greater results later

More time taken to explain, plan, delegate, coach, review progress in the short term equates to more time gained in the long term. The challenge is to act on this approach within the cut and thrust of our daily lives, knowing that there isn't really any sustainable alternative. As I have found, committing myself to at least 20 minutes mindful meditation each or most days has resulted in me being able to make far better use of the time I have left.

The drive from all directions seems to be to squeeze time, expand time, and respond to ever-increasing demands on our time yet, beyond certain efficiencies, time remains a constant. Many individuals in senior positions have reached a point where their effectiveness is diminishing to a point of near 'grid lock' because of the demands on their time. They may be doing a lot more things and responding to more telephone calls, more emails and attending more meetings. However, the core competencies and skills that many of them are being paid large salaries to deliver on are being squandered by being 'chained' to a never-ending treadmill of their time being used by others. The sense of personal responsibility and choice for their time, one of our most fundamental resources, has been 'removed'.

So what's the solution? The answers must lie within the individual and yet an additional clue would probably be gained from looking at certain professions. For instance, eminent surgeons in their chosen field probably earn a lot of money by many people's standards and, given the length of time they take to train and the benefit they bring to people's lives, few would doubt their worth.

Nor would they question the rationale to make the best use of their time: performing operations and talking to their patients.

Lend me your watch and I'll tell you the time...

Imagine that a group of consultants comes into a hospital and decides to increase efficiency by suggesting a flatter structure. Surgeons and doctors must dispense with secretaries, do their own emails and appointment setting, even set up the theatre before operations and help clean it up afterwards.

Most would think this to be a crazy use of the surgeons' time. Saving surgeons from more menial tasks would be nothing to do with surgeons being put on some hierarchical pedestal or being seen as better than others. It just makes common sense to have such highly skilled people freed up by others to concentrate on that which they do best. Obvious stuff, yet compare this scenario to many businesses. The drive by most organisations to deliver shareholder value is usually calculated by a range of often-rigid criteria, such as head count, often regardless of total salary bill. This means that the number of junior staff who could free up managers to manage and directors to direct is stifled. We seem to have lost the connection between the title of a 'manager' or 'director' and their ability or the time it truly takes to really *manage* people and *direct* the business. Being more mindful will help, but there is a limit, short of spreading certain loads more evenly.

There are many core skills to being an effective manager of people. **Context setting, delegation** and **troubleshooting** others' problems (not solving them) are three such skills that many managers have never been taught and therefore don't know how to use in their day-to-day life. Without these three and other related 'people management' tools, it is unsurprising that, when asked, the vast majority of people feel as though they are unprepared to manage people well when promotion comes, as has increasingly been my experience over the last twenty years.

> "It just makes common sense to have such highly skilled people freed up by others to concentrate on that which they do best."

Setting the scene, painting the picture, setting a context

This obviously converts into a very patchy experience when it comes to those who are managed. Some people are naturally gifted in managing people and getting the best out of them. For others, the seemingly obvious (be it how to describe making toast, or other tasks) will need to be broken down, taught and practised.

For instance, context setting: the old adage of 'Tell them what you're about to tell them, tell it them, then tell them what you've just told them' has a lot of relevance in day-to-day management. However, the biggest stumbling block, apart from lack of time, lies in the assumption of the context setter, regarding what the person you are talking to does or *should* know already. More context than is assumed as being necessary is often needed.

One of the acid tests in context setting is to take the result of your communication as being the true indicator of the message you want to get across

For example, if I explained and got agreement that it was really important for me to have a thorough report on my desk by 10am on Wednesday and a half-hearted report appeared on my desk at 9am on Thursday, it would be easy to blame the person I'd asked to do it. However, if I imagined that my life depended, *literally*, on that high quality report being on my desk by 10am on Wednesday *and* it was impossible for *me* to do the report, then I'm left with these questions: 'How else could I have explained what I wanted, what extra information could I have given, what question could I have asked?' In short, how much more of a mindful context could I have set to *guarantee* that the outcome resembled what I had asked for?

It is only by taking this degree of personal and mindful responsibility in context setting that you can hope to avoid blame, while achieving the results you require.

There is little point in having a pre-defined expectation of what you *think* it should take to communicate a message and sticking slavishly to that expectation, regardless of what result it produces. In all instances, a successful communication takes what it takes; often more time and mindful explanation is required in setting the context if you're going to get the result you want, to be essentially the same as the result you get.

Delegation: a fancy word for dumping on others?

To many, delegation has become a euphemism for dumping unwanted stuff on others. Yet explaining what you want somebody else to do, ensuring you explain the benefit to you *and* the likely benefit to them are important keys to delegation being more of a benefit to *both* parties. Again this process follows the key principles: you explain, it raises **awareness**, they 'get' the benefits on both sides, and they take greater **responsibility**. They 'run with it' and they will feel pleased to be **accountable** for the outcome.

It's important to explain exactly what outcome is required and, if it's a big task, at what stages you want a report, or a more simple 'heads up' on progress. In addition, it's key to establish what freedom they may have to deliver the outcome in their own style. It is only at this point when you've both agreed what is required – interim reports or check-ins, timescales for delivery and critically, their *willingness* to do it – must you then do what is for some the most difficult thing: back off and give them space to do what you've asked!

Treat them as volunteers with choice and you'll get choice-led responses, with all of the sense of their personal commitment that this implies.

Troubleshooting is not 'Mission Impossible'

At this stage, the third skill set of troubleshooting comes into play. You've set a **clear context**, you've gained their **agreement to delegation** and set them off on the tasks they've agreed to fulfil.

Yet they may hit a problem.

For some delegators, this is one of the reasons that stops them from delegating in the first place. However, remember managing is partly concerned with bringing others on, not doing everything yourself. So when they come to you feeling stuck or asking for advice, it's so tempting to wade in and take over again. This feels like the shortest route, the time-saving option.

However, do this and not only are you taking on the problem/issue that you've handed to someone else, you're also robbing them of the opportunity to learn for the future. So the art of troubleshooting is to ask a set of simple questions when they come to you with their issue or problem.

1) Ask them to explain in detail what the issue is; this gives them a chance to repeat and clarify. It also allows them to blow off some emotional steam, a positive thing that will clear the way for more rational, mindful discussion.

2) Ask, "Where did you expect to be in the process at *this* point in time?"

This is important as it focuses on where they *are now* in relationship to where they *expected* to be now, as opposed to the final end result at a future point in time. For example, if somebody had taken on a sales goal of £300k over three months and at the end of month one they were panicking because they'd only secured £50k, it would be useful to ask where they expected to be at this point. You might get a panicked answer of, "Well I've got to get £300k of sales in and I've only got £50k so I'm £250k adrift!"

Your job is to help them realise that this is a three-month goal. So a realistic goal for month one may be £70k, month two £100k and month three £130k. So at this point, the end of month one, the difference between £50k and £70k (month one's 'target') is the actual current problem: a £20k shortfall, not one of £250k.

3) The next question is, "What have you done so far to close the gap for month one?" Draw out a range of answers.

4) Then ask, "What else could you do to close the gap for month one?" And you'll get another set of answers.

5) The following question makes use of the answers to the previous two, "If you were to continue what you've been doing" (the answers to 3), "plus what you think you could do" (the answers to 4), "do you believe it's likely these combined actions will produce the result?" The answer is usually 'Yes' and if so your response should be:

6) "Will you get on and do these actions?" and finally:

7) "Do you need any help in doing them?" In most cases they will feel buoyed up and happy to go off and continue until the next planned check-in or report.

If the answers have produced a 'no, I'm still stuck', then you may have to review the goal, their resources or their ability; however, in most cases this is rarely the outcome. A sense of more mindful empowerment for the person you are supporting is usually the end result, plus satisfaction for you.

Time is of the essence

This may all sound pretty simplistic stuff, so what stops us setting adequate contexts, effective delegation and troubleshooting problems when they occur? I'd be surprised if any of these ideas are totally new to you. It boils down to our simplistic misguided belief that things should take less time than they do. The uncomfortable truth is that *managing people effectively* **takes time.**

If the notion of managing people like this takes more of your time, then you may be thinking, "Where do I get the extra time from?" Firstly, it's worth considering the alternative.

If you *don't* spend the time upfront, setting context, delegating tasks, troubleshooting problems along the way, then you're going to spend *more* time doing things yourself, mopping up issues and wondering where your day disappears to.

Mindfulness meditation, even 10 to 20 minutes a day, can help as when I am stressed everything appears to be more difficult, and often more time consuming. When I am calm I have a greater sense of being able to see the wood for the trees, to see more clearly where best to spend the time I have.

Time to change

"If the notion of managing people like this takes more of your time, then you may be thinking 'Where do I get the extra time from?'"

The principle of understanding the time it takes to manage people is even more important when it comes to managing change.

To illustrate, there is a conundrum that seems to afflict most building projects, from the living room extension to a large civil engineering project. The conundrum lies in the fact that with modern project management software and the raft of experience of what it takes to do each small component job within a building project, what prevents accurate estimates being given?

In most cases, the timescale is under-estimated and, for that matter, the budget too, because most people don't like to accept the time things *actually* take.

Another example: everybody's approach to moving house is probably different. Some like to move into their new home, live with boxes unpacked and the basics organised for a while, to get a feel for what they want to do before they set about redecoration. This for some can take months or even years before they are clear or ready. At the other extreme I've known people who've bought their new home but didn't move in; instead they rented for a couple of months so that they could decorate and make their new home exactly as they wanted it, before they finally moved in, with the new curtains hanging and every room decorated just as they'd wished.

These two extremes and all the shades of grey in between are indications of the fact that people have different appetites for change and absorb the new in different timescales. Try and force people to do things at a faster rate or in a manner that is way outside their comfort zone and they'll grind to a halt.

The same is true of people in an organisation: the speed of change needs to be done at a pace that people can absorb. They have to feel some sense of **choice**, by their own **awareness** to changes being raised, so they can take some **responsibility** for owning and being **accountable** for the new.

This is especially true at work as, in nearly every case, people will have their day jobs to do as well as their commitments to the change process. In addition, if the change to process or systems or job role and structure are agreed and yet implemented too fast, then it is likely that bad habits will creep in, confusion will grow and the knee-jerk reaction to reject the unfamiliar will become overwhelming. This principle really needs to be understood, it's not something that can be simply glossed over. (This process of HOW is explored throughout Part Two: the practicalities of change).

Soul time

There are very few occasions when an introduction to someone new, with the question, 'And what do you do?' is met with an answer as exciting as 'Hello, my name's David and I am a professional explorer'. I was once introduced to this guy, David, who proclaimed to be just that. I was somewhat envious and intrigued. I was eager to hear some of his stories.

One story was about the time he'd spent in the wilds of Kenya, 30 years ago in the days before mobile phones or any communication infrastructure existed in this area. At a certain stage in the project he was involved in he had to get an urgent message to those who employed him. The radio wasn't working so this meant a forced march for two days and a night across open bush to deliver the message.

David set off with an interpreter and three Masai guides. Initially the speed was swift and, although fit, he and his interpreter had to 'dig deep' to keep up with their Masai companions. However, progress continued to be good and after a day and halfway through the first night, they were bang on schedule. They snatched small rests here and there but kept on going. At some point in the middle of the night and without warning, the three Masai stopped.

The interpreter stopped too so David complied and had a little rest. They ate a bit of food, took some water and prepared to move again, but the Masai showed no signs of movement. They had not eaten or drunk anything, just adopted a stance he hadn't seen before. They were standing with heads bowed, eyes closed, leaning on their spears and appeared to be in some kind of trance. This went on for quite a long period of time and David became increasingly frustrated and concerned that the good time they'd made up until then was being frittered away. Yes, they were all tired but he felt that if they kept going they would just about get to their destination in the timescale needed.

Go with *their* flow...

Eventually David couldn't contain himself anymore and rather than just complain and moan to his interpreter, demanded the interpreter shake the Masai to get them moving, as talking to them had produced no movement. The interpreter looked alarmed at this suggestion and bounced David's request back at him with a tone of disbelief. "Do you really want me to physically shake three Masai warriors as they lean on their spears?" David did re-consider this and, on second thoughts, resigned himself to his fate and sat on a rock, expecting failure to come with the dawn.

To David's surprise, an hour or so after the Masai went into this apparent trance, they suddenly stirred without warning and the life came back to their bodies; they stretched and breathed the air in deep sighs. David rushed to his interpreter to beg for an explanation. After a moderate pause, the leader of the three took a deep breath and simply sighed his short reply, "We had moved too far, too quickly. We needed to allow time for our souls to catch up with our bodies." This is surely mindfulness in action, deeply infused into the Masai culture from birth: an acute awareness of the intuition of harmony within the individual's body, and the willingness to 'listen' to what the body is wanting to tell us.

At the time, David recalled that their answer didn't make much sense; he was just relieved that they'd come out of this trance or whatever it was and were prepared to start moving again. They continued, and they did get to their destination just inside the timescale needed and David did successfully send his message.

However, David also recalled that while he and his interpreter were exhausted, the Masai seemed strangely untouched and refreshed at the end of their ordeal.

As David told me this story, the final line made me shudder as I recalled the many times in my own life when, on reflection, I probably would have liked to have had the courage or made the time to let *my* 'soul catch up' with my busy mind; a mind full, rather than it being mindful, or a stressed-out body, yet the echo in my head was often along the lines of 'You haven't got time, just keep going'.

This is true for so many in the West, even though perpetual movement, constant activity and stressful thoughts quickly become counter-productive. There is no short cut; either you spend time to 'be', to become more mindful of thoughts and feelings in the now without a knee-jerk reaction, allowing you to more effectively plan, context set, absorb and implement, or, you keep going at a constant high speed and

"We had moved too far, too quickly. We needed to allow time for our souls to catch up with our bodies."

in many cases experience the law of diminishing returns. So much is talked about 'work/life balance', so few do much about it.

The 'Masai' marketing director

During a tour of the offices belonging to a major European car company, and before I discovered mindfulness through Vipassana meditation, the CEO introduced me to several of his directors as we passed each of their offices. We came to the marketing director's door, which was ajar but the room was dark. The CEO assumed the office was empty, walked in, turned on the light and, as he was saying, "This is the office of our marketing director", he was stunned into silence as he saw the said person lying prostrate on his desk.

Before the marketing director could say anything, the somewhat embarrassed CEO had ushered me out and was waffling some excuse about the fact that his colleague probably didn't feel very well.

Next time I was at the offices, I found my way to the marketing director's door to see if he still worked there. He did, and happened to be *sitting,* behind the desk this time! I couldn't resist asking him for an explanation as to what was going on that day, and what happened as a result.

He explained that the role in his contract was Creative Marketing Director and that he liked to get at least half an hour each day to think creatively as he can't *be* creative unless the distractions of the day are put to one side. So most days he liked to put his telephones on to voicemail, drop the blind, close the door and lie on his desk for 30 minutes or so to allow his brain to think. I was amazed at the guy's courage and just as I found myself judging him for being mildly eccentric, I remembered the Masai story and I smiled. He was being mindful, creating time to 'be' in the now, which allowed him to be more productive with the time he had to 'do'.

I don't lie on my desk, but I do carve out some time each day to think and allow myself to catch up, as well as time to meditate. This need is a human norm and increases at times of stress and change. It's a fact of life, there's no point arguing with it, it's a bit like jumping off a cliff and arguing on the way down that gravity isn't fair; it won't care. Likewise, there are certain principles that apply to a human **being** that we ignore at our peril.

Set aside the time it *actually* takes to manage people and manage change, as opposed to making do with the time we have left over for these tasks after all the other busy-ness of our day-to-day lives. This is a powerful principle that simply isn't worth arguing with if we want to stay effective and well!

Manager + managed = more than the sum of the parts?

'Getting things done via other people' is one of the most basic definitions of management. I once looked up the word 'management' to see where it originally came from. It is a derivative of the Latin word *manus,* which means 'hand'. The dictionary went on to describe this as meaning *'giving the experience of extra hands'.* 'A curious notion' I thought. How many times have you experienced people who have managed you as giving you the experience of 'extra hands'? Or managed and manager as together being more than the sum of the individuals?

Now clearly everybody's style of management will be different depending on personality and outlook. It's also worth noting that being a 'manager' isn't the preserve of those with that word in their job title. If you are a parent, carer, youth club worker, student or work with people in any way, regardless of whether you officially have people in your care to manage, I would assert that you are a manager, i.e. you get things done (or not!), via other people.

Very little happens in life without a degree of communication and negotiation with others. We also use the word in different contexts, which gives us a clue to its additional meanings. For instance, you may be going to your car in a multi-storey car park and as you approach your vehicle, you see somebody laden with bags and, as a bag starts to rip, they struggle to keep control of their load. You may instinctively rush towards them uttering words like, "Can you manage?" It means 'Can I help you to do what you were doing?' It rarely means 'Can I take over, make you feel stupid, give you no help at all, ignore you?' or other such mainly negative connotations that the word 'manage' often means in a work context!

Some have a natural personality that is more controlling than others, some a more collegiate involving style and yet the simple truth is, when you're on the receiving end of being 'managed', most like to feel a balance

> "Getting things done via other people is one of the most basic definitions of management."

between freedom to think and deliver in their own way and a degree of guidance and clearly understood boundaries and expectations.

There have been many words written and spoken over the years about differing styles of management: democratic, autocratic, meritocratic, hands-on, delegatory, etc. The one style that has probably been much over-used and, in many ways much misunderstood, is that of empowerment.

'You *are* empowered, just clear with me *all* that you're doing before you do anything'!

I've struggled with dyslexia for much of my life. In my early years this meant that reading was a bit of a chore and not something I did for pleasure. The positive consequence of this is that when I came to enter the world of change management, there were many words that sounded like jargon to my ears, which were used repeatedly in the work place, that often left me wondering 'Hang on a moment, what does this word actually mean?' I was talking about this with a friend one day and he said, "You ought to get an etymological dictionary." I think my first response was, "How do you spell that?!"

I did get one and, to my amazement, found that looking up words, as a 30-something year old, was actually exciting. Discovering what words actually meant and where they actually came from, as an adult, was far more illuminating to me than struggling to understand the meaning of words while I was at school. So to learn that the word 'power' comes from the French *pouvoir* which simply means 'the ability to do or act' seemed revelatory to me.

Consequently, to 'empower' is to '*enable* people, to do or act'. The key here is 'enable' not instruct, dictate or force. I've heard so many senior managers over the years talk about empowerment of their staff as if they were wielding some kind of weapon. I have the same kind of caution to empowerment as I do to 'team building' or 'happiness'. *Feeling* part of a team or *feeling* happy are usually experiences that come about as a *result* of several things, over a period of time, that aren't overtly designed to create teams or happiness. In fact, the happiness example sounds so obviously crass. Imagine suggesting to a group of people, 'Let's get together in order to get happy' (no substances allowed!).

Now I'm not suggesting being happy or experiencing happiness from time to time isn't a laudable aspiration, or even a natural expectation on occasions, but it's rarely something you can achieve 'head on'. I don't say to my friends, "Let's get together on a Friday night to get happy". I might suggest we meet for a few drinks and go out for a meal. By saying this I'm equally not suggesting that they are overtly thirsty or necessarily hungry and can only have those two functions fulfilled in the company of others. They are social euphemisms for sets of actions people need to do and yet, when done collectively, enable us to talk, interact, etc. which might collectively, on reflection, be described as having a good time or enjoying yourself.

Likewise, if a manager were to come to you and say, "I'm going to empower you," particularly if you are in a senior position, it may sound patronising or to some I've heard it described as a veiled threat, as if they are going to be 'done to' in some way outside of their control.

Set the conditions for empowerment then back off

The best description I've come across regarding empowerment is to have the experience broken down into its two main component factors: authority and accountability. To *enable* somebody to take power, to feel confident out of choice, to 'do or act', they will need to have the *authority* to do so. (There's another word I explored, 'authority': to be the author of, to feel as though the individual wrote his own script.)

Ultimately people either take authority or not. They may be invited but ultimately it is an internal **choice**. If somebody sees an injustice in the world, their **awareness** of that injustice has been raised; it's often the ordinary person who decides to take **responsibility** and *do* something about it and that often may inspire others. Ultimately *they* decided to **take authority**; it isn't something that others could give them.

Secondly, empowerment requires a degree of **accountability**. A *willingness* for the individual who is prepared to take the authority, in turn to be measured, to be 'held to account' for the outcome or consequences of the actions they have 'authored'.

Set up the environment

Now a good manager or director can do a lot to create an environment of trust for his people whereby staff feel increasingly confident to *take* authority for certain actions, also to understand the parameters of the authority they can take and where those parameters stop. They must also understand that with authority comes accountability, they go hand in hand. So empowerment is not something that can be given but is something that a good manager of people can help set the conditions for, by creating a set of circumstances whereby people in their care, be it children at home or employees at work, feel confident to take power and be accountable for their actions.

The benefits of this style of management far outweigh the time it takes to set up the conditions, via context setting, delegation and troubleshooting etc. If people *do* feel confident to act on their own, and are prepared to take the consequences, good and bad, for their actions, then it plays to the need of all human beings to feel useful, contributive and satisfied.

If people aren't empowered, if they are directed without reason, corralled, or end up feeling taken for granted, then self-esteem drops, productivity falls. You know, you've been there, I've been there; this argument is probably a no-brainer in the cold light of day when you're reading a book.

All I'm attempting to do at this point is to remind us that **time taken to manage people well and empower them to *do*, is time well invested.**

The alternative is to end up spending more time mopping up the consequences of poorly set context, poorly delegated actions, confused and de-motivated people.

It's another choice, it often feels like a no-choice situation, but time *is* finite; spend it well at the beginning or squander it poorly towards the end of a task. Time doesn't care, a bit like gravity!

CHAPTER 6

Be mindful in your change, walk your talk

What does the experience of the cinema mean to you? It's an experience that still fills me with a degree of excitement. Buying treats and a drink before I go in, sharing the experience with friends or family and then discussing the experience afterwards.

It's a treat that I remember from boyhood, one of those Pavlov's dog experiences that when the lights go down and the adverts come on, I'm transported into another world. I'm also one of those people who like to go at the beginning of the programme. For me watching the adverts and trailers is as much a part of the whole experience as watching the feature, it gets me in the mood. Occasionally, an advert shot for the cinema, which can take advantage of the extra time the media can afford, as well as the big screen experience, can have a powerful impact.

A point of view

One such experience occurred several years ago. It involved a series of shots from different perspectives, all filmed in slow motion and without sound, apart from a voiceover. The first short scene was of a man in a smart suit walking along the pavement carrying a briefcase. The accompanying voiceover simply commented, "A story seen from one angle tells a story"; the screen faded to black.

Then the next slow-motion scene showed the same pavement but the close-up was of a young guy in his 20s with a shaven head, rolled up tight jeans, braces: overall, the garb of a skinhead. He was running flat out. It then faded to a third scene, a fairly tight close up, this time of the side of the young man in full flight, running along the pavement as he caught up with the man in the suit, all still in slow-motion, whereby the skinhead proceeded to wrestle the smart guy with the briefcase off the pavement and into the road. The accompanying voiceover said, "And a scene shown from a different angle can tell a different story."

The screen faded to black again and then came back, but this time with the focus pulled right back to reveal a wide-angle shot of the young man repeating his run, this time I could see why he was looking upwards. The man in the suit was walking under the crane on a building site next to the pavement. The palette of bricks at the end of the crane's cable had slipped and the bricks were tumbling downwards in the original path of the suited man. The young man grabbed the gent in the suit and wrestled him to the ground out of the way of the falling bricks, in an attempt to save him from injury, which appeared to be the outcome once the brick dust had settled.

The final voiceover to this last sequence said, "It's only when you see the situation from all angles can you know the full story." Now I'm not sure the advert made me buy the newspaper it was designed to sell, however I've never forgotten the ad.

In later years this ability to stop, draw back, reflect, and see a broader perspective became enhanced when I started mindfulness meditation.

By understanding that the route to true clarity lies in being more open to what is *really* happening NOW, not what one's pre-judged experience of the past, or projected expectation of the future might be; seeing things as they truly are only comes from stepping back and adopting a wider less attached viewpoint. In fact 'to see things as they truly are' is the literal translation from the ancient Indian Pali word, Vipassana.

> "It's only when you see the situation from all angles can you know the full story."

'Oh, would that God the gift would gee us…'

One of the biggest stumbling blocks to successful change, be it within an individual's life or within business, is often the inability of those trying to bring about change to step back and see the full picture. In some respects it is a contradictory notion, as they are an integral part of the thing they are trying to change, part of 'the water they swim in'. **Self-awareness** and **personal responsibility** in this up close and personal setting, is hard to grasp.

Several years ago I met a business coach and found myself explaining the set-up of my change management company and what we were seeking to achieve for our clients. The coach was interested in our discussion as, in many respects, what we were doing had obvious overlaps with her area of expertise.

A friendship grew and it became clear to her that some of the ways in which I was managing the company were at odds with what I wanted to achieve and, more alarmingly, I simply couldn't see this. It was a blind spot and the term 'cobbler's children' became uncomfortably true. Now I'm not sure whether the children of boot makers are still running around in poorly-repaired shoes, but the analogy is one that I was aware of in theory, but had lost sight of in respect of my own situation. It was rather sobering to realise that change consultants could also go blind to what needed to change!

The friend's objective viewpoint turned out to be an extremely refreshing and valuable contribution to the development of our business. Probably her most valuable input was the reassurance that the very limited ability to *really* see yourself as others see you is not something to be ashamed of, it is something to be embraced as a reality. However, this simple truth has massive knock-on consequences in our daily lives. As Robert Burns wrote, '*Oh, would that God the gift would gee us, to see ourselves as others see us.*'

Mind the gap

We all know that there are times when the impact we have on other people is slightly, or even grossly, at odds with the impact we want to have or think we are having. But rarely is this 'impact gap' fully understood in terms of its knock-on consequences.

Acknowledging that there may be a discrepancy between how you want to come across to other people and the actual impact you have on them is probably a laudable goal, and one that a developed sense of mindfulness can help achieve.

We worked on a change programme where the managing director of a large multinational company was fairly proud of the fact that his nickname was 'The Bear'. After a while working with the organisation it became apparent to me that there seemed to be some misunderstanding. The MD thought 'The Bear' referred to cuddly/teddy bear which, as he was quite a big chap in height and in girth, was seen to him as a term of endearment. However, for those using the term, it referred to 'grizzly bear', as many experienced him as someone who 'tore people apart' with his verbal outbursts and 'undermining attacks'.

The further we got into the change project, the more I was able to build quite a trusting relationship with him, to the point whereby I felt confident in suggesting a series of one-to-one coaching sessions.

It was in these sessions that I gently started to point out that there seemed to be a discrepancy between how he thought he was perceived and the stark reality of how others experienced him. After several hours of talking, including videoing him and playing it back, I found myself sitting opposite a man who was visibly upset and who slowly started to realise that when the 'boy inside the man' was frustrated and he was expressing this emotion, he'd failed to realise that to the outside world that 'boy' wasn't visible and they were left seeing a 17-stone man with a big booming voice!

These outbursts, which to him were passion and firmness, were for many experienced as anger and rigid control.

Mirror, mirror...

There was a further irony in that he had grown up with a father who was extremely bullying in an underhand way and so he had decided to ensure that he would be firm and upfront in his feelings. This was to ensure that, where he could, people were in some way protected from others bullying them by his clear and upfront approach. To realise that to the majority of people his firm and fair approach was being received as aggressive and bullying was doubly upsetting, an impact gap indeed. So what was he to do about it?

The key for him was to have his *own* **awareness** raised relating to this discrepancy; only at that point could he start to take any **ownership** for his behaviour. He started to understand that, at times, changing the delivery of his message was more than enough to change the impact. He didn't have to be a different person and, in most instances, he didn't even have to change many of the words or the course of actions he believed in, it was simply the *style* of delivery that needed to change, and an increase in his mindfulness to be able do so.

Over time he also acquired more honest feedback from others close to him, through him getting more used to asking open questions to check for understanding, rather than his usual assumptive stance that because he'd said something, people had understood it!

As in the three key principles, this MD couldn't be **accountable** for an impact he didn't take any **responsibility** for and in turn he couldn't start to own something when he wasn't aware of its existence.

There was another chapter to this particular story. It was not a coincidence that there was an impact gap for the MD to deal with, highlighted within the process of change, particularly when you realise one of the change parameters was to create an organisation that was more responsive to customers and the market place.

The more his goals were explored, the more people within the company came to the conclusion that the management style needed to be more inclusive, more empowering which, in turn, meant that the board of directors would need to *manage* in this style. This style was one the MD and his board were more than happy to pronounce but they, and in particular the MD, were doing so in a dictatorial and, to many, a threatening way, i.e. the antithesis of the style they were 'demanding' from others. In short, they weren't being mindful of what they needed to do differently on a day-to-day basis.

So how do you be the change you want to bring about?

When Ghandi made his famous quote, "You must *be* the change you want to create", he was saying so out of a profound realisation that to bring about change via any other route was simply counterproductive. Nobody is saying this is easy to do. I remember finding myself intervening in an argument between my two children once and, towards the end, suddenly realised that I was screaming at the top of my voice whilst spouting the words, "For goodness sake stop shouting!"

The biggest challenge is to get a realistic perspective on the differences between **intention** and **behaviour: become more mindful of this and much will change.** A friend once told me that in order to have our goals achieved we individually had to 'be' the future in all that we do right now, so that we achieve or 'have' the results that are rightfully 'ours': 'be' - 'have' - 'our'. OK so it sounds a bit contrived as a lot of these expositions can be, yet there's a kernel of truth in this. It's so easy to expect an outcome without understanding the contradictory effect an individual's *be-havi-our* can unwittingly have on achieving the outcome.

The Northern Ireland Peace Process was tortuously slow for those that lived through it and yet I expect that history in years to come will condense the timescales, as history must do, and future generations will be left with the key events. In very simplistic terms, it may run something along these lines: 'Two traditions, apparently diametrically opposed, tried to resolve their differences through force for 30 years and eventually sought and achieved a political solution.' Thus it ever was in conflicts over the millennia.

What's been curious for me having grown up with this situation rarely off the news I listened to, or watched, was the fact that on a human level the Protestant struggle at its most basic was largely to do with a fear that their values and way of life were under threat and, therefore, needed defending. Ironically, on this same very simplistic and fundamental level, exactly the same could be said to be the driving force behind the struggle of the Republican community.

"The biggest challenge is to get a realistic perspective on the differences between intention and behaviour: become more mindful of this and much will change."

So you had two groups of people with a basic desire to bring about security for their own way of life, but set on a course where they'd come to believe the only way to achieve that security was to destroy it for the other community. This was quite clearly unsustainable for both and yet both sides, with all the justification of blame and righteousness, perpetuated this behaviour and grief-fuelled anger, on both sides. They weren't able to be the change they wanted to see.

The disconnection between intention and behaviour

This extreme example is one I picked deliberately; as I've said, the *intention* on both sides was fundamentally fuelled by a desire to create a secure future for their own tradition. Yet out of that identical desire, both sides exhibited *behaviour* that for thirty years or more did not produce the intended results. It was only when both sides learned to be-have differently that they created a chance to fulfil both sides', or 'our', underlying intention, i.e. secure futures for communities all round.

There also seems to be a dynamic at play; if you articulate your **intention** *before* you start to do anything, then when you start 'doing' or 'be-having', it tends to highlight any discrepancy between **intention** and **behaviour**. A classic example of this was John Major's famous *Back to Basics* speech.

The Tory leader spoke of the importance of family values and basic moral decency. He didn't do an audit of what his fellow politicians were 'doing', he just *talked* at length about the importance of returning back to basic family values. Of course this was a red rag to the media's bull, to find every marital infidelity and moral indiscretion among Major's cabinet!

There is a corporate version of this political discrepancy. It has been a fashion in recent years for companies to come up with a mission statement which often has a set of values attached to it. In so many cases, this simply doesn't come across as real. It's not that companies or individuals don't genuinely believe in a common set of values, it's that they are so easy to pick holes in when compared to various examples of company behaviour.

'Oh mine's a pint and a packet of nuts. By the way, what's your value set?'

I remember once visiting the huge expanse of offices of another major pharmaceutical company. The reception area was on the ground floor of a six-storey building which was designed to have all the offices above, facing inwards, so the centre of the building, above the reception, was a series of six balconies up to a glass atrium roof. Hanging off seven horizontal poles from the top balcony were huge long posters, each with one of the following words on it: *integrity, respect, open communication, customer service, innovation, team spirit, and honesty.*

As I waited at the reception desk, while the receptionist dealt with three telephone calls without her eyes even flickering an acknowledgement of my presence, I looked up at the wafting flags extolling the company's set of values: *respect* caught my eye. When eventually I was acknowledged and I had said that I was here for my meeting, the receptionist was pleasant enough but was rather confused as the person I'd come to see was away on holiday. My eyes flashed up at the *open communication* banner.

A telephone call produced the news that the second-in-command understood some of the reasons for my appointment and would be happy to meet me. So I waited for another 30 minutes, without any warning that the meeting would take place late. As I sat there having been initially ignored, then felt 'lied' to and finally kept waiting without explanation, the company values on the flags above my head seemed to be the living embodiment of a set of contradictions.

The curious thing is that the meeting went well; I got to know the people involved during the following weeks and over time the change project was heralded as a huge success. However, I may have been a lot more forgiving on that first day if the values weren't there for me to compare against the behaviour I experienced, even though it was unintentional.

Now I'm not suggesting that a large proportion of the people didn't hold these values as important; the difficulty was that there was a huge disconnection within the culture, or 'what people did around the place', between how they behaved and what they said they stood for. The problem lay initially in the fact that few within the company were mindful of this discrepancy; they honestly believed that they stood for these values and yet found it difficult to accept that daily behaviours were different from the underlying intention.

This didn't just translate as an internal discrepancy but this blind spot meant that when market feedback confirmed that a large proportion of their customer base viewed the company as being insular and unresponsive, the management team fired the market research company that came up with the data!

If it's worth defining, it's worth measuring

Defining specific behaviours that in some way will reflect each value is a sobering way of tackling this discrepancy. This was done with the pharmaceutical company, ending up with twelve behaviours to collectively reflect the seven values. Then a way of measuring the degree the behaviours were exhibited was designed - and by the management team! This created a much more mindful approach by individuals to their behaviour.

(More on *how* this was done later in the book.)

Importantly, we were a good way into the project before we did this as measuring behaviours is an **accountability** tool, and personal **responsibility** needed to be gained first with the senior management team, once their more mindful **awareness** to this discrepancy had been raised. They then felt they were changing how they behaved, by **choice**. (Always follow the three key principles and in the right order!)

The senior management team realised that unless *they* defined and exhibited the specific behaviours they were prepared to **role model** and to have measured, it would be unrealistic to expect the rest of the company to behave in the same consistent ways. For example, when we looked at the value of *respect*, many argued that it was obvious; the problem was that respectful behaviour to one was seen as disrespectful behaviour to another. So whereas the concept of respect was a common-to-all 'no-brainer', how it looked was more difficult to agree.

The answer to this specific value example lay in a cultural norm that was annoying to most there and common to many companies. It was a largely consensual culture, which required many, many meetings and the electronic diary system had meetings starting on the hour and finishing on the hour.

However, nobody had bothered to factor the reality that the campus was vast and it could take up to 15 minutes to get from one meeting room to another. This resulted in lateness for meetings being endemic, as it compounded the 'normal' reasons why people are often late, such as catching up on telephone calls, replying to a few emails, going to the toilet, etc.

Meetings, bloody meetings!

The overall effect of these pressures was that meetings rarely started on time, people wandered in and out and, to my fresh eyes,

> "Whereas the concept of respect was a common-to-all 'no-brainer', how it looked was more difficult to agree."

meetings in this company were incredibly disrespectful of people's time and input; they were also very inefficient.

The initial response to this cultural norm being pointed out, as an example of the 'respect value' being flaunted, was a torrent of excuses: 'You don't understand how busy I am'; 'I have too many meetings to go to, but they are all important, so I try my best'; 'Surely it's better to get to some of a meeting than to miss it altogether?'

It took quite a while for people to start to mindfully realise the visceral connection between what they said they stood for, their intention, and their day-to-day behaviour. When this dawning occurred, via the detailed staff feedback we collected, they then started to realise that their resistance to accepting their behaviour versus what they stood for was seen as arrogant: 'impact often trumps intention'!

This realisation led to the acceptance that the company being perceived as having arrogant traits wasn't the fault of the market research company that pointed it out, but something they had to deal with by changing their own, individual behaviour, not just trying to change perception through denial and spin.

The behaviours around meetings were eventually seen as an obvious area to address. This was tackled in two main ways, again **all defined by *choice* through the collective agreement of the management team.**

Firstly, a list of basic guidelines was drawn up to make meetings more efficient. Each meeting had to have an agenda, sent out before the meeting. Each point of agreement (not just 'we discussed it', but what was the final agreement) or an action to be done (including by whom and by when) was recorded in the meeting 'output notes' (not detailed minutes) and then sent to all within 24 hours of the meeting. These notes were reviewed at the beginning of the next meeting and if actions were not done, realistic new dates were to be agreed. People had to stick to the agenda and only change it by common agreement. All individuals had to commit to work with the chairman so that the meeting would end on time.

New behaviours locked into place

All of these points were ticked off on a checklist at the end of every meeting and the checklist was posted on the team's private intranet site. Every person who attended a meeting could access these check lists and alter the 'ticks' if they felt they weren't true.

This might sound very 'nit-picky' and draconian, but *they* decided it was needed if they were to be serious! However, if you think this was detailed and a bit harsh, wait till you hear about the second 'rule' they adopted: to deal with lateness!

Firstly, they agreed that all meetings were to be set for 50 minutes or one hour and 50 minutes (or less). The PAs were told and the meeting room booking system changed to support this. These measures helped get around the 'not enough time to get to the next meeting' problem. The other part was that whoever was chairing the meeting would lock the door five minutes after the due start time. No admission was accepted after the door was locked.

I feel it is crucial to keep repeating that these behaviours were thought up and agreed by the team; it was their mindful choice. They had become totally committed to the change process and to the realisation that their day-to-day behaviours made an impact within the overall change objective. This kind of commitment was a sure sign that the three key principles had been followed well and in the right order.

Values into actions

These behaviours around meetings were born out of exploring what day-to-day actions would demonstrate the adopted value of respect. They weren't intended to encapsulate *all* that respect might mean, that would be unrealistic, but it was an indicator. When all of the twelve behaviours (an arbitrary, yet concise enough number) were agreed as a rough reflection of all the seven values, they were role-modelled by the senior management team *only* to start with. Next came measurement via transparent peer review – another very brave, yet choice-led accountability procedure. The overall result was that most of the staff observed a tangible, positive shift in perception of this leadership group during the space of a few months.

It also meant that meetings became more efficient by more decisions and actions taking place; in turn, the company started to be run more effectively.

So what started out as a 'value' with arguable worth in any practical sense ended up as a vital part of the overall change process, delivering tangible, strategic results, and in the process it raised mindful awareness within individuals as to the impact of their behaviour regardless of intention. This is one example of how to *be* the change you want to see, to consciously walk the talk.

CHAPTER 7

What stops us 'being' our change?

'Know thyself' is another old adage with a lot of obvious relevance to this subject of intention versus behaviour, 'walking your talk'. It's also brought into sharp focus when combined with another saying, 'A little knowledge can be a dangerous thing.' It's easy to be selective about the knowledge we hold true for ourselves and it can be difficult to see ourselves as others see us and more difficult to accept it as true.

In this chapter I will be inviting you to focus even more on the effect *you* may have on those around you, especially when it comes to change. It's time to get personal! There is some theory to explain and some examples to relate to yourself. All of this is important within the context of the psychology of change and what stops us.

The connection between you, your personality and your communication style cannot be divorced from any change you wish to bring about. Gaining a sense of mindful **choice** via the three principles is particularly relevant in this chapter. Without you raising **your awareness** of the effects you have on others, especially when scared or stressed, you won't be able to take **personal responsibility** for your impact. And without that, being held **accountable** by others for your part in holding back change, especially change you set out to achieve, will be even harder for you to accept.

Perception really *is* our reality, as long as someone else's perception about me isn't too wide of *my* mark! So where do you draw the line?

You can't be all things to everyone. The best you can hope for is to gain a balance between being **authentic** and being **appropriate**. These are two more words that came up a lot in my early change management days and so I found myself going back to my etymological dictionary.

As I mentioned previously, 'authority' comes from the word 'author' and so, in this context, being 'authentic' speaks of being real, being true to what is *so* for you. However, nobody gives me the right to say my truth regardless of how I deliver it. I have to earn that right and, if I achieve it, it will be done through delivering what's real for me in a way that's appropriate for others.

The expression 'be appropriate' means behaving in such a way as 'to gain or to achieve the desired outcome'. A little saying I used to have in the back of my mind when I first learned this stuff went along the lines of, 'Am I doing or saying what it takes right now to be appropriate and realise the outcome I want?'

There's a much more fundamental litmus test that can be applied to discover whether the right combination of authentic and appropriate is being used. As we touched on earlier in the book when we discussed context setting, when a communication has been made, what was the result and how did I feel? If what I got back as a result of a communication was very similar to what I asked for, then I could argue that the communication was appropriate, especially if both the person I had spoken to and I felt OK with the outcome.

Blame or choice

If however I asked for one thing and got something else, I'm left with a choice. Either I blame the person I'm talking to, or the situation, or myself, or alternatively I take responsibility for the outcome and attempt to communicate in a different way to get the desired result. So if a managing director thinks he's being firm and fair but the world around him tends to reflect the fact that, to them, he comes across as rude and aggressive, he can either

> "Nobody gives me the right to say my truth regardless of how I deliver it."

blame them or change his behaviour so it's perceived to be more in line with his intention.

It also follows that if a company is perceived by the press or its customers as being aggressive and dominant, and yet it perceives itself as being innovative and successful, then it's only a matter of time before customers vote with their feet.

To put it bluntly, if you are being truly **response-able, able-to-respond**, then it's a good idea to examine all aspects of your life – your relationships, your financial state, your working life – and accept it all, good, bad and indifferent, as a reflection of what you have put out into the world, *regardless of your intention.*

Responsibility: the ability-to-respond, not just react

Now this is a big philosophical standpoint and not everyone will necessarily agree and yet the challenge may be, 'What's the alternative?' Even if I find it hard to believe that this is *actually* true, that my world is a reflection of me, if I decide to act in my life as if it *may* be true, then I'm less likely to blame.

It's also important *not* to end up blaming myself, because this stance isn't about saying everything in my life right now is my *fault*, but it is my responsibility, i.e. do I have, or could I muster, the ability to respond to the situations I find myself in? This goes to the heart of the ideas in Chapter One about choice and, specifically, finding choices within what appear to be no-choice situations. **What gets in the way of this, in most cases, are various derivatives of fear.**

Now these are bold statements that demand some explanation, so here goes: I talked earlier on in the book about the body sensations generated and felt as exhilaration and excitement in the aliens landing in the skiing resort analogy being the same as the body sensations generated, but felt as fear or frustration, in the 'going to see the bank manager for a loan' analogy. It's worth understanding where some of these responses come from and how they shape our personality, the way we communicate and the ways we therefore attempt to achieve things in our everyday lives. This is critical to comprehend if we are to understand, on a personal level, how we affect the process of change.

Most of us are familiar with the basic survival mechanism of flight or fight and, as I mentioned previously, when we find ourselves in any situation all the sensory input may lead to a change in the body's production of adrenalin. The adrenalin produces shifts in breathing patterns, heart rate, body temperature, muscle tone, etc.

Depending on the context and our previous experiences, our thought process kicks in and 'tells us' that the situation we're in is one to be treated as excitement (if you're going downhill skiing and you happen to like skiing) or apprehension (if you're told by your bank manager that they can't give you the loan you want). Yet why should the *intensity* of these feelings bear little correlation, often, to any *physical* threat? People do pay and queue to ski, even though skiing has associated physical threats and yet the challenge of the bank manager is something that few would pay good money for! It boils down to our *sense* of threat to survival.

A random survey was carried out on the street so people didn't have much time to think about the answers. The question was, "Which of the following activities would you find the most physically threatening: rock climbing, hang gliding, addressing a theatre full of people or white water rafting?"

It may be no surprise, as you read this, to know that the 'addressing a theatre full of people' option came out as top of the list, by far! And yet the question said 'physically threatening'. To the survival part of the mind, it is likely that 'the most threatening on any level' is what most people interpreted the question to mean.

Ask a group of people to list the basic survival needs and you'll tend to get the following: air, water, food, physical comfort (not too hot, not too cold, not too wet, not too dry) and security or love. I've asked this question many times to many groups of people over 20 years and although it's not something we think about when we're down the pub with friends, those basic five categories tend to come up, time and time again, in various orders. The interesting thing is that to the question, "What are our survival *needs?*" the answers reveal four physical and one emotional, i.e. love or security.

Is love or security a survival need?

There was an experiment carried out in the 1920s in 'foundling homes', the American name for orphanages. The experiment itself is revealing in how our changing perceptions of what's acceptable behaviour constantly shifts, as this experiment would not be allowed today. However, things were different then.

The experiment took groups of children between five and eight years old in each orphanage and they were divided into two groups, the control group and the experiment group. The researchers took great lengths to ensure that both groups of children were treated exactly the same on a physical level, i.e. they were in the same warm surroundings, they both had the same kind of clothes, the same food, etc.

The only difference was that the control groups were allowed to function pretty much as they'd always done, with plenty of interaction between themselves and reinforcement from the adult carers. However, the experiment groups were kept separate from each other and had no verbal input or eye contact from any carer; they were simply given their food and allowed, without context, to be on their own. Now you can see why the experiment wouldn't be allowed today.

Over the ensuing weeks, the behavioural changes of these children were studied. They showed signs of frustration, anger, sadness and eventually withdrawal. The symptoms they started to exhibit were very similar to those which were captured on film in the early 1990s when orphanages that had been neglected were discovered in Romania.

The children in those film clips and also in this experiment tended to stay in one place, be it their bed or the corner of their room, even if there was a large expanse of room around them. They would rock gently back and forth, sometimes violently; they would appear to stare into space and not engage with anyone who came into the room as they had eventually learned that this would never bring a response.

Not just emotional needs

What eventually led to this experiment being stopped was the fact that, beyond these emotional responses, the children in the experiment groups also started to show signs of *physical* deterioration. If they became ill they were given medicine, the same as the control group, but the response time was delayed and in many cases they didn't show signs of much recovery at all.

In other instances, children exhibited hair thinning and even teeth loosening; as one researcher commented, "It appeared as though these children were giving up the will to live." Now if we try and look beyond the natural revulsion to the experiment and try to see what might have been going on in practical terms, none of the four *physical* survival needs were being breached. The children had enough air, food and water as well as their physical comfort being taken care of. It was only the retraction of love or emotional security that caused not just the emotional distress, but the *physical* harm.

For thousands of years, mankind has directed most of its efforts towards avoiding *physical* threat to survival and for a large proportion of the planet that is still the case. Yet for the majority of people within the Western world the survival challenges are not on the same level as they were even a hundred years ago. You only have to read Dickens to see how, for the majority of people, the daily grind of putting a roof over their heads and food in their stomachs was tough. There was no social security or health service safety net attached.

"Children exhibited hair thinning and even teeth loosening; as one researcher commented, 'It appeared as though these children were giving up the will to live.'"

'Disposable income' only entered the dictionary in the 1950s

To put this into further perspective, only in the early 1950s, in an American dictionary, did the phrase *disposable income* first officially enter the English language. As a boy born in the mid 1950s, over the years I can remember the introduction of central heating, double-glazing, antibiotics, etc. In fact, if you list the real *physical* threats that we face today, what are they?

Violent crime or terrorism is in the media a lot but in statistical terms affects a very small number. Getting an illness for which there is *no* treatment has also become less prevalent with medical advancements. On the 'non-physical threat' list, if you lost your job it may be horrible or uncomfortable but would you starve to death, would you be evicted within weeks as in Dickens' time? You might, eventually, have to downsize or change your lifestyle but would your *life* be in danger?

The simple truth is that most people in the Western world have now achieved a level of 'survival' that is way above the daily grind that our forebears faced for thousands of years. Yet the adrenalin rush that accompanied the threat of being attacked by a sabre-toothed tiger, or an infection that was untreatable, or food price rises leading to not being able to buy food at *all* are, for most of us in the developed world, fears of the past.

However, as society has become ever more complex and pressurised, these physical survival needs have been replaced with ever more subtle and pressured fears of an emotional nature. We may have our basic needs covered but they have been overtaken by a 'need' to eat the right food, go to the right schools, live in the right home, in the right area, do the right social activities, drive the right car, be the right shape, etc., etc., etc. And when we don't hit any number of these 'rights' we can often feel failure, guilt, fear, frustration, in other words a whole host of emotions that are to do with our emotional sense of well-being and esteem.

In many ways our physical survival needs have been overtaken by an ever more complex web of *emotional* survival drivers. So how do we cope with these non-physical yet just as 'real' pressures on our sense of security?

As I mentioned at the beginning of this chapter, understanding our coping strategies for dealing with fears and stress is the critical first step. Awareness of this will also help us be aware of these coping mechanisms in others. Without this mindful self-**awareness** we can't do anything about our impact, we aren't **able to respond**, we just react and then fight being held **accountable**, as it 'wasn't my fault!' All sense of **choice** goes out of the window. This sequence is what will contribute to stopping us from being the change we want around us.

Defence mechanisms against perceived threats

As the American experiment with orphanages showed, our drive for emotional security is as powerful a survival need as the way we are programmed to survive physical threats.

Where did all this start? How much of this is down to genetic programming and how much is down to learned behaviour, is a perpetual debate. Suffice to say, it is a mix of both and as the 'clasp hands' exercise showed, at least some of our behaviour is learned and so can be re-learned. Most of us are aware that learned behaviour started in childhood, yet it's worth reminding ourselves just how much the growing up process has shaped who we are today.

A baby or young child will look up to its parents or caretakers to provide everything: food, shelter and security. In fact, up until a certain age, small children may cry when the parent leaves the room as for them if they can't directly experience something in the now, then it doesn't exist. The concept of something being in the next room is literally that, a concept.

It's rather ironic that Buddhist monks take a lifetime to develop the mindful discipline for staying in the here and now, when for young children it's the only thing that really exists. As we grow up, at some point in our teens or 20s it's likely that we look at our parents and think 'gosh they're *not* all powerful, they're not the god-like characters we thought them to be when we were growing up'. We start to see them as ordinary people who did their best; at some point we take them off the pedestal. For most this is a natural process.

An exercise on the past

Here is an exercise you can do on yourself to get a sense of how some of your defence mechanisms got formed during this period of your life and what form those defence mechanisms may take. It's an exercise in mindfulness and one I use a great deal in my work with others, as it may help you realise how the past is shaping your present and that it does not need to continue doing so.

As you're reading this, think about an incident that happened to you in your early childhood, around or before the age of eight or nine. An incident where you were playing, having fun and you either did something that your parents perceived as wrong or you caused an accident. (I suggest you don't choose anything too 'heavy', there are lots of fairly ordinary incidents as I've described in most childhoods.)

Think of an incident where the response that you got back at the time (not with the benefit of hindsight) seemed confusing or disproportionate. Notice how you felt at that time; you may even have a little of the feelings now as you think about that situation.

I've taken people through this exercise many times in a coaching situation and I'm still surprised at just how many incidents people come up with. Some, however, find it hard to recall or then, when they do, often preface the recollection with the words, "I can't really think of anything, apart from this, not sure if it's important, but here I go." They then proceed to say something like they spilt paint on their trousers when they were seven and thought they would wash them, so put them in the washing machine and managed to turn it on. They didn't realise that there was a pair of white sheets already in there, waiting to be washed. The paint ran out of the clothes, ruining the sheets and rather than getting a 'well done' for washing their clothes, they got shouted at for ruining the sheets! I have got lots of my own examples and I suspect you may have too.

Most of us are still children at heart

Although this kind of experience is just part of growing up, it is important for where we are heading to pause a little and try to re-capture a sense of how these kinds of experiences can affect us. One way to really 'get' the impact of this kind of situation on us, as the children we were (and still are in many ways) is to translate a similar story into the world of us as adults.

Imagine that you invite some friends round for dinner. You offer them drinks and you give one friend the glass of wine he asked for, in one of your expensive glasses. He accidentally breaks it. You shout at him and then send him up to a bedroom for the rest of the evening without having supper. How might your friend feel?

In most cases the friend would leave and that might be the end of the friendship! This may sound a ludicrous example, yet this story is exactly the kind of thing that, to varying degrees, has happened many times, over years, to most children. Add in the fact that when this happened the person reacting to your behaviour was, at that time, a person in authority over you, literally wielded a sense of authorship over your life, and we start to realise the effect these incidents can cumulatively have on our sense of security and self-esteem.

We are emotional 'blotting paper' when we are young

Now I'm not saying in any way that parents are wrong; as a parent I've found myself reacting like this on numerous similar occasions. However, as to being a child at that point, when the one person who feels like God in your life withdraws his love, because that's how a sharp response often 'lands', it can feel as though the emotional plug has been pulled on the child.

This kind of incident happens thousands of times in our lives and most of them, in retrospect, feel pretty innocuous. Yet they can have a cumulative effect on the way we respond to that feeling of having love withdrawn or being made to feel insecure.

Back to the exercise:

It may be interesting for you to think of two further incidents in your life, one at say the age of between 10 and 13 and one between 16 and your early 20s: these age brackets are important development stages.

Again, with each incident, recall when you did something perceived as 'wrong'. Even if at these ages you may have realised you were doing something wrong; choose incidents where the negative response you got from those in authority felt *over the top* or unjustified. Or maybe you were falsely punished for something you didn't do. The authority figures may now include teachers or other key people to whom, as someone growing up, you looked up to, or who had authority over you.

> "When the one person who feels like God in your life withdraws his love, it can feel as though the emotional plug has been pulled."

Take yourself through each incident separately. Each time recall what you were doing, what the unexpected or confusing reaction from those in authority was, how it made you feel.

As you take your time to think and feel your way through these sequences you may also start to realise something else: that a pattern in your own behaviour may have started to emerge in terms of how you responded to the feelings of being let down or exposed or 'made' to feel vulnerable.

Just before we draw conclusions as to what we do with these experiences, here is another piece of evidence which supports the effect that authority figures have on us as the children we were/are. (I still feel about 20 max, most of the time. How old do you feel on the inside?)

A group of student child psychologists in northern California carried out a simple experiment, yet the results were profound. The student psychologists sat at the back of school classes with children from the ages of eight through to 16. They had two mechanical counters, one in each hand. Every time a child received a positive message of any kind from teachers, they gave a click to the counter in the left hand. Every time a child received a negative comment, a click was made to the counter in the right hand.

After several weeks of observation, the number of 'clicks' was added up. On average, the children received 326 negative comments to 41 positive comments, per DAY. That's week in, week out, for years. This is in addition to the responses to accidents or doing something 'wrong'. All in all, it's no wonder that for many of us our sense of worth or self-esteem is poor.

A simple test of your self-esteem as of now: get someone to record you on video in natural conversation. Then play it back. How does that make you feel? Now compare how it feels to watch a friend of yours in the same situation on tape. Is there a discrepancy between how you feel in response to the two tapes?

Behaviour patterns in response to being 'made' to feel insecure

Most people end up compensating for or defending this accumulated sense of poor self-esteem or emotional exposure by adopting a mixture of **three broad categories** of 'defence' responses.

The first one: if you feel unloved or exposed in front of those who are really important to you (as you grow older this could be anyone you feel has authority over you in your life) then you may have developed a response of '**seeking** approval' - trying to be what you think people *want* you to be. Saying 'yes' sometimes when you mean 'no', smiling when you're in discomfort, doing those little actions to win favour in the hope they'll be spotted and acknowledged!

Approval seekers, when feeling vulnerable, have a never-ending search to have their self-worth confirmed by other people. They tend to show the softer range of emotions for fear of upsetting people or gaining others' *dis-approval* although when really pushed they can lash out and show emotions that would be described as out of character by many around them. (If you're feeling uncomfortable right now this may be your preferred option. If you don't know what I am talking about, read on!)

The second type of defence mechanism is in many ways a collection of opposites. The word to best sum up these behaviours, again mainly exhibited under pressure and with people they feel are important to them, is **control.**

Controllers are people who seek to control what emotions they show and in some ways control those around them to make the controlling individual feel more in control themselves. They tend to show the anger or dismissive range of emotions when under pressure, rather than the softer end of the spectrum. They like to be right, like to have the last word, again can wear a smile but it's often one that seems to be disdainful or supreme rather than a smile of 'please like me'. These traits will kick in more in situations where they feel vulnerable.

The irony is that controllers *need* people to control, so often gravitate towards approval seekers. Whilst approval seekers rarely *believe* the approval they seek, they will often gravitate towards controllers as they are destined never to give the approval the seeker requires.

'Psychobabble' or kernels of uncomfortable truth?

Mad or what?! Yet I imagine you will be feeling a sense of uncomfortable recognition of one of these two types of defence responses unless you are thinking 'what a load of psychobabble rubbish, I wouldn't do any of that!' In which case you're probably a controller!

If neither of these two defence mechanisms works, then the third option is to simply **withdraw**, either emotionally or physically, maybe losing oneself in a TV, phone or computer screen of some sort. It's a bit like getting to a point where you pick up your metaphorical bat and ball and walk off life's pitch. It is rarer for someone to occupy this defence response as a first port of call; some timid folk do but more likely it is a place we go to when nothing else seems to work. The vulnerability or tiredness with the emotional battles of life just seems too great for a while.

This whole area of defence mechanisms and personality traits is one that can be explored in greater depth and could form the heart of another book. Suffice it to say for the purpose of this section of *this* book, how we respond to insecurities has a crucial effect on our behaviours within the context of role modelling change.

Overall, from the brief descriptions given so far, I imagine you were able to identify more with one of the three defence traits than the others. To what degree your childhood experiences governed your leaning towards approval or control and at what point you tend to withdraw is a debating point that may not be answered easily via a book; as mentioned earlier, it's partly nature and partly nurture. Whatever the causes, it still leaves us with a question as to what to do about it, if anything.

It all comes back to behaviour versus intention and the gap between the impact you want and the impact you give.

I know that *my* fundamental leaning under pressure, particularly with people that I feel have some kind of authority over me, is to seek their approval when I'm feeling insecure. I know that if I smile when I'm not feeling comfortable, or try and sell myself to make up for a sense of insecurity, that these traits are likely to come over as insincere. Likewise, somebody who controls by bottling up emotion or only coming across as aggressive can leave those around them believing that they're only capable of being tough.

Neither of these traits is fundamentally *stronger* than the other. Their effect is just different and, crucially, if these are the *only* habitual responses, especially if unconscious as they tend to be for most, then it is no wonder that the intention/behaviour gap exists. Consequently, many people get mis-judged for who they *truly* are or what they *really* stand for.

We all need love/security to survive. The lack, or perceived lack of it from those important to us, can leave us feeling that, 'Who I am is not enough'. This creates a problem: how to be or appear to be enough, or simply avoid exposure.

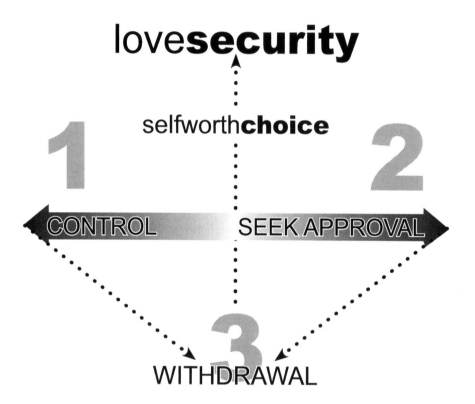

The more I use one of these three above, the more likely I am to react or blame rather than own my part in emotionally testing/exposing situations

The more I 'choose to have' the uncomfortable feelings, when I am feeing insecure/exposed, the more I'll reinforce my self worth, rather than mask my perceived lack of it through one of these 3 defence mechanisms.

The observation of these dynamics in others will help me to be able to separate other people's behaviour from their true intention.

Richard Branson, Alan Sugar, Tony Blair and Margaret Thatcher

Here are some examples of well-known people and their 'defence' leanings. Richard Branson and Tony Blair exhibit more of the approval seeking traits than control. Yet they are strong leaders and eminently successful in their fields, although curiously both have been accused by various commentators of being insincere, even sycophantic.

On the other hand, people like Alan Sugar and Margaret Thatcher exhibit(ed) classic control traits. It wasn't until those who are close to them got to know them well did their softer and more caring side become strongly apparent.

The danger is that if you remain oblivious, NOT mindful to the effect that any defence mechanism can have on your impact, you may be unwittingly communicating one set of traits that is often at odds with the words you are using. This in turn will create conflicting communication which, unless you can spot why, can feel very undermining and confusing, both to you and to those you are communicating with. **This can stop you 'being' the change you want to achieve.**

The route forward is, once again, to follow the three key principles. Become **more mindfully aware** of the voice inside your head. You know the commentator, the one that right now may be saying things like, "What voice, what's he talking about?," or "I could do with a cup of coffee," or "When does this chapter end?," or "…" – yes, that stuff. If it's anything like my voice it babbles on in the background of my head, churning out inane comment on most things most of the time.

However, when I'm in a situation that makes the adrenalin flow, my voice goes into overdrive as it starts commenting on what the adrenalin *means*, in terms of feelings and emotions and whether I should be excited and get involved, or scared and fight or take flight. It usually 'instructs' me to take the safest option, not always the one that will best serve my growth, or ultimately what I really want to achieve.

In these situations, if instead I can **raise my awareness** of compensatory habits that I

> "If these are the only habitual responses, especially if unconscious as they tend to be for most, then it is no wonder that the intention/behaviour gap exists."

may start to use, like smiling when I'm uncomfortable or being aggressive when I'm scared, then I may have a chance to **take responsibility** for my feelings and thoughts. I may be able to pause, take a deep breath and see different choices as to how I might respond, not just react blindly.

I may then be able to communicate a bit more of what is *really* going on for me, rather than me being blindly driven by habitual reactions. So I will be **aware** of my reactions internally, more **response-able** to the emotions I'm feeling and talk from that standpoint rather than trying to hold it all in, or cover it up. I will then be more **accountable** to those around me for the impact I actually have, rather than me blaming the world for getting the wrong end of my stick.

What is real, what makes our reality?

Most of our moment-to-moment reality comes about via our senses: touch, taste, smell, sight and hearing. There is also a sixth sense, our thinking. Our mind responds to thoughts (whether they come from inside or outside our head) just as our hearing responds to sound or our taste to flavours. If you are unsure about the inclusion of this sixth sense then try a little experiment.

Close your eyes, sit comfortably, clear your mind as best you can. Then, bring to mind something that in the past has upset you, or maybe angered you. Or something that excited you, or brought you a thrill. As you think of these experiences, notice whether your breathing changes, and whether your pulse rate changes. In most cases these two physical changes, at least, take place. And they are changes in reaction to just a thought, without the need for any external stimulus. A strong indication of the power of the mind to affect the body, and as I have mentioned earlier in this book, once the body has reactions, adrenaline is pumped around our system to get us ready for flight or fight, the survival response.

The left-hand side of the diagram opposite is a product of our mind pre-deciding how life should be, according to the rules, rights, and social codes we subscribe to. It's a product of the survival mind, the part of our brain that fears not knowing and would prefer to have answers even if they may not be the right or appropriate ones!

How does this sequence take place? Something happens to trigger a reaction from one or more of your six senses. This is likely to trigger a thought, often,

'I like this', or I 'don't like this'. And behind the thing or situation not being liked, is a *sensation* that is unsettling. If I like the sensation I may want more of the stimulus and the feelings or sensations that go with it. If I don't like the sensations and feelings that go with the stimulus, then I may want to get rid of them.

WHAT IS REAL?
Two very different approaches to dealing with 'reality'

SENSATIONS
Your thoughts are causing you unwelcome feelings.
You have TWO OPTIONS depending on your level of CONSCIOUSNESS.

IN-THE-MEMORY	IN-THE-MOMENT
Mind-led	**Intuition-led**
REACT TO THE SENSATIONS I am unaware of my thoughts and feelings. I feel uncomfortable. I share my opinions.	**OBSERVE THE SENSATIONS** I notice my thoughts and feelings. I know nothing for sure.
SEEK EVIDENCE AND AGREEMENT I seek to justify my opinions by making evidence fit and canvassing support.	**CHOOSE YOUR FEELINGS** I'm having feelings. I know what I am feeling. I'm okay with having the feelings.
MAKE DECISIONS I make decisions based on my opinions and attachments to ideas and people.	**RESPOND TO WHAT'S SO** I take responsibility for the sensations I'm feeling. It's my thoughts causing them.
ABDICATE CONTROL I attribute blame where I see fit. Things are out of my control.	**RECOGNISE YOU'RE IN CONTROL** I'm in control. I am able to act to review and, if necessary, revise my thinking.
THINK OF REASONS YOU MUST BE RIGHT What I did was the right thing. To be perfectly honest, I'm feeling a bit righteous.	**NOTICE THE RESULTS OF BEING ALIGNED** I have responded appropriately to the situation. I'm feeling satisfaction.
This column illustrates an effort to make sense of reality through your expectations, preconceptions and past judgments.	This column illustrates the key to getting what you want by going with the flow - being in control by relinquishing control.

If the sensations and feelings are generated by an external stimulus, a situation like the weather changing when I didn't expect it, a traffic jam, a loss of something I wanted, or someone's behaviour, then in these cases these sensations may lead me to form an OPINION.

If the stimulus that gave rise to my reactions continues, then any opinion I might form is likely to become stronger and become a BELIEF or EXPECTATION.

After a while I will start to look for EVIDENCE as well as AGREEMENT from others to support my belief. For example, I think someone isn't pulling their weight at work, so I ask a colleague and, even as I ask I am listening out for words in reply that back me up. Or I ask around until I find those that agree with me, "Ah", I say to myself, "I knew I was right".

After some selective evidence, and agreement from others, my beliefs will become consolidated in the form of a DECISION and I'll become ATTACHED to my stance, because, in my belief-bound mind, I am the sum of all my decisions; they are what defines me, they are who I am.

A teacher once said to me, "If homicide is to kill someone, and suicide is to kill oneself, then to decide is to kill off other options".

Once I have made a reactive decision, one born out of not wanting to own my *sensory* reactions to a situation, then all I can do is BLAME.

Although I may feel justified in a self-satisfied kind of way, I am actually out of any real CONTROL as the situation is doing it to me! All I can do is to keep telling myself (and probably others that may share my viewpoint) just how RIGHT I am, how justified I am in feeling aggrieved, and constantly rehearse all of the REASONS why I am right and the situation is wrong!

We've all been there. A reactive reality, leading to RIGHTEOUSNESS, is part of being human.

> "A reactive reality, leading to RIGHTEOUSNESS, is part of being human."

However, we also know that we don't have to live in a 'reactive reality'.

We all have the ability to reflect, to call on our 'reflective consciousness'.

It may take a moment, a minute, an hour, a day or longer, and, at some point if we choose to look beyond our sensory reactions, we may see another parallel reality.

The right hand side of the diagram is based on responding to 'what is' rather than what should be - leading to the natural ability to respond to life out of an intrinsic sense of integrity or wholeness. This is an in-the-moment process and by definition *cannot* be pre-decided. An anathema to the survival part of our mind, which prefers to imagine it knows what's going on; it prefers the 'in-the-memory' model.

It takes sensitivity and being aware of feelings and levels of energy to live life out of the in-the-moment model. In this state, *observation and awareness* of one's beliefs and expectations will happen automatically - so giving the best of both worlds.

Being locked into the in-the-memory model will radically limit options and creativity. The in-the-memory side is first and foremost a reactive machine, which will in most instances attempt to kick in first.

The more connected to emotions and energy we are, plus the more awareness we have of our reactive side, the more quickly does reactivity decline and give way to a much wider range of options - an experience of being in control and able to *respond* to everything in our life as though we 'wrote the script'. This is true responsibility.

Honing this awareness and mental discipline is at the heart of mindfulness training, and acquiring the muscle memory to observe our 'reactive reality' more quickly is a lifetime's work!

The link between energy and emotions

How can we achieve this sort of ownership of difficult feelings in live situations? To start with it helps, I have found, to understand a little more about what we often term 'negative emotions'.

Negative emotions tend to fall into five distinct groups:

APATHY: includes boredom, can't be bothered, disengaged. Very low energy.

UPSET: includes being upset, disturbed, crying, through to grief. More energy than apathy.

FEAR: from slightly worried through to frightened and terrified. More energy than upset, i.e. think about times when you've been upset, then times when you were frightened - often more energy in the latter.

ANGER: includes the range of emotions from irritation to frustration, to anger to hatred. Tends to be more energy than when frightened or feeling some forms of fear.

STUBBORN PRIDE: includes resistance, blind righteousness, and immovability. Lots of energy in this category!

Beyond these categories of emotion, most of which we don't want and don't like, lie the emotions we *do* want, sometimes crave: calmness, happiness, joy, love, etc.

So what is the most effective way of getting from a negative emotion to a more positive one? Well we all have lots of ways to do this! And, do they all really work?

A clue to a fundamental route to moving out of a negative emotion is to observe how the five stages have more energy in them the further you move from apathy to fear and beyond.

Another observation is that all the negative emotions are really various forms of fear. Apathy? Fear of moving forward or getting engaged. Upset? Fear of loss and moving on. Anger? Fear of being out of control, not seeing how to get want you want. Stubborn pride? Fear of admitting you might be wrong!

And what about fear itself? There are many expositions of this word and my favourite is using the word as an acronym:

False Evidence Appearing Real: F.E.A.R.

Unless the fear is in relation to a physical and an immediate threat, most forms of fear are triggered by the mind's desire to keep us safe from anything and everything that feels like a threat to itself. Fine if I can discern the difference between a threat to my mind's sense of itself and the threat from a speeding car suddenly appearing around the bend of a road I am crossing; in this case I may need my body to react quickly with adrenalin so I can get out of the way.

The adrenalin is less helpful if it's because I feel the fear of embarrassment, or guilt, or of not feeling worthy in front of my peers. This is often 'false evidence appearing real'. False in that it often has no actual meaning other than that I ascribe to the feelings, and yes, the feelings or sensations are *real* as my body is experiencing them.

So what is real beyond the range of negative emotions? **Well, some scholars would say it is a state, a state of being, one of being-at-one with everything going on. In short a state of love.**

Now you may not have expected love to be talked about in this book, and I won't expand on this in much detail here as it is a very personal concept. However I will say most would accept that love can take many forms and feelings, and yet the *state of being* called love is not born out of particular feelings and not out of certain desires being met, but it is a state of mind, a state of being or a heart-state that is born out of a state of *acceptance*, not victim-led resignation, but an equilibrium: mindfulness lived.

So how to deal with the emotions or energy that feel negative?

A powerful way to deal with them is in ways that replicate how best to respond to other forms of energy like electricity or gravity. This may sound a strange link but bear with me.

If you think back to school days and some of the basic rules of physics you may recall, principles such as these:

1) 'Energy cannot be created or destroyed, it can only be changed from one form to another.' [Einstein]. That is, if you burn a piece of paper the latent energy contained in the paper is transformed into heat, light, smoke and ash when burnt. All of those elements add up to the latent energy contained within the sheet of paper.

2) 'What is resisted will persist with equal and opposite force.' That is, the downward pressure you are exerting via gravity on the space you are occupying right now is equal to the force from the floor supporting you, otherwise you'd sink beneath the ground or be propelled into the air!

3) 'Energy will take the path of least resistance.' That is, electricity runs to ground, water and other liquids find their own level, etc.

OK, and how are these three laws of physics applicable to the energy of emotions? Well in many ways the same principles seem to apply.

"How are these three laws of physics applicable to the energy of emotions?"

Feel the 'pain' and do it anyway

If I am feeling a negative emotion I cannot make it disappear by sheer force of will. However if I really feel it, breath into it, embrace it, almost give up to it, it tends to transform into a more positive emotion, as in the first law above. For example if I can talk about how I feel and not blame anyone or thing for how I am feeling, there's a chance I can turn anger into passion for instance, or apathy into action.

The second law is easier to spot in relation to negative emotions. Most realise that the more a negative emotion is resisted, the worse they feel. For example if I am feeling frustrated or worried and I say nothing, do nothing but bottle up the feelings, I can end up with tension in my body, a headache or even become ill. We humans are not designed to be batteries or storehouses of negative emotion. It will take as much energy to hold down or suppress negative feelings or negative 'energy', as is contained within the negative emotion being suppressed. Not healthy on any front.

Then there is the third law of energy: taking the path of least resistance. In simple terms, if I do not find ways to appropriately express my feelings, especially negative ones, then the energy contained within them will find a way out. I'll take out frustrations on others, or the cat, or when driving, but it is unlikely to be 'clean' or directed in ways that will serve either me or those around me.

This is all very well, but are there things to practise to develop such acceptance and expression of difficult feelings?

There are many techniques to manage and express negative emotions in appropriate ways. Here is a mindfulness exercise designed to transform negative emotion or energy into positive energy. I have used and taught this exercise for many years, often with amazing results:

AS YOU SIT WHERE YOU CURRENTLY ARE, FOCUS ON A PROBLEM OR DIFFICULT SITUATION YOU HAVE IN YOUR LIFE, SOMETHING THAT IS ONE WAY, BUT YOU WOULD LIKE IT TO BE ANOTHER WAY, AND THE DIFFERENCE IS CAUSING YOU TO FEEL A NEGATIVE EMOTION. (Don't make this up. It has to be a real problem for the exercise to work.)

CLOSE YOUR EYES AND GET IN TOUCH WITH HOW YOU FEEL RIGHT NOW IN RELATIONSHIP TO THIS SITUATION.

DESCRIBE YOUR BODY SENSATIONS NOW, EITHER OUT LOUD OR TO YOURSELF SILENTLY, USING THIS CHECK LIST:

- IS YOUR BREATHING FAST OR SLOW?

- AND IS YOUR HEARTBEAT, FAST, SLOW, ABOUT NORMAL?

- IS THERE ANY TENSION IN YOUR STOMACH?

- WHAT ABOUT YOUR SHOULDERS AND NECK? ARE THEY STIFF OR RELAXED?

- ARE YOUR HANDS SWEATY OR DRY?

WHAT NEGATIVE EMOTION OR FEELING DO *ALL* OF THESE BODY SENSATIONS ADD UP TO?

RESPONSE (SAY OUT LOUD THE FEELING OR NEGATIVE EMOTION, NOT A THOUGHT).

NOW ASK YOURSELF THIS QUESTION WITH THESE WORDS:

"IN THEORY, *COULD* I LET GO OF WANTING TO CHANGE MY (state the emotion*) ABOUT THIS SITUATION YOU'VE FOCUSED ON?"

RESPONSE   "YES/NO" (Gut response, don't think about it or try and understand the question any more than you do)

"THANK YOU. (then say this next question with some energy) NOW, *WOULD* I LET GO OF WANTING TO CHANGE MY (FEELING) ABOUT THE SITUATION I BROUGHT TO MIND RIGHT NOW?"

RESPONSE   "YES/NO"

"THANK YOU. HOW DO I FEEL? DO I FEEL LESS OF THE EMOTION OR MORE? HEAVIER OR LIGHTER?"

RESPONSE   (Be honest with your gut response to this last question)

REPEAT THE PROCESS ON THE SAME ISSUE IF THE NEGATIVE EMOTION OR 'CHARGE' IS STILL THERE.

If you go through the sequence more than twice with a 'no' to either question, say 'yes' to both, with energy, next time around.

If the response is that the feeling or charge hasn't gone up or down and is about the same, then repeat the sequence again replacing the feeling stated with the word "STUBBORNNESS".

You can also do this exercise with someone you really trust asking you the questions.

OK, this strange-to-some series of self-searching questions needs some explanation. To start with most perceived problems in life can be traced back to a negative or difficult feeling generated around or because of the problem. Think about it, if you didn't feel anything negative about a situation, would you even recognise it as an issue, as a problem?

Secondly, going through the various body sensations slowly, *mindfully* will help you get in touch with what you are *really* feeling, as opposed to what you were thinking, or a feeling on the surface.

Then, what follows, is my explanation of those two strange questions, "Could you let go of wanting to change this feeling"? And then "Would you let go... etc."

The survival part of the human mind does not like to be wrong, and so wants to get rid of things it doesn't like, to be right about most things especially threats. And yet as the three laws show, what is resisted will persist with equal and opposite force.

So, the "In *theory*, could you let go of..." question is a 'consultative' question to the mind, a softening up manoeuvre, if you will, meaning if you *could* let go of wanting to *change* this feeling, not that you're going to, this is just in theory, honest! It's a kind of trick question to trick your survival-oriented mind into just considering loosing its grip.

Then, when you ask yourself, "*Would* you let go of wanting to change this negative feeling?" you are effectively asking your mind to stop resisting, and *have* or *FEEL* the feeling. And as you say yes and allow your body to do so, the feeling passes through, transforms from held or stuck feelings, to lighter more positive ones.

And... best not analyse this. Just do the exercise several times, on real situations with real feelings, and see what happens. This is a good example of core mindfulness in action, being with 'what is': being in the now, whatever that may feel like.

> "Would you let go of wanting to change this negative feeling?"

There is no 'I' in Team

So far in this chapter I have talked predominantly about the importance of *you* being mindfully aware of your *own* feelings as well as your impact, especially when it comes to communication and in particular when you want to 'be the change' you wish to bring about.

Getting other people to do things differently is very difficult if you are a key influencer or manager and you're not able yourself to do some of the things you are asking others to do differently.

Again, it's one of those obvious things when we think about it in the cold light of day but, as we've explored, the kind of impact we *actually* have on other people is the only impact the rest of the world sees; it's not privy to the thoughts inside our head regarding how we think we'd like to come across. In this respect, the physical world around us has perfect integrity, it doesn't lie, it reflects back to us the impact we actually have, rather than what we'd like to have. Sometimes this feels cruel, depending on how out of touch we are with the effect that we're really having on our world.

Raising personal awareness and taking responsibility for our own impact is also a critical first stage to bringing about change to others. Mindfully role modelling that which you want to be different, through your daily actions and behaviours, and offering yourself to be accountable for those behaviours to your colleagues and friends is the only way to inspire and be taken seriously as a change bringer.

So how does this approach fit in with the notion of team?

I recently delivered a leadership workshop for the board of directors of a media company. Many of them had worked with each other for a number of years and most individuals were big characters with larger than life personalities. They kept talking about wanting to make the board a 'higher functioning team' and yet few understood what was, at the heart of them together, preventing this.

At the beginning of the workshop, in response to me starting to talk about the effects of the individual within a team, one of the directors simply said, with a sense of categorical assertion, "There is no 'I' in team." By the end of the workshop when he had examined his relationship with other board members, he had changed his mind.

There is a lot of stuff talked and written about team. I find some of it irritating. As I mentioned before, team, like happiness, is the result of doing many things, it is not an instant outcome to be imposed on anyone, or any group of individuals.

Generally, I have found that there are two types of team, where team exists: one is based around task and the other based around relationship.

Task-based teams

A few years ago I was driving home late at night and I drove round a bend to see, just in time, that two cars had collided moments before. I managed to pull up without damaging my own car and a couple of vehicles behind me also managed to stop without incident. We went over to the vehicles, could see that people were injured and that the damage to both cars was substantial.

Things then became a bit of a blur in my memory. All I recall is that one person had a flashing light and a safety triangle in his boot so he put these up as a warning sign ahead of the bend and stood there signalling traffic to slow down. Someone else in the group who had stopped to help was a first-aider and started to help where he could. Others had mobile phones and called the emergency services. We all just went into action without any discussion or argument. We all did what we felt we could do best to make the situation as safe and comfortable as possible for those concerned until the emergency services arrived.

The police arrived first and took over the role of traffic control. They took names and addresses and did what they could for the injured until the ambulance got there and finally the fire engine with cutting equipment. When all the services had arrived, I found myself with the other drivers who had initially stopped, huddled together, as our tasks had been taken over by the professionals. We stayed and chatted a while, a couple of us even swapped numbers. It was a powerful experience. Eventually we drifted away, drove off and, for my part, I never contacted the two people whose numbers I had taken and they didn't contact me. I meant to, but life got in the way and the reason for calling seemed to diminish until the incident became a memory of something I did once.

When I look back, for that relatively brief period of time that we were all engaged in doing what we could, we were a team. We were a team galvanised around a set of tasks that were obvious and clear; we just did what we could and got on with it. However, when the tasks were taken over by the professionals, the team eventually dispersed as there was no common basis for it to continue other than the passing thought that we might reconnect. In the event, as far as I know we didn't reconnect because the tasks were done and there were insufficient reasons for coming together again.

Relationship-based teams

It's funny how every few years some technological or social development starts to happen and those in society who are probably more change averse tend to make comments like, "The children of today can't have as many friends as we did, they don't go out and play like I used to," or "Why do young people spend so much time on their computers? I don't know how they have time for friends."

These points could be argued a whole range of ways, and yet there seems to be a fundamental drive within people in general to create and maintain friends, regardless. My kids have probably got a larger social network now, through the various networking sites on the internet and through text messaging on their mobiles than I was able to maintain as I was growing up; it's just different. They will probably end up with the same small number of truly close friends – hopefully; five or six is the average I'm told.

As the years roll by, it's interesting to me that out of my close circle of friends there are three or four with whom I keep in contact, not just out of historical habit. We still relate stories of our *current* trials and tribulations, challenges and excitements, not just recalling stuff from back in the old days. These are true relation-'ships'; big, sturdy, well built vessels that can weather most storms and wouldn't capsize through a 'heavy downpour' of disagreement or a 'strong wind' of misunderstanding. These are my 'telephone in the middle of the night' friends, a potential team that can spring into action whenever a common task becomes apparent but, in the absence of such a task, they are happy to jog along and share each other's company, relate to each other's life.

> "These are true relation-'ships'; big, sturdy, well built vessels that can weather most storms and wouldn't capsize through a 'heavy downpour' of disagreement."

'Task-based' takes a team so far. 'Relationship-based' goes the distance

When it comes to building a team in the workplace, or on the committee you serve, or even in the family you are in, a team built *only* around task will take you so far but a team built around relationship *plus* a common task will carry you a lot further. The difficulty in many company situations is that people aren't always given the opportunity or don't always know how to build real, gritty and robust relationships with each other before the common task is introduced. Even worse, in many cases the task or goal doesn't feel common to everyone and without that true commonality, compounded by poor and weak relationships, the chances of a sense of a strong team emerging are extremely low.

So what is the best way to build a relationship-based team? As I mentioned, 'team' and other notions such as 'happiness' are experiences that happen as a result of doing several things, often not initially embarked upon with the intention of 'team' or 'happiness' as an outcome. Imagine being single and going up to someone you like the look of in a bar and saying, "Would you like to get happy with me?"

No! Madness! Yet so many people are thrown together at work and told to 'be a team'!

The key probably lies in *individuals* being able to have an impact on those around them that is *congruent,* i.e. what you see is what you get, individuals that walk their talk **and express their emotions.** In other words, developing the trust needed to be real 'in the round' with those in the 'team'.

In addition, each individual needs to be a **relationship and, therefore, a team builder:** someone who reaches out, builds bridges and relates with those around them. If the majority of people in a group are willing and able to do this, then a sense of team will naturally emerge.

Traditional team building activities like getting barrels across a stream are things that might pull me together with a group of people for a day or so. However, understanding over time the desires, hopes and fears of those I work with, safe in the knowledge that my desires, hopes and fears are of some importance to my colleagues as well, will create a far more powerful foundation for a natural sense of team to emerge.

Being more mindfully open, honest and real with people around you, 'being' the change you want to see, is the most powerful way to create the conditions for relationship-based teams. It is also this sense of team that is needed to drive and withstand the bumpy road that is delivering change.

The whole of this first section in Chapters 1-7 has been exploring the nature of mindful change, its dynamics and our psychology in relationship to it.

The second section explores the practicalities of bringing it about.

A more detailed summary of this first part is contained within the concluding chapter.

PART TWO

THE PRACTICALITIES
OF BRINGING ABOUT
MINDFUL CHANGE

Introduction to Part Two

The themes, especially the three key principles, explored in Part One are referred to in Part Two as the psychology of change and they underpin the approach to the practicalities.

In Part Two, I explore our change-by-choice approach to bringing about change, starting in the next chapter, Chapter 8. I discuss the notion that there is no single 'silver bullet' for making change happen, contrary to many of the change fads over the years. Change is brought about by doing many small yet integrated things.

In the following chapter, Chapter 9, the 'five golden rules' relating to the practicalities of implementing mindful change that have become apparent to me over the years are outlined in brief. Then each golden rule is explored, in some detail, during each of the following five chapters.

The final chapter summarises the key themes throughout the whole book and brings them to a conclusion.

CHAPTER 8

There's no 'silver bullet'; Change is realised by doing many small things

Eddie Izzard popped up on my son's iPhone, which was being bluetoothed into the car stereo as we drove along, as part of the random shuffle mode; it was sandwiched in between a German thrash metal band and The Prodigy.

Because iTunes had randomly selected a track within an hour-long Izzard CD, the rambling muses that came over the speakers seemed even more wonderfully bizarre and thought-provoking as there was even less context than if I'd been listening to him from the beginning. He was rambling on about religion and talking about different gods in different cultures. He then went on to say that he felt the best religion had to be Hinduism as it had got *thousands* of gods which, he concluded, had to be good news as including every deity would ensure that "…no god would feel left out!"

I'm not trying to convey his wacky humour; it's one I like but, as with all comedians, humour is a personal taste. What the sketch reminded me of is the sense of confusion I had when on several occasions I've spent time in India and tried to understand the Hindu religion.

Hinduism has always struck me as a religion that couldn't have come from any other country than India. I'd always been fascinated by the idea of travelling through the sub-continent and when I first did so 20 years ago, I spent six weeks on trains and buses being completely subsumed by a riot of colours and smells and vast numbers of people and huge open spaces and poverty and richness and… an all-consuming intensity of vibrant life! This was my experience of India and when I've gone back it has never failed to give me a similar experience.

So Hinduism, with its thousands of gods and rich tapestry of colours, pictures and ceremonies, always strikes me as a wonderful all-encompassing explanation for the complexity and contradictory experiences of life. The religion seems to reflect, in part, an acceptance of the Indian way of life that, to a Westerner, strikes me as a strange mix. On the one hand there seem to be the ideals of flow, harmony and rhythm and yet, on the other, helplessness and an inability to affect the outcome of anything. At times there seems by some to be an acceptance of life, bordering on resignation.

Mark Tulley, the one-time BBC India correspondent, gave a radio talk once that summed up some of India's contradictions. He explained how he had been in the back of a taxi through the madness of Delhi's daily rush hour; the stop/start of the traffic had been replaced with no movement at all. This static position was slowly accompanied by a rising cacophony of shouting, horns blowing and general noise.

Tulley recalled that it didn't perturb him too much as this was India. So after a while he got out of the cab to stroll in the direction of the hold-up, expecting to see a cow munching on a vegetable that had fallen from the back of a truck, as such things were commonplace in bringing even dual carriageways to a grinding halt, as is still sometimes the case today.

Fate or destiny

However, on this occasion cows were not the culprit. As he got to the crowd surrounding what appeared to be the cause of the hold up, he pushed his way to the front to see a sight that he found quite horrifying. A teenage girl lay virtually motionless, but still alive, in a pool of blood. She'd been hit by a car. What made the sight unusual to Tulley's Western eyes, even having lived in

"Why was nobody comforting the girl? The replies were along the lines of, 'This is her fate, it would be wrong for us to interfere'."

India for as long as he had, was the fact that nobody was attending to the girl; everyone was simply standing and watching.

Tulley said that he had, in somewhat panicked terms, asked if the ambulance was on its way, what people were doing, why was nobody comforting the girl? The replies were along the lines of, "This is her fate, it would be wrong for us to interfere". Eventually someone did call an ambulance but the girl was dead when it arrived.

Mark Tulley offered this story as an insight into a mindset he still found excruciatingly difficult to understand, while stressing it was not universal within Indian culture. He acknowledged that having come from a Western sensibility, where all things that aren't 'right' can and should be fixed and often in a singular 'righteous' way, profoundly different approaches seem an anathema. This approach to 'the way of doing things' lies at the heart of what some bands of missionaries set off with, as their guiding principle. In many cases, it resulted in destroying other cultures, mainly because those cultures were simply different, not worse.

The Western mindset is so hard to understand when, like me, you are a Westerner, as it's the water I swim in, it's all-pervading, it's all I really know. And yet through glimpses into other worlds, different mindsets, it's possible to realise that there are different ways of understanding the world.

The Western way is often reductionist, rational, and frequently works on the premise that there is, or should be, a single optimum solution to most problems, hence the emergence of the 'silver bullet' theory. There is something so deep within this way of thinking that we'll often assume there is a *one* way, a best way, a singular way to affect what are often very complex and subtle situations. Even with the benefit of history and a littering of countless 'right' ways that often didn't work, or may have done for a while but were slavishly stuck to for too long, we still don't seem to learn very well.

Surfing and corporate governance?

Fad Surfing in the Boardroom by Eileen C. Shapiro has to be one of the most eye-catching book titles I've come across. The book simply lists in chronological order most of the management and change management fads over the years. Who came up with the idea, what they were supposed to address, which period of time were they held as being 'most in favour' and at which point did the idea decline in popularity.

The book starts with a time and motion study in the 1920s and goes through such things as transactional analysis, total quality management, right through to business process reengineering, downsizing, strategic planning, etc. I remember the colleague who brought the book into the office, who was also a change management consultant. He sat down, threw the book to me and, as I flicked through it, we both found ourselves giggling uncontrollably. We also recognised that there was a nervous discomfort behind our laughter.

It was only when looking through the whole panoply of management ideas and fads that two conclusions become very apparent. Firstly, within the descriptions of each fad and particularly with the guru or consultant who developed or branded the fad, there was, in most cases, a sense of 'eureka' style enthusiasm that *this* time, *this* person, had found *the* answer. And yet as we read the book our experience at the coalface made their 'silver bullet' idea seem either stale or obviously inadequate.

The other conclusion was that reading all of the fads in this précised format left us with another conclusion that *collectively* the effect of *most* of these ideas on an organisation would almost certainly have a *profound* effect if targeted towards specific objectives.

In other words, it was the multi and varied approaches that couldn't be neatly written down in *one* theory, but **together,** that seemed to ring true. Simply, a holistic approach seemed to be the realistic one to produce believable results and yet, if the route could not be explained in a simple 'monotheistic' theory, then it somehow seemed to fall into the 'Hindu religion' end of the religious spectrum in trying to be 'all things to all situations'.

Whole or hole

It's curious how the word 'holistic' seems to have got a bad press, or at least a wishy-washy press. Maybe it's because holistic medicine has connotations of alternative, non-scientific ideas, aspects of which people can easily pick 'holes' in. Perhaps that's it. Perhaps spelling holistic in the same way as we spell hole is the problem; perhaps it ought to be 'wholeistic'.

Again it probably boils down to a view (some would say a predominantly Western view) that the way we best make sense of our world is to compartmentalise things and keep all the components separate. We have traditionally done this with our health.

We go to see a doctor if there's something wrong with our bodies; church or its equivalent fix our souls, and education develops our minds.

We do intrinsically know that the three aspects of us as human beings are connected and yet we often find it is difficult to accept the interdependence of how affecting one aspect of who we are does affect another. It's almost as if for a problem there must be a single cause. It often takes extreme situations to see that this is usually a simplistic and unrealistic position to take.

For instance, I watched one of the many makeover programmes on television recently. It had 'extreme' in the title which I remember injected a sense of caution for me and my finger hovered on the remote control button, wondering whether I was prepared to watch.

It followed the fortunes of a morbidly obese person and in one scene the individual was engaged in a heated argument, berating his doctor for not making him well, whilst refusing to accept that curbing the intake of vast quantities of food was any business of the doctor's, nor was it related to his state of health! I hit the remote button as it felt too painful to watch such a gross state of denial.

This extreme example only sought to point out what happens around us most of the time, the refusal that many of us unwittingly have to accept the subtle and multi-various ways that affect a situation being the way it is. This multi-various cause must in most cases be matched by a multi-various approach when trying to bring about change for the better.

Sustainable change is rarely brought about by one big silver bullet; it is usually achieved by addressing many small things in a mindful and targeted way, over a prolonged period of time. This realisation became clearer to me recently when I took a friend to Tate Modern. She was someone who believed she hadn't a great interest in art and didn't feel 'qualified'

"It is difficult to accept the interdependence of how affecting one aspect of who we are does affect another."

to wander around the galleries. I suggested that it might be interesting for her to suspend notions of what art was and her own judgment about herself in relation to art, and simply stand in front of pictures that interested her in any way.

I then suggested she observe what emotions she felt in relation to each piece. She tentatively agreed to do this and I was exhilarated to observe a freshness of response to the paintings she felt drawn to. Her face lit up or contorted, she stepped forward or moved back to each 'naïve' or 'pure' reaction.

Impressionist making an impression

One of the paintings that she was most taken with was *The Lily Pond* by Monet. She, like many, was used to seeing the image on a postcard or a poster but to experience the painting in the flesh was quite a visceral experience. She came to realise that the 'complete' image in her mind was only fully achieved depending on how far away she was from the canvas.

Too close and she saw "all those jagged and disconnected brush strokes with strange shades of paint that you don't see on lily pads." As she stepped further and further away from the painting, the individual stroke that seemed disconnected and in some cases wrong when viewed close up, slowly merged to produce the rich vibrant image she was familiar with but which appeared more powerful when looking at the original.

After a long time transfixed by the painting, standing at what she felt was her optimum distance, she turned to me and said, "How did he know where to put all those disconnected brush strokes?" She went on, "He didn't paint lily pads, he seemed to scatter paint in a disconnected way; how clever of him to know that it would produce this beautiful image."

This experience reminds us that most things we see in life, be they the making of a car and all its thousands of component parts, the building of a 'home' from plumbing to brick work to decoration and soft furnishings, or the creation of an organisation from its people, to desks, to processes, to output; all of these examples are collages of individual 'brushstrokes' that produce the illusion of a company, or a car, or a home. Yes, it exists but the closer you get to it the more you can see the brush strokes and the more you should be able to understand its component parts and how they fit.

This truth is particularly important when it comes to bringing about change within a group of people, be it a family, a company or any form of organisation.

As we discussed earlier in Part One, 'organisation' is connected to 'organic' and 'organism, a body with connected interdependent parts sharing common life' – one of my favourite dictionary definitions. It sums up beautifully the connection between the separate parts and, crucially, their interdependence in producing the whole. In fact, when we see any 'thing', they are all things that we see or refer to, with our over-arching label, yet when we start to think about them we know that all of those 'things' are only the sum of the individual parts. It is easy to forget that affecting one or two component bits of the whole will have an overall effect on the whole entity. Some component bits are more obvious in affecting change than others.

More than the sum of the parts

A lot of people would think of a car as a discrete item rather than stopping to realise than it is made up of thousands of component parts. If, for example, a family saloon wasn't being as efficient in its fuel consumption as you'd expect, unless you are of a mechanical leaning you may take your car to the garage and ask them to look at the engine. I remember doing just this in my youth, expecting them to do something with the carburettor or other bits I'd heard my more mechanical-minded friends identify as being critical to optimum efficiency.

To my surprise, when I went back to the garage, the mechanic who was slowly wiping his hands on his oily rag announced in a knowing way that my engine was in good nick and nothing needed adjusting. He paused for a few seconds to enjoy my expression of confusion and disbelief, as his news sat uncomfortably with my experience of the car's fuel efficiency having been poor.

With perfect timing of someone who knew his trade, he spoke just before I uttered my confused question. "TT," he said. "Sorry?" I replied. He said quietly, "Tracking and tyre pressure."

I had no understanding that my tracking was out and was even more surprised that the steering pull as a result, which I was unaware of, would affect my fuel efficiency. Likewise, I didn't realise that insufficient air in my tyres meant using more petrol.

Many years later I found myself, metaphorically, playing the role of the oily-ragged mechanic. I was trying to explain to a confused board of directors that the primary cause of the inefficiency they'd asked us to investigate was to do with building architecture and their use of space, rather than systems and process, which is what they were expecting.

The company had started the change project, due to their market share starting to decrease. Their overall efficiency was also identified by the company as an additional target of change, in order to make the company more competitive again.

Interdepartmental communication was a vital part of this efficiency drive, as the differing disciplines and departments had become relatively insular and siloed in their mentality. It was not surprising therefore that the directors felt that improving process, i.e. the actions that each department did and how those actions connected between departments, should be the key focus of attention.

So a lot of time and effort was spent trying to improve these processes but, a bit like the silver bullet, it was a mistake. All their eggs seemed to be put in one basket and the results were poor.

To us, coming into the organisation from the outside, certain things seemed blatantly obvious, which to them was part of their 'wallpaper', or the water they swam in; they were blind to them in many ways. For instance, the managers all had small 'rabbit hutch' offices with nameplates including the letters of their degrees after their name on the doors. Some departments were in different buildings and email was the preferred communication; picking up the telephone was rarely thought of, let alone going to see a colleague from another department, unless it was pre-planned. There were so many 'mini-meetings' that it was amazing anything ever got done.

Physical environment affects behaviour

We were aware that the company as a whole was expanding and a new building on the organisation's campus was close to completion, at least as a shell. We proposed that the three key departments that needed to work more closely together move from their separate buildings into the new building and that the rabbit hutch offices that were planned were replaced with a greater mix of open plan space and small meeting rooms to be used on an as-and-when-needed basis.

This proposal was greeted as though a cultural bombshell had been dropped but, more worryingly, most of the senior management couldn't see the connection between the proposal and the problem. Their mindset was so ingrained in believing that the way they were physically configured was right for no other justifiable reason other than that's the way it had always been. So following the principle of mindful **awareness** then **responsibility** *before* **accountability,** we backed off from trying to convince them and spent time talking to the majority of people within the departments.

The majority view of the rank and file was that the only way to overcome interdepartmental misunderstandings and rivalry was to get to know each other better. They also felt that better processes and slicker systems, by themselves, would probably make little difference. After this weight of opinion, the departmental directors were still unsettled by the potential infringement of 'departmental fiefdoms'.

However, they eventually saw that the benefits outweighed their fears and so the departmental directors eventually agreed to moving the departments into the new building, as long as it could be seen as a nine-month experiment. If it was proved, as many senior managers believed it would be, that the departmental learnings would be lost and the sense of identity within each of the three disciplines would be diluted, then the departments could go back to their old buildings and the proposed occupants of the new offices would be allowed to take up their promised residency.

Interdependence needs to be *experienced* as crucial, not just as a theory

During those nine months after the moves had taken place, processes *were* improved *and* a new interdepartmental system installed but, to the amazement of many, the biggest contributing factor to efficiency and a re-energised culture was the natural 'mingling' of the three departments within the same building. People had to walk past the desk of someone from a different department in order to get to a colleague and on the way would stop and have a casual chat about what they did.

> "The departmental directors were still unsettled by the potential infringement of 'departmental fiefdoms'."

These ad hoc inter-departmental conversations revealed that perceptions of what people did was, in many instances, at odds with how the person had previously 'held' the other discipline. Many of the chats started to take place and the cumulative effect led to a sense of understanding, not just of the other departments, but of the true interdependence of the three disciplines. The overall conclusion was that what each department was there to achieve was, in very practical terms, pretty worthless unless it dovetailed with what the other departments were doing. Obvious to most on the outside of any organisation, yet this clarity is so often lost when you're in the middle of it all.

Understanding the subtlety of the component parts within change is not always easy and often requires objective help from those not in the cut and thrust of the areas that need to be affected.

No 'silver bullet' diet, either

In recent years there has been an explosion of programmes on television and articles in the press to do with health, fitness, variation of food, what's healthy, what's not, etc. At last, most of us seem to be getting the point that being fit and healthy is achieved through addressing a whole range of issues; there is no one silver bullet to fitness, either.

Mixing sachets of powder with apple juice plus taking supplementary vitamins and minerals three times a day for a week was considered an acceptable, if radical, form of weight control in the 1980s. I remember a friend of mine explaining with a degree of evangelical zeal that all his fitness issues would be solved by this miracle seven-day regime. It sounds bizarre now.

'Three to five thirty-minute sessions of aerobic exercise per week' is a phrase that my teenage kids are aware of, such is the mindset shift of today regarding fitness and health. I've also heard my children regularly saying that they've just had a banana or an apple instead of another bag of crisps, as they have 'only had three of their five a day'. So finally, many of us are getting the point that guidance such as 'eat a balanced healthy diet', 'everything in moderation' and 'a little bit of what you fancy does you good' is placatory and probably misleading if we are to be truly fit and healthy. Defining what 'fit' and 'healthy' means in specific terms and how to affect it in the round is the key.

It's not always the obvious

When companies try to bring about change, it's the subtle and often that which isn't obvious that will need to be addressed. This, alongside the obvious, all done in integrated and considered ways, over quite a long period of time and with the **willingness** of those involved, is all necessary if change is to be sustained. It's this 'wholistic' and integrated approach that will ensure the organism/organisation is addressed in a rounded way.

In conclusion, the desire for progress can mean an unhealthy emphasis on progression of the obvious, sometimes at the expense of changing the useful and subtle. Of course it all depends on what you are trying to change or what the driver is for change. And does it feel choice-led or imposed?

On an individual level, moving house or preparing for a planned family are changes that are quite different from negotiating your way through a divorce or changing lifestyle because of illness. **Mindful choice** in the change process, as we have discussed, is a key factor.

When it comes to bringing about change within an organisation, again mindful and choice-led, rather than imposition is key. When companies come together, the words 'merger' and 'acquisition' are often used in the same breath, as though they are interchangeable. And yet, working with many companies who have gone through this process, one always feels like the acquirer, i.e. dominant and the other always feels like the acquired, i.e. more powerless. Other planned changes will generally be felt as positive, i.e. expansion, moving into different markets, etc. or negative/threatening, e.g. the industry sector has become lacklustre, new practices mean a reduction in staff or the market has shrunk and so has production.

So there are no single silver bullets, there may be many of them if used collectively. It's important not to simply change the obvious as opposed to the important. This approach can create the illusion of change, as effective as just moving the furniture around.

Organisations are made up of many component parts and it is understanding what to affect and when that will make the difference to the desired outcome; if not, change may be reduced to a frothy and disruptive diversion.

> "The desire for progress can mean an unhealthy emphasis on progression of the obvious, sometimes at the expense of changing the useful and subtle."

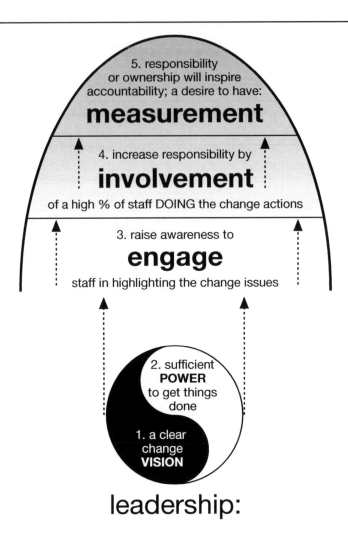

5. responsibility
or ownership will inspire
accountability; a desire to have:

measurement

4. increase responsibility by

involvement

of a high % of staff DOING the change actions

3. raise awareness to

engage

staff in highlighting the change issues

2. sufficient
POWER
to get things
done

1. a clear
change
VISION

leadership:

THE 5 GOLDEN RULES FOR
choice-led change

nos. **3**, **4** & **5** are the application of the **3** key principles

CHAPTER 9

Implementing mindful change: Introducing the outline of the five golden rules

'Looking back on it, hindsight is a wonderful thing.' I missed the irony of this phrase for quite a while when I was young. Given my surname, a variation of this phrase, 'In Hynd-sight', has sometimes been suggested to me as a title for an autobiography, should I ever think of writing one; on second thoughts, a bit cheesy! Driving between clients gives me an opportunity to listen to the radio and Radio 4 has become quite a companion for me over the years. Recently there was a discussion programme exploring the art of the good autobiographer.

One of the points that came up time and again in the discussions was the observation that when a life is researched and written down it can often assume a form or pattern that appears to be pre-destined or orchestrated. There are of course some extraordinary individuals who map out their lives in great detail and manage to follow the map. For most, however, there is at best a series of general directions followed to a greater or lesser extent, dependent on changing desires and objectives.

This is how the ideas in this book evolved. It has been through a series of circumstances and observations that the ideas we've looked at so far were 'uncovered'. Sometimes by trial, sometimes by error, and then by retrospective observation to make sense of it all.

It is this retrospective observation of client engagements over the past 30 years, rather than laboriously constructed academic theories, that has given rise to the key principles and now the five golden rules I am about to explain.

The first two golden rules are so intertwined that it is difficult to explore them in isolation.

VISION and **POWER** are needed initially for change to *start* and for change to be followed through.

A musical interlude

There are some bands or tracks of music that are evocative of a certain period in your life. They can take you back to your youth or certain events and as rock and roll and popular music has become the new establishment, there are almost five decades worth of genres and memories to draw on.

However, there are many bands and albums that are so much 'of their time' that, regardless of their success, they don't seem to translate into the nostalgia market. The Beatles, The Rolling Stones, Glen Campbell, The Jackson Five: these are all incredibly diverse and yet regularly featured on the BBC Radio 2 playlist of music down the years. Quintessence, Camembert Electrique or Gentle Giant are, in case you didn't know, names of bands that in their time were also quite iconic in their own field and yet obscured now by time and profound changes in musical fashion.

Occasionally an album comes along that achieves tremendous success in its time but within a few years has almost been forgotten and almost certainly wouldn't get airtime on drive-time radio. *Tubular Bells* was one such album.

When Mike Oldfield had the idea of writing, playing and producing *Tubular Bells*, record labels didn't seem interested. Such music seemed a risky departure for many, but for the fledgling Virgin Records it was manna from heaven. The long-term success of this record label was founded on this unlikely album and for many 'young' labels replicating such success with other artists would have been vision enough.

Vision: ability to see what others often can't

Power: ability to make it happen

The ability to combine hobbies or personal interests with business is a great gift; to others, Richard Branson's interests of music and flying seemed disparate bedfellows. The history of the Virgin success is well documented and yet there is just one aspect I want to focus on here as it illustrates these first two golden rules of vision and power very well.

As the Virgin empire started to expand, the fledgling Virgin Atlantic, Virgin Records and Virgin Megastores were all doing well. Such is the nature of an airline, Virgin Atlantic needed a huge investment of capital if it was to make the break from small time operator to medium-sized carrier. The classic route in such circumstances is to float the company and raise the required expansion capital via the City and shareholders. So when Branson decided to float Virgin Atlantic it seemed the logical and, to some, the only route.

Of course every action has a range of consequences and one consequence of a flotation that many entrepreneurial starters of businesses struggle with is the transition from being their own master to that of being answerable to shareholders. Richard Branson struggled with this, as have many entrepreneurs. He wanted to steer Virgin Atlantic in the direction of *his* vision, what he envisaged it to become. It became increasingly apparent to him that this was at odds with the kinds of risks shareholders and the City were prepared to stand. **What happened next is a classic example of someone finding a choice in what appears to be a no-choice situation.**

Branson's solution was unusual and brave, although at the time many thought it was foolhardy, even naive. He decided to sell Virgin Records, the vehicle that had provided his initial fortune and was felt by many to be a much more stable business; but sell it he did and with the proceeds of the sale he bought back Virgin Atlantic.

Not only was this a brave move but he must have realised that there was no going back. The capital investment needed to expand and sustain a privately-owned airline in a world where state-owned airlines were still the norm was immense. At that time, the recently de-nationalised British Airways, although not state-owned, had the power base of a national carrier and was a formidable opponent; it looked like a David and Goliath situation but before the sling shot was used!

The rest *is* history. This move by Richard Branson and his subsequent determination and tenacity is a perfect example of somebody having both the **VISION** and the **POWER** to bring about change. Although every change opportunity in business may not be as dramatic as the Virgin example, experience shows that all change projects rise or fall on the combination of a clear and unwavering vision, i.e. the ability to see a tangible, measurable future balanced with enough power or clout to bring it about.

Taking your people with you

The remaining three golden rules govern the ways in which the key principles of awareness, responsibility and accountability manifest and play their part in delivering change that is real and sustained.

So, you may have a clear leader or sponsor who can see that things have to change and also has a pretty clear idea as to what the outcome might look like. This is not enough; they also need to have sufficient political and individual 'nous' or power to get things done. However even these two are rarely enough by themselves. Mindfully taking the rest of the organisation, or a critical chunk of it, with you is key, and so finding ways to turn raised **awareness** into **ENGAGEMENT with a swathe of the workforce is the third golden rule.**

Many companies these days talk about 'their people being key to their success.' This and other similar phrases are so easily eroded by various perceived gaps in impact between what a company says and what is experienced.

The first brochure that my company produced had a cartoon on the cover. It wasn't based on any two particular individuals but was an amalgam of sentiments that had been expressed 'behind closed doors' to me and my colleagues by several directors of different companies.

The cartoon featured the face of a managing director talking to the face of a financial director. Both had a speech bubble and both also had a thought bubble. The MD was saying to the FD, "People are our most important asset," and the FD's spoken reply was, "I couldn't agree more". However, the MD's thought bubble read "I wish my shareholders believed this" and the FD's thought bubble read "...Yeah, I wish it was an asset whose depreciation I could write off against tax."

Now this level of cynicism will vary and some would argue that they would, or do, champion the importance of people within their organisation. The problem occurs when it comes down to *engaging* people in change. As the speeding analogy in the first part of the book established, people need to be **aware** of change *before* they buy into it. When it comes to *their* jobs, *their* working practices, *their* culture, simply telling them about changing anything, or even the need to change things is, by itself, unlikely to achieve real buy-in. It has just occurred to me what a curious phrase 'buy-in' is. What would it take for people to become so aware, so engaged with the need for change within their organisation whereby they would pay money out of their own pocket to literally purchase or *buy-in* to a period of change? There have been some *rare* examples of difficult periods of change where staff have volunteered to forgo wages for a period of time in order for a company to survive, but this is an extreme situation.

Help people find their own vision within the context of the leader's vision

How change is achieved (and I'll explore this in more detail in Chapter 12 on Engagement) must be directly proportionate to the change outcome and have a real relevance to the workforce as *they* see it; their vision, if you like. This is sometimes regardless of how powerful the leader is or how inspiring is their vision. Without a critical mass of people feeling as though they *want* to engage in the changes required, out of a sense of mindful choice, to things they have helped see or identify, then resistance and resentment to varying degrees are unavoidable. The chances of the two 'visions' being very different are slim; more on this in the next chapter, Chapter 10 on Vision for change.

INVOLVEMENT is the fourth golden rule and it mirrors the second key principle of ownership or **responsibility**.

In many ways, the real hard work, if done properly, will have been achieved in the previous stage. If a critical mass of the workforce has been successfully **engaged with the process of change** and, as a result, has helped identify *what* needs to change, there is every chance that they'll have created an enthusiasm and willingness to be **involved** with bringing those changes about and implementing the doing of things differently. This will usually dovetail with the vision of the sponsor of change, the one with the power and sense of desired outcome.

Chicken feed

Sun Valley Foods (owned by Cargill, the world's largest privately-owned food company) was the largest producer of chicken in Europe when we worked with them in the 1990s: from the farms they owned, to the processing plant, to the industrial-scale cooking and packaging factory. They produced chicken for KFC, McDonald's and Marks and Spencer.

Several of the directors had started to realise that managerial efficiency could and should be improved and lay at the heart of evolving the business. The problem was that the middle managers thought that where there was a problem it lay with the directors and the directors in turn believed that the middle managers were mainly to blame. After working with senior directors for several months, we finally convinced them to conduct a survey across all the senior and middle management of the company.

We wrote the questions in ways that related to the values set which the company had recently launched. This meant that the questions had recent relevance to a set of values which had been defined by the input of most of the company. The questionnaires were filled in anonymously and we were the only ones, initially, who got to see the results. The statistical analysis of all the answered questions was done in such a way as to give a percentage favourability figure to each set of questions and, in turn, each group of questions relating to all five company values were also laid out, with their percentile scores.

We then assembled the entire management – middle, senior and directors – into one room. Rather than focusing on the change issues that we'd been called in to address, which had led to the blame 'ping-pong' between senior and middle management, instead we went through the survey results.

Wanting to be involved in implementing changes

The favourability scores revealed figures that hovered between no more than 73% and down to as low as 22%. The percentage scores were an average of *all* management. The average scoring of *all* the groups was also calculated, producing a figure of X%. After explaining all of the scores to each section of questions and then how the single average figure was arrived at, we simply put the X% number on a flip chart and asked, "Do you want to be an X% successful company in the eyes of its management?" This had a dramatic and stunning effect.

As the results were unveiled, one by one, a murmuring rose out of the gathered throng that was quite different from the 'tit for tat' blame of the previous few months. People started to use phrases like "*We* have some serious issues here" and "I didn't realise *we* had so many things to address" followed by "*WE* have to sort this lot, *WE* can't allow this to continue."

That single morning's session was a profound turning point. We had gone from the problems being identified but no-one being prepared to take ownership for them, to a situation where the collective 'we' had overtaken managerial dividing lines. Individuals were offering themselves to be responsible, to take unilateral ownership if necessary to change things for the better. *This was mindfulness on a collective scale.*

They went on to recruit others in the company into various working groups, to tackle the different aspects of what needed to change. They then followed through into implementation of these ideas, in many practical ways and over several months. The collective effect was to bring about the changes the company needed, rather than managers disagreeing on where to start, which was happening when we arrived.

MEASUREMENT is the fifth golden rule, and is the manifestation of the third key principle of **accountability.**

Once a sense of ownership or responsibility has been translated into practical **involvement** in change, then the final golden rule of measurement/ accountability tends to follow fairly easily. The alignment of people **engaged** with identifying the problems and the solutions, resulting in them wanting to be **involved** with actually bringing about the changes, is at the centre of creating mindful choice-led change.

Why 'choice-led' change? As we've explored previously, business may not be a democracy and yet taking the time to engage people in a problem, and involving them in fixing the solutions, will produce far more sustainable results than imposing changes upon a resistant and confused workforce.

> "I didn't realise we had so many things to address" followed by "WE have to sort this lot, WE can't allow this to continue."

Holding people accountable for changes in, say, 'working practice' when they didn't want to bring about the changes in the first place is always going to be an uphill struggle. But if you get people *so* **engaged** that they feel they've written the script, and **involved** in delivering changes in ways that give them tangible satisfaction, then they will want to offer themselves to be **measured**, or held accountable to their peers and to their bosses as a way of wanting to be acknowledged for tangible progress, a job well done.

The managers at Sun Valley Foods weren't aware of these five golden rules. The MD had the **vision** and he also had the **power**, both by personality and position. But it was the raising of awareness leading to **engagement** of the vast proportion of his managers, and the **involvement** of many more in the practical actions of change that they all drove out of choice, that led to tangible and **measured** results. **These were aspects of mindfulness in action and on a collective scale.**

It was only in retrospect, when I pointed out the five stages, that they were recognised, but as with most business models, I happen to think that they are only useful when drawn from observation of what tends to work, rather than thought up as a theory for people to conform to. These five stages and how they overlay with the three key principles are born out of observation of how and when change has worked.

During the next five chapters I will be exploring in some detail the practicalities of how these **five golden rules** have been put into practice.

CHAPTER 10

The first golden rule: Vision for change

It sounds obvious and yet it's worth stating that, in order to embark upon a piece of planned change, it's critical to define why you are doing it, what it is you hope the change will achieve.

There have been lots of definitions by consultants, gurus and writers on the definitions of purpose, mission, vision, strategy and many other words used to describe what people and organisations are about, want to achieve or stand for.

Getting some clarity on the distinction between what an individual and an organisation stands for, its reason for being and what it wants to achieve in the foreseeable future is particularly important in relationship to planned change.

Here are definitions that I have found useful for these three: purpose, vision, mission and strategy.

PURPOSE

'Purpose - a reason for being': probably the most succinct definition I've found yet a few more pointers may help us to get a sense of what this short phrase means and doesn't mean:

1) A statement that describes what a group of people or a company is about, its reason for being.

2) It should always have an emotionally inspiring component if it's to engage people.

3) It should be aspirational and never ending.

4) Everything the organisation does should be tested against the statement.

NASA is often quoted regarding vision, which I'll come on to shortly, yet few know NASA's purpose statement: *'To explore the universe for the benefit of mankind'*. This short phrase ticks all four boxes above. It says what NASA is committed to do, what it's about, i.e. to explore the universe. It has an emotionally engaging component with the words 'for the benefit of mankind', but crucially for the 'never ending' bit, it does *not* mention rockets or any inkling of *how* this purpose will be achieved, as this would be self-limiting, rather than 'never ending'.

Purpose is all about essence, not form

A manufacturing company producing electrical components for domestic consumer goods was started in the 1930s and, when we came to work with them, it was still being run by the son of the founder. The business had since been sold to become a branch of a large multinational, and yet the feel of the company was distinct, it had a strong culture. They had a statement which they called their 'statement of intent', but it was what I would define as a purpose statement as, again, it ticks the boxes above. It was simply this: 'We produce goods that our customers will be proud to use and that we are proud to produce'.

One of the things that made this statement live was a habit the owner's son had, who was still retained as the MD. As he walked round the factory, he would simply go up to people when they appeared to have done a good piece of work, *or* they'd done something that perhaps wasn't as good as it might have been and, without passing direct comment, would ask *with warmth*, "Are you proud of that?" He had the knack of saying it with a warm smile and holding the moment between himself and the employee. It was never patronising or accusatory.

"NASA's purpose statement: 'To explore the universe for the benefit of mankind'."

Just before the silence became too uncomfortable and, in most cases, before the person replied, he would simply say, "Thank you," and move on. When I first witnessed this, it struck me as strange. I couldn't wait to find an appropriate moment to talk firstly to an employee and then to a middle manager who had been on the receiving end of this question. What did they make of it?

They both said similar things: when it first happened they felt it a bit strange and also thought that perhaps he was trying to catch them out. They weren't sure whether it was a statement or a question, but they also both said that they took it now as an opportunity to pause and reflect and be their *own* judge, as they knew in their heart of hearts, when asked, whether the thing they were doing was something to be proud of or not. The MD never expressed *his opinion*, nor were they encouraged to answer the question out loud. It was simply an opportunity to pause and consider whether, at that point, their actions were making the statement of purpose real.

VISION

This is probably one of the most misused words when it comes to 'management speak'. "We are totally committed to serving the needs of our customers, whilst engaging in relationships with our partners to produce the highest quality of service, so that we can continue to be a world class player in this highly competitive global market"! OK, so this one isn't completely real, yet it is an amalgam of three statements from real companies: one was called a vision statement, one a mission and one a purpose statement and to me it all sounds like complete bullshit!

It manages to contain some of the key words the corporate speak experts seem to favour: 'partners, successful, global, customers' and yet it doesn't *move* me one jot, I don't know what they are about, what they will *actually* deliver, or how. A statement of purpose, even if it follows the guidelines outlined above, by itself is not enough to inspire and motivate.

It could be argued that human beings are here to grow, evolve, make some kind of difference. But without knowing what each individual is committed to *do*, within this broad canvas, it's hard to get too excited. The clue to vision lies in reminding ourselves of its literal meaning: *the ability to see*. A 'visionary' is one who can see the future, 'visual' is something I can see in front of me, or in my mind's eye, 'visible' equals apparent – they are all capable of being seen, therefore are tangible, measurable, and verifiable. So a vision should encapsulate something that can be achieved, that can be seen and so measured and verified and within a timeframe people can get their heads around.

'A man on the Moon and safely returned by the end of the decade'

Staying with NASA; its purpose was given direction and drive when in 1962, driven by the US government's purpose, *'to prove the superiority of the American way by beating the Russians to the Moon'*, JFK made one of the most famous pronouncements in recent history, *"We will formulate a mission to put man on the Moon and return him safely by the end of the decade."* (Notice the use of the word 'mission', more on that in the next section.)

The language JFK used was clear, tangible and measurable; in other words, people were in no doubt that by 31 December 1969 America would either have an astronaut back on earth who claimed to have walked on the Moon, or not. No ifs, no buts, no "We will strive to launch people near possible planets as yet unspecified, as soon as we can, and hopefully bring them back alive, as is our world class commitment to you, our customers"!

Not only was JFK's vision black and white, but the timing of the attempt was also important. Seven years is probably on the longish end of the time spectrum for most projects. Three to five years in corporate terms is the length of time that most people nowadays will tend to think of, both in terms of their own career and the 'visible' time window of the company they work for.

This project also stacks up **when held against NASA's purpose statement**. A man on the Moon and back safely by the end of the 1960s was one good way of manifesting the commitment of 'exploring the universe, for the benefit of mankind'.

MISSION

The word 'mission' is probably the most misused of the three words used in corporate mission statements, i.e. purpose, vision and mission. The majority of the hundreds of mission statements I have read tend to describe an open-ended statement of intent which is more akin to the definition I have offered of 'purpose' rather than **'mission: an operation designed to carry out the goals of a specific program or vision'.**

In the case of the JFK vision of a man on the Moon, the subsequent 'mission' NASA developed included the means to achieve JFK's vision by a certain date; the vital 'how', the 'Apollo Mission'. **So a 'mission statement' should really be a statement of HOW to deliver the WHAT.**[5]

A formulated **Mission** and the necessary tactics becomes a key part of the overall **strategy** to deliver the **vision**, within the on-going context of the never-ending **purpose**, or reason for being.

"You are invited to a strategic strategy conference"

In the early 90's we were delivering a change project for Microsoft UK. We hadn't been there long when a colleague and I were invited to attend "a strategic strategy conference." My colleague and I looked at each other and burst into laughter. We then simultaneously blurted out, "What does that mean?!" More importantly when we got there it became apparent that most in the room didn't know what it meant either! I later discovered that the conference convener had read the phrase in a management book. Typical of mindless management speak I thought.

At its core, the meeting was about how to work out or formulate their strategy, or the route by which they needed to achieve their goals and overall vision.

Strategy and its derivatives such as 'strategic' are much over-used words and often applied in ways that do not reflect their true meaning. In simple terms, I like to think of **strategy as a fancy word for route.**

In summary, whilst evolving a sense of direction a company should define a tangible and date-bound vision, (where it is going), then assess the truth of where the company is now, (often overlooked), then plot a route, (or strategy) between the two.

In this book I am not going to go into the detail on how best to write strategy, however remembering that 'strategy is a fancy word for route' is a good levelling phrase as a reminder for plotting a route or a 'shopping list' of stuff and actions to achieve the goals and targets needed to accomplish the

---

5 Another example: Desert Storm was the name of the mission to achieve the vision of a Kuwait free of Iraqi troops by the beginning of Ramadan.

mission. The list is likely to include staff or resources (staff levels, equipment, office space, investment etc), as well as actions (improved process, systems structure and attitude). How to include a critical mass of staff in co-creating aspects of strategy is detailed in the next two chapters on golden rules 3 and 4: ENGAGEMENT and INVOLVEMENT.

Another word on vision

As mentioned, visions do need to be **achievable and achieved, and then they must be replaced with the next one.** Too many 'stretch goals' that aren't achieved will become de-motivating. Conversely, once a vision *is* achieved, it's important for there to be a new vision, another description of how the next chunk of the organisational future will look. The next bit of the never-ending 'purpose', made real.

In the 1970s NASA were close to becoming a victim of their own success. The mistake they made was to realise their vision in July 1969 with the landing of the triumphant astronauts and their safe return, without envisaging what would come next, i.e. a new vision. All they knew how to do was to continue extending versions of the same vision and keep going back to the Moon. The increasing elaborateness of the expeditions, including electric cars on the Moon, playing golf on the Moon, all justified with important scientific experiments, started to wear thin on Congress, as public opinion started to become indifferent to yet more live pictures from the Moon, on endless television broadcasts. NASA had made the mistake of not coming up with an inspiring vision that could take the place of the one they had delivered.

You're only as good as your last vision

"NASA had made the mistake of not coming up with an inspiring vision that could take the place of the one they had delivered."

Fortunately for NASA, they realised their 'mistake' in the nick of time and started lobbying Congress for a budget to develop a reusable spacecraft. It was touch and go, but eventually agreement to fund the development of the Space Shuttle programme was agreed. They didn't make this mistake again.

It may be helpful to think of a mission statement as referencing a point on the horizon. It needs to be no further away than a speck on the absolute edge of people's horizon. If it can't be seen, it will be of little inspiration; too close to their field of vision and it will become overwhelming. Once I've bought into something I can see, probably within a three- to five-year time horizon, then the closer I get to it the more the need for a replacement vision on the 'new horizon line'.

Companies often fail to do this. Fulfilling 'next year's sales targets' or 'agreed percentage growth figures dictated by commitment to shareholder value' isn't a vision, that's just a fact of life. Replacing an inspiring goal as the last one is achieved is the key to an organisation maintaining visionary status.

NASA learned its lesson and as the Shuttle vision was becoming a reality they started to create the next 'horizon' in the form of the Hubble Space Telescope. At every point since then they have ensured that there is a new horizon not far behind the completion of the current vision, to ensure Congress keeps inspired enough to keep funding them, to manifest tangible chunks of their never-ending purpose.

Few of us, Elon Musk and Branson with his Virgin Galactic aside, are involved in organisations that send men into space or, some might argue, directly do anything for the benefit of mankind, but all of us can benefit from having a vision in mind.

Where to start?

How do you arrive at a vision that is inspiring and verifiable? Well, the start point has to be with purpose. If you're not clear about the company's reason for being in *essential* terms, apart from making money, then ask yourself what are *you* about? What *do* you stand for? I realise this isn't a question we spend a lot of time debating. As I mentioned earlier in the book, when was the last time you went down the pub with a few mates, ordered a round of drinks and said, "Right then, what's your purpose, what do you stand for?" It's probably unfortunate that the only time we universally get to reflect on what an individual stands for is at their funeral!

Notwithstanding a degree of natural self-effacing embarrassment, see if you can recall right now the charities you've subscribed to, the causes you have supported or would be prepared to do something for. It may be you have helped out at your kid's school or youth activity, that you've raised money for charity via a marathon, be it 26 miles or sitting in a bath of beans. It may be as simple as expressing your frustration and sense of injustice at items on the news, even if you realise you end up doing little about it.

All of these instances will be indications of what you are about.

Some people tend to express their statement of purpose in terms of their *values.* For the time being, achieving some mindful clarity about what you *personally* stand for is a sufficient departure point for you to start to formulate a vision, as the two need to be compatible for them to be real.

Several years ago, we were approached by the IT director of Barclays de Zoete Wedd, the forerunner of Barclays Capital. He knew things needed to change and couldn't quite formulate what and how. By a process of many conversations, over a couple of months clarity began to emerge.

The problem was that the IT division of any investment bank provides all the screens, all the software, the email, the fax and the telephone lines for all the traders to do their work. The problem was that the traders thought of IT in disparaging terms: reactive fixers when things went wrong. The IT director knew that their value was greater than this. The trick was to come up with a vision statement that would be sufficiently inspirational, while also realistic for a large IT workforce; initially it was not targeted at the traders.

Working backwards from a date-bound goal

After weeks of playing with words like 'we strive to be the provider of choice' or 'we will provide outstanding service for our traders', which made our skin creep, our attention turned to ways in which that industry measured itself because without a way of measuring improved service, changes made would be hard to see in visual terms. It became clear that the City is very much a place of 'emperor's new clothes' and that perception and confidence, to a large extent, rule over substance and hard facts. The purveyors of perceptions were, in many cases, pedalled by the journalists writing in the financial sections of newspapers.

> "I don't know what all the fuss is about. If I have a problem, I make a phone call and some T-shirt with a screwdriver comes and fixes it!"

One phrase became apparent to us at the time; in the majority of cases when a journalist wrote about Goldman Sachs, they would add in 'Goldman Sachs, the City's leading investment bank…' We enquired by what measure Goldman Sachs acquired this pre-eminent status. When we asked people we had worked with at other investment banks, as well as BZW, the conclusion seemed to be that over and above Goldman Sachs being one of the top *achieving* banks, its *number one* position was broadly agreed because journalists and other commentators were prepared to keep saying so!

So we devised a vision statement: 'By the end of 1997 the IT division of BZW will have had an unsolicited article, published in a financial broadsheet, declaring it to be the best in the City.'

Now this vision statement wasn't the most elegant and wasn't designed for public consumption; even the traders didn't get to see it but for the members of the IT division it suddenly started to crystallise what their actions had to be. They could work backwards from this statement, knowing what journalists are like and knowing what it might take to produce an IT division that was so outstanding it would warrant such an article.

They also started to realise the knock-on conclusion, that perception of them was a massive part of reality; so getting the traders on board would be a critical part of realising their vision of an article in the financial press. A simple one-page questionnaire was developed and it was sent electronically to all 4,500 traders. The accompanying context asked for feedback about IT and how to improve the service. Most questions were in the form of tick box replies with room for comment at the end.

It's hard to summarise the overall sentiment that came back, but one comment on one of the questionnaires gave us a benchmark for most of the other comments. It simply said, 'I don't know what all the fuss is about. If I have a problem, I make a phone call and some T-shirt with a screwdriver comes and fixes it'! This reply was indicative of the general mood of traders and seemed a long way from the glowing article the vision statement aspired to.

What's 'visually' inspiring to your colleagues, what would they like to see?

The clues to success lay in reading between the lines. The dismissive tone derived from the fact that most traders saw IT as subservient, mainly because they provided a predominantly reactive and fix-it service, in the absence of knowing what else to do. The turning point came when it became apparent that IT could offer 'tailor-made software packages' and/or bits of IT kit that would increase the percentage return of deals the traders were doing. Suddenly IT went from fixers of stuff that breaks to providers of tools that can make traders more money.

This took the IT guys into another universe for the traders. They started to perk up and dialogue started to happen between IT and the traders. In the end, the fixing and maintaining role of IT was not only improved but, over time, was taken by the traders as a given. What IT were interested in was the added value that their more proactive approach could produce to their company's bottom line.

The IT division went on to execute one of the biggest wholesale moves ever undertaken within the City, to Canary Wharf - a feat achieved without a single hour of trading time being lost. They were acknowledged in several newspapers as being 'outstanding' and 'one of the best IT divisions in the City of London'. These comments were printed before the end of 1997!

Other changes that may trigger a change management programme don't always lend themselves to a clear vision. Being merged or acquired is a prime candidate for a planned piece of change, so is expanding into a new market or having to diversify and expand sideways. In some instances, it's simply the case that the culture has become dull and needs re-energising.

The problem with all of these triggers for change is that, by themselves, they aren't automatically translatable into an inspiring outcome that is capable of being envisaged. Merging or acquiring another company to achieve what, apart from potentially increasing shareholder value? Expanding into another market for what specific benefit? Even re-energising the culture may seem more obvious but, for the cynics and the 'jobsworth' mentality within any organisation, the lack of a point to it all that they can see can leave them feeling as though the re-energised culture is an attempt just to shake everybody up for a while.

The key is to come up with a vision that will inspire.

There's another important factor to be aware of in relation to articulating a sense of vision statement.

The map is not the territory

The Long Mynd is a small area of rolling hills and moorland in Shropshire which, to my amazement, having grown up with it quite close to my native Birmingham, is an area many people aren't aware of.

Being the closest area of 'wild outdoors' to where I lived in my youth, it was the first place I was taken to with the Boys' Brigade to learn the skills of camping, hiking and map reading. The area appealed to the romantic side of me in my youth that wanted to believe that Tolkien's Middle Earth existed somewhere! To me, the Long Mynd has something of a time that is lost about it.

Many of the names of the Long Mynd seemed to echo my desire for this fantasy world to somehow exist. Names like Rattling Hope, The Wilderness, Wentnor-Prolley-Moor and The Devil's Chair all helped, along with little gated chapels in the middle of fields and thatched pubs, accessed only via single-track lanes. The problem for a 14-year-old BB member like yours truly, however, was often that of finding a way through miles of relatively featureless rolling moorland to get from one hamlet to another.

I remember having a heated debate with a couple of my fellow Boys' Brigade hikers on a practice expedition for our Silver Duke of Edinburgh's Award. We were tired and wet, we had been walking most of the day after a fitful night's sleep in a damp tent. We were desperate to get to our agreed second night camping place and yet the mist prevented us from seeing the full extent of the view from halfway down the hill we thought we were on.

The argument that ensued revolved around two of us trying to convince the third member of our party that the one building we could almost see in the distance *had* to be a village church and perhaps it was marked on the map as being a church *with* a spire before some storm or other had removed it, as appeared to be the case! Also, it was argued, the ridge to our left probably appeared much flatter than the one on our map because of the swirling mist. My friend and I overruled the lone voice of our third member and we continued along the route we believed to be the right one.

This heralded the beginning of a very long walk, halfway through the night, until we finally discovered that the spire of the church hadn't blown down and that in fact it was a stone barn belonging to a farm on the other side of the hill we thought we were on!

You can't plot a route to where you're going if you're not clear where you are.

This was one of many painful lessons in my youth that was summed up by the words of our Boys' Brigade captain who, with a sense of irritation and righteousness, greeted us when we eventually got to the campsite, with the comment, "Never make the landscape fit the map. If the map doesn't fit the landscape, you're in the wrong place!" This lesson and many other examples over the years, particularly when I came to pursue mountain running which involves orienteering, proved to me the importance of establishing *exactly* where you are, without deluding yourself, before you can plot any kind of course of future direction. This principle is as true in the context of conjuring up a vision as it is to traversing the Long Mynd.

So many companies conceive of a vision that may well be laudable but when it's seen in relationship to the position of where they *actually* are as of now, it can often be seen as unrealistic and therefore de-motivating. Having ambitious goals, targets and visions can be inspiring and motivating but there is a fine line between a stretch goal and one that breaks people's faith along the way.

And as mentioned, if strategy is a fancy word for route, then you can't plot a route or strategy without an accurate starting point, no matter how clear the end point might be.

This leads into a final thought: as well as establishing a clear vision in relation to a piece of planned change, formulated by the sponsor of that change (this usually means the leader such as a CEO or MD), **it's also important to help a critical proportion of the workforce to establish their *own* vision.** This statement may well sound contradictory to most of what I have just been talking about.

Experience has shown that these two approaches cannot only be *complementary*, but also critical if any vision is to be *agreed*.

"Never make the landscape fit the map. If the map doesn't fit the landscape, you're in the wrong place!"

How the vision of a leader/sponsor can be dovetailed with a broader view of a proportion of the workforce will be explored as part of the third golden rule.

CHAPTER 11

The second golden rule: Power

Power is one of those words that has acquired a range of negative connotations, such as 'power over someone', or 'power hungry', or 'all powerful', often meaning too much in the hands of too few.

For the purpose of understanding 'power' in this context, similar to what we talked about regarding 'empowering others', the word is offered out in its literal sense: 'power: the ability to act, or get thing done'. Having a vision of how a change will look is one thing but without the accompanying power or ability to get things done, the change will remain a vision unfulfilled.

Time out

Time is a fascinating concept. From a scientific viewpoint, intervals of time can be measured with seemingly ever-increasing accuracy. There are now atomic clocks which are so accurate that their *inaccuracy* requires so many decimal points over so many years that, for this relatively unscientific mind, it seems incredible.

However, for all our ability to measure time, our *experiences* of time can often be quite different. I have been in many work situations where, no matter what I do, there don't seem to be enough minutes in the hour, or hours in the day, to get everything done.

At the other extreme, as mentioned in the introduction of this book, I have attended many ten-day Vipassana Buddhist retreats to develop mindfulness. They were all conducted in silence, without eye contact, with no reading or writing materials, no interpersonal communication nor music devices and a regime of meditation from 4.30am, with breaks, until 9pm. Time in this setting can, at some points, feel never-ending! When I first read about this regime from a friend who had done the course, I received the information with a mixture of intrigue and 'this is madness'. Yet being someone who loves the challenge of a new experience, I decided to take part, although it took me *eight years* to get around to it!

It was a rollercoaster of a journey and ultimately extremely powerful. The point in mentioning it in this context is that, as I drove to the retreat, the thought of ten days with nothing to do and no distractions seemed, at the same time, a wonderful relief to escape from the world, but also terrifying. Time seemed to stretch in front of me like a never-ending void.

As I developed the mindful experience of living more in the now, time seemed less relevant as the past is time gone, and the future is time not here yet. Yes we can learn from the past and plan for the future, but if either of those are at the expense of living in the present...

Time: it's not what we have, but what we do with it

There are many experiences in life between the two extremes of lots of time on our hands and the more frequent experience that there are not enough hours in the day. Time, although finite, is one of those things, like money, that we often think we can somehow stretch and bend. Although this is an experience we can sometimes achieve, it will always have consequences. Managing time in your personal life and in a business context is a constant challenge and the outcome can leave us either feeling **powerful** or feeling like a victim. In many ways, social convention can derail our sense of reality around time.

How many meetings have you attended when you turned up late, or other attendees arrived late? And what do I mean by 'late'? There are many instances in my life when I've physically been where I agreed I would be within the time window, defined by the second hand on my watch, but experientially I didn't manage to 'arrive' until ten or fifteen minutes afterwards.

In most cases, being late is a function of reasonable excuses and insufficient intention. I'll understand if you bristle at those stark phrases and the voice inside your head makes comments such as 'what does he mean? I can't always get to where I need to be on time, I lead a very busy life, he obviously doesn't realise how much I need to do.' If it's any consolation, the voice inside my head spouts similar self-affirming excuses on a regular basis. It's only when I think of situations where being late is simply not an option, do I realise that I have choices even within those apparent no-choice, time bound situations and I mean *choices* other than just being late! The innate power to exercise degrees of intention that will overcome most 'reasonable' excuses is what needs to be harnessed. This is mindfulness once more.

Personal power to get things done

A great example is an airport. I know people do occasionally miss flights and yet most realise that if you get to the airport with insufficient time to spare, the aeroplane will take off without you – no ifs, no buts, it's just a fact. The aeroplane doesn't care. For most, doing what it takes to get to the airport on time is so ingrained that it's a non-option. And yet this 'power', this *pouvoir*, the ability to do or act when it comes to getting on an aeroplane, suddenly escapes us when it comes to being present, ready to engage, at the meeting that starts at 10am.

This point was rammed home to me by a Zen-like teacher I had when I was being trained to take large American-style personal development seminars in the 1980s. One of the disciplines being taught was what they called self-actualisation. It literally meant that you were encouraged to live what you said or talked about, literally, with *no discrepancy*.

When this came to time, if you agreed to be somewhere to start an activity at 3pm and you weren't there, in place, ready to kick off by at least 2:55pm, the door would be closed and you didn't dare enter! Excuses were useless; you weren't made wrong, as your physical actions were taken as a pure translation of what you **actually** intended, i.e. **not** to turn up on time. That intention was 'honoured' as your choice, with all the consequences that a 'choice' not to be there

> "You have free choice and the physical evidence doesn't lie, so how you actually show up in the world is your truth."

would imply. A phrase used a lot was, 'You have free choice and the physical evidence doesn't lie, so how you *actually* show up in the world is your truth, not what you talk about.'

Try, and get things done

This initially seemed a very harsh way of doing things! Until one day my teacher, somewhat frustrated at my lack of grasping this point, dropped a pencil on the floor in front of me. She then invited me to 'try and pick up the pencil'. I felt a bit confused, I knew there had to be a trick somewhere but I couldn't spot it. I looked around at my colleagues for clues but they looked as bemused as I felt. So after a little hesitation I bent down and picked up the pencil. The response was immediate, "No, no, no, I didn't say 'pick up the pencil', I said 'try and pick up the pencil!'" She took the pencil from my hand and put it on the floor with the same repeated instruction.

Now I was really confused! I bent down, my hand hovered but eventually, not realising what else I could do, again I picked up the pencil. Another instant response and similar to the first one, yet fortunately this time there was a slight glimmer of a smile on her face. She said, "You still don't get it do you? I asked you to *try* and pick up the pencil, like this," - and she proceeded to take the pencil from me, put it on the floor and stretched out her hand a few inches above the pencil. She then made lots of groaning and straining noises. After a while she stopped and said to me, "That's *trying* to pick up the pencil." She then calmly said, "Now please pick up the pencil," which, after a pause to think about the possible trick, I did. This time, once I had picked it up, she simply said, "Well done."

Power boils down to an internal mindful decision

The discussion that followed was long and detailed. We talked about an internal mindful decision that has to be made when you decide to do something, the intention and tenacity it takes when somebody declares they will walk unaided to the Poles, or they will cycle unsupported around the world, or they will bring about a specific piece of change within a company.

Or even what it takes to turn up to a meeting you agreed to on time. The difference between trying to do something, and actually doing it, is often a world of difference and requires a sense of POWER that has to be *claimed* and not assumed by dint of role or position.

I've worked with many holders of a vision for change who weren't natural or ultimate decision makers in the organisation. Likewise, I have also worked with a number who were in a position of power in terms of their title, CEO or MD, but who seemed unable to overcome all the logical reasons thrown at them preventing them from change, such as budget constraints, politics and fear of upsetting those around them.

Tenacity and a drive, **power** to get things done, despite a whole range of obstacles, are critical qualities that go hand in hand with a sense of **vision** if any kind of change is to be translated into sustainable actions.

What puts somebody into a position of power; is it a role or title? Is it an assignation? What proportion of it is grit or rank?

In the late 1970s and through into the early 1980s there was a mushrooming of personal development seminars in this country. The British media greeted many of them with a mixture of concern and contempt. These reactions were understandable as the British reserve was a lot stronger years ago and the notion of personal understanding and expression of things like 'emotions' and 'energy' were words that generated more cynicism in the British psyche than anything else.

Powerful is as powerful does

However, a friend of mine took a personal development course and rather than trying to sell the experience to me, which would have got my back up, she happened to point out a couple of things about me that nobody had ever said out loud before. In those days I had a habit of wearing a smile most of the time, even when I was talking about things that made me feel upset or angry. Of course, I didn't realise this discrepancy and yet, when my friend pointed it out, she did so in a very matter of fact and non-judgmental way. She suggested that if my facial expressions were more consistent with how I felt, i.e. to smile when I'm happy or relaxed, contrasted with the appropriate expressions when I'm feeling different things, I would come across as more real, more believable.

I was sufficiently intrigued by these simple observations to find out more about the workshop she'd attended, which I ended up enrolling on and taking part in. This proved to be a momentous decision for me, in that I became friends with one of the workshop facilitators and my fascination with the mixture of 'pop psychology', personal understanding and direct personal feedback was something that played to my long-standing interest in what makes people tick.

The courses needed people to assist in organising the logistics and to be trained as assistant facilitators. I enjoyed taking on these voluntary roles and, particularly, found it fascinating to observe how the facilitators worked with the individuals and marshalled these large groups.

After a year or so, the facilitator I befriended talked to me one evening and asked when I was going to put myself forward to be trained as a facilitator. I remember feeling slightly shocked and my reply included thoughts such as, "I don't know enough about psychology; I don't think I'm qualified to do what you do." He said that my training and experiences as a professional actor for the nine or ten years to that date gave me skills of presence and ability to communicate and that the psychology and philosophy behind it could be taught, if I was willing. I still felt a resistance to the idea born more out of fear than a lack of desire.

Are you powerful, or just practising?

At this point he took a long pause, looked directly at me and asked,

"At which point in your life do you want to be a master practising, as opposed to you practising to become a master?"

I probably choked on my crisps or whatever I was munching in the bar at the time; this phrase sounded a bit too profound for me. It took several repeats and some explanation before I got a sense of what it meant.

It started to dawn on me that this facilitator appeared to me to be a 'master' at what he did – not perfect, not flawless, but extremely accomplished and confident and yet I was surprised to learn in these discussions of his own insecurities and, at times, restrained confidence. Yet what lay at the core of his 'ability to do' what he did so well was so often driven simply by an internal decision that he *could* do it.

Nobody would ever give him the authority to 'be the master practising'; he had to give that authority to himself, while realising that he would be forever practising. We went on to discuss that many people spend large chunks of their lives practising or preparing to take the plunge, to take the power and do the thing they've always said they would but find that, in the absence of the authority or POWER to act being given to them, they are ultimately loathe to give themselves that authority.

Leadership really does boil down to individuals having the courage to act and make something happen despite their insecurities and failings. It can often appear that leaders are flawless and all powerful which is simply unrealistic and, in fact, undesirable as such a person would be arrogant and therefore dictatorial rather than inspiring.

So for a piece of planned change to take place, if you have the vision to see that it needs to happen, but nobody else you feel is doing enough about it, then what would it take for you to claim the authority, **to take the power to get things done**? Once this internal decision is made, then it becomes a question of *how*, rather than *if*.

Once you've decided, it's just a matter of how, not if

There are many 'hows' to overcome. One of the biggest obstacles is often that of budget. It is rare that a budget for change has been thought of in advance and, in some instances, it will not be politically acceptable to create a budget for change. In such cases, being creative with redefining existing budgets or arguing cost benefits over expenditure are challenges that need to be taken on if an individual's power is to overcome the many obstacles.

Having the power or courage to take on the arguments surrounding change is also important. Exploring the disruptive elements of change and the financial costs in the short term will be off-putting for many, regardless of the long-term value. In addition, how to battle through the politics of change and how to stay focused for the long term and avoid change getting derailed by the urgent over the important. These 'how' questions

"Many people spend large chunks of their lives practising or preparing to take the plunge but they are ultimately loathe to give themselves that authority."

are ones to which an individual who has taken the **power** and has the **vision** has to find his own answers, but they all start with the initial decision that things staying as they are is not an option.

One of the hallmarks of great leaders is their ability to be power-ful, i.e. full of the ability to act or get things done. The bad press surrounding the word comes into play again; many will hear the word and think that it infers 'power over' someone, as in the phrase 'power struggle'. It doesn't always have to be this way. Yes, there are many examples of world leaders who have tried to exercise power in an autocratic way: Hitler, Stalin and Mao are three examples of power that led to extraordinary suffering and negativity.

However, there are counter examples: Nelson Mandela and Mahatma Ghandi are two examples of people who were extraordinarily powerful in that they got a lot changed and done but without exerting power over other people. In many ways, their route to bringing about their vision was by being un-wavering about the outcome, but equally committed to creating the conditions of **empowerment** for those around them. Literally helping many people involved and committed to the cause to feel a sense of authority and accountability to each other, rather than the dictatorial power of control and fear by dictatorial leadership.

Having a leader who has a clear vision but also enough power to *enable* things to get done are the two intertwined factors needed if change is to be successful. They set the scene for the next stage of implementing change: **taking your people with you.**

CHAPTER 12

The third golden rule: Engagement

The third golden rule is where the rubber hits the road, where the nitty gritty, or the nuts and bolts of change, really starts.

The first rules of having a leader or sponsor of a piece of planned change who has a clear **vision** of what the change outcomes should produce, plus the **power** and therefore the ability to drive it through, are prerequisites. Beyond these two, getting as much of the organisation to help make the change happen is critical; without this, vision and power are of little use.

This third golden rule of **engagement** parallels the first key principle of awareness. We discussed earlier that if individuals truly understand what the real situation is, and they understand what may need to change, then awareness is more likely to be translated into them owning and taking responsibility for making the changes happen rather than them being driven from the top down. The question is how to raise this awareness, *sufficiently*, how to **engage** *enough* people within an organisation?

As a parent you learn many tricks to get your children to do what you want them to do. Striking the balance between helping your kids make informed choices and steering them towards the choices *you* want is a pretty consistent balancing act for most parents. How do you get the balance between giving a child complete freedom of choice on the one hand and avoiding a dictatorial command on the other? Of course it all depends on the situation; both of these two extremes have their place.

I remember trying to get one of my children to come on a walk one very blustery, autumnal Sunday afternoon. I initially made the mistake of saying, "Do you want to stay inside and watch television or come out with me for a walk down the lane?" As the words left my lips I knew I'd handed my child a no-brainer. No matter how much I sold the benefits of the walk, the cosiness of staying in and watching television was always going to win hands down, on this occasion!

We're going out... where do you want to go?

The following week a more seasoned parent gave us some advice, which we tried with reasonable success. At a suitable break in the television programming we turned off the television and announced we had an exciting choice for my five-year-old. It was waiting at the front door. He bought the bait and raced me to the entrance to find a choice of red Wellingtons or blue.

With as much excitement as I could muster I announced, "We're going on a walk down the lane, which colour welly boots do you want to wear?" Now we got away with it on that occasion, but it wasn't long before my children became far more savvy and those kind of tricks were overcome. But the principle of creating a sense of real choice in the face of what will *have* to happen is an important principle.

Over the last ten years or more my colleagues and I have experimented with various methods of creating engagement and strong buy-in for mindful change within companies. The following description is an amalgam of case histories that have taken place with a range of corporate clients.

If the vision for change is fairly obvious, i.e. the company is just about to be acquired or is just about to be merged, or maybe the company is to expand over a set timeframe which will mean obvious changes in the way they do business, then in those circumstances announcing a vision as a statement of *intent* will be a good starting point. However, in some instances the vision, as seen by the leadership or sponsor of the project, is more subjective, more subtle.

For instance, we have worked with several organisations where the vision for change was to 're-energise the lacklustre culture'; in other instances it was to 'differentiate our brand within the market place'. In these cases, the general awareness among the majority of the workforce of these objectives being tackled was not obvious or previously established so a slightly different approach was needed.

How to combine the first key principle of **awareness** with **engagement;** to engage enough of a workforce so they are *driving* change, not resisting it?

Traditionally, where there is an attempt to involve people within an organisation to feel engaged with the process, it is usually carried out within the context of gaining buy-in. People 'buying into change' is generally accepted as a good thing; however, as I mentioned before, **the *depth* of buy-in required** is often grossly underestimated. It's not necessarily the way in which buy-in is attempted, it's more to do with the level of understanding and commitment that is achieved.

How much buy-in do you need? Enough so they're demanding change!

Examining the methods generally used to create buy-in will help shed light on how effective they are. For example, conducting some form of employee opinion survey can be a valid attempt to find out what people within the organisation feel about the *status quo* and proposed areas of change.

Setting up focus groups or management forums where the areas of impending change can be discussed can then facilitate a two-way exchange of ideas.

Or in some cases it can be a series of carefully crafted top-down communications, explaining the context and background for the period of change that is to be embarked upon, while also explaining the perceived challenges and benefits hoped for. All of these methods will have an effect.

There is also an alternative approach to the list above involving an outside perspective. There can be benefit in bringing in the objectivity of external consultants who specialise in helping organisations see what they may have become blind to. With both these approaches there is a danger that, be it managers explaining change or consultants facilitating the notion

> "The depth of buy-in required is often grossly underestimated."

of change, in both cases it can still feel as though change remains an imposition, no matter how well it is framed.

If you have children, or you can remember back to your own childhood, then I expect you will have had an experience similar to this one. A parent tries to get the child to do something; it spirals into an argument, descends into a battle of wills and reaches a point of stalemate. A short period of time later, someone from *outside* the family talks to the child. During the conversation this stalemate is discussed. The outsider draws out the options from the child and the child concludes a course of action. The child then explains the course of action to the parent. Then, the parent throws up his hands in disbelief, while uttering words along the lines of, "But that's almost exactly what I asked you to do in the first place!"

'But I thought of it first!'

Now at this point the parent should have the grace to allow the child to continue to think that the similar, or even identical conclusions as the parent's are the *child's* conclusions. The fact that the child reached those conclusions in their own time, in their own way, and possibly with some outside help, should be allowed and acknowledged as totally valid. It is the reaching of these conclusions *in the child's own way* that is *precisely* the kind of awareness and consequent **ENGAGEMENT** with the issue that the parent initially sought to achieve. It's just that getting the outcome via the *child's* route, whilst a bit annoying for the parent, is engaging for the child; this is the key.

With the above analogy in mind, we developed the following process on a large scale within companies.

Firstly, we talked with the sponsor, the person with the power to implement change, over a period of weeks until they were clear what their reasons for change and vision of their future looked like.

There then needed to be a carefully crafted communication to the company, explaining that there was a planned piece of change on the way; for example a merger, acquisition, expansion, etc., and that 'objective specialists were to be used to help guide the process'.

Alternatively, if the reason for change was less specific, i.e. the culture needed to be re-energised or there needed to be clearer differentiation in the market place, then the communication would be more along the lines of 'We are using a group of external specialists to objectively assess how we are doing as a company.' This communication needs to stress that it is useful every so often, to carry out what may feel like a '20,000-mile service check' on the company to get a grasp of how the organisation is doing, according to the *people within* the organisation.

Draw out what *they* see as needing to change

The next stage is to carry out a series of confidential one-to-one discussions with, ideally, an external change expert, to achieve confidential objectivity. These need to be across a broad representative cross-section of the organisation. It needs to be an external company carrying out this process as it is very difficult to achieve confidentiality and real openness if the conversations are conducted by people within the company.

Likewise, it's critical to find a change consultancy that has good experience in the art of people and culture change and is experienced in interviewing people in supportive and constructive ways.

The selection of people chosen for the conversations is also important. It needs to reflect the organisation as a whole in microcosm, i.e. a proportionate mix of gender, all disciplines, all managerial levels and non-managerial, as well as people who have just joined, plus medium- to long-term servers. When compiling the list, ensure there are a few cynics as well; it's important not to try and skew the outcome by filtering these choices. The number of people interviewed is also important; between 30 and 40 within a workforce of 500-1000 would be a suitable number.

Finally, the chats should be free flowing; no scripted questions other than variations of two questions: "What works here?" and "What would you change?' An open dialogue around these two questions for up to an hour. Some will add to what they have said by email or with another shorter chat once they have reflected on things; this is to be welcomed and encouraged.

Where this approach was developed

We shaped and developed this process initially through being asked by Microsoft UK to develop a questionnaire that would fit within a European-wide survey of all employees. The key part of the brief was to overcome the entrenched cynicism and the feeling of being 'done to', that many in the organisation felt would be the response to a questionnaire if penned by senior management or outside consultants.

To get round this perception we proposed a fairly radical approach. We conducted a series of one-to-one discussions, each lasting up to an hour, without any script or questions. My colleagues and I had all been trained in NLP (Neuro Linguistic Programming) and other techniques to put people at their ease and draw them out.

The open questions we used were very broad and along the lines of: "Please tell me about your company, what works and what doesn't?" or "What would you celebrate and what would you change here?" In most cases, these initial prompts were more than enough to get people talking for all of the hour about most aspects of the company. Some of us wrote down everything we possibly could, others recorded the discussions.

Clear themes emerged: *their* questions, *their* themes

We then spent many weeks comparing the notes from these interviews and realised that there were very clear and common themes arising, of what employees wanted to change plus, in many instances, ideas of how to do so. They were also fairly consistent about the areas that they wanted to keep and even enshrine. It was from these notes that it became very clear to us, which questions needed to go into the survey.

We also put in at the end of the survey the question: "What *proportion* of these questions do you feel represents the most *poignant* areas of change within the company at this time?" They were given the choice of 'less than 50%', '60%', '70%' or '80% +'. The overall scoring of these questions from the final survey results was something *over* 80%, which told us the proportion of people who felt the questions used in the final survey were 'on the money'. So even the questions asked had been 'written' or at least guided by the employees, which meant that buy-in to the survey seemed to be high.

This whole approach was communicated in great detail, time and time again, over the months we were involved. It generated a waiting list of people who wanted to talk to us; people asked when the results of the questions written would be shared and also how soon the questionnaire would come out. It became a buzz of conversation within the company and the final results were greeted with a sense of excitement, a true sense of **response-ability** or ownership being created, in them *wanting* to do something about what had been mindfully **raised** in the survey; the workforce had become **engaged** in the process, BIG time and on their terms.

Re-energise the culture

We constantly develop and refine this approach for engagement.

An alternative approach, especially for smaller organisations, has been to dispense with the questionnaire part, which is still very useful for large numbers of employees, as long as the questions are written as a direct result of what comes up in the interviews. However, in some instances the interviews *themselves* can produce sufficient 'ammunition' to engage the company and provide clarity for action.

OMD UK is a media agency owned by the Omnicom Group. It is part of a vast international advertising and media network. The buying of advertising space across all media and the clever placement of the advertising message, within an empathetic environment, has become an extremely competitive spin-off from what the full-service advertising agencies used to provide.

Media agencies have to have extremely shrewd and clever negotiators to broker the competitive purchase of advertising space in such diverse environments as television, press, radio and the internet. Whereas the creative work of the advertising company is more easily appreciated, the more subtle art of creatively deciding where these ads are placed falls mostly to the media agency. Placing a Nike football ad in the middle of a premier match would be an easy one to work out, a holy grail, if it could be afforded. But where best to place yet another detergent ad, in what media and at what time of day?

This is the world that OMD UK inhabits and the MD, after many discussions with us, concluded that the main objective for change was to 're-energise the culture and find ways to differentiate the brand'. OMD UK was highly successful and yet, in a crowded market, needed to stand out more and with even 'fresher' energy.

We decided that this aspiration wasn't specific enough, visual enough or tangible enough to be a vision statement, so we felt that it was not quite right go public to the staff with it, initially. So the second of our recommended options, that of **keeping this vision 'quiet' in the initial timeframe**, was agreed upon. Trying to engage the workforce to re-energise their culture and become more 'stand-out' in the market felt like it might be a bit of a top-down pressure that would feel mildly patronising to some or, for others, not even needed.

A communication from the MD to the workforce was crafted, stating that I and some of my work colleagues would be available to chat to a range of employees covering a cross-section of the company, 'to gauge opinion on the general health of the company'; a '20,000-mile check-up' type communication. Some 45 one-hour chats were undertaken, covering a wide range of disciplines and positions.

A 45-hour stream of staff consciousness: 'farmed mindfulness'!

The 45 hours' worth of frantically scribbled notes was then dictated and typed. The process of dictation is a useful one, particularly to the colleague who wasn't at the interview, as between the interviewer and the person typing, clarity can be improved upon. A key point of this process is to preserve the colloquial language used, so when somebody said, "For f***'s sake, when are the management going to get clear about the direction of this company?" that is what I would scribble down and that is what was typed. What we ended up with was 45 hours' worth of random comments on a range of things that were good, bad and indifferent.

> "For f***'s sake, when are the management going to get clear about the direction of this company?"

The next part of the process was to sit diligently in front of the computer screen, with the collective stream of consciousness on one side and a blank document next to it. A colleague and I would then spend many eye-watering hours reading the stream of consciousness, having taken out all the names so we didn't get influenced by memories of *who* said what.

All comments that seemed to be about a particular theme or area would get cut and pasted into the blank right hand document, under a working title of what that theme might eventually be. For example, the themes could end up being on communication, management, leadership, the physical environment, etc. It all depends on what the comments say, and what commonality among emerging themes there may be.

The power is in the detail of this process

Depending on the size of company and the size of sample/number of interviews, this cutting and pasting process can take several weeks. What we end up with is *all* of the comments cut and pasted into a number of themes; the exact number will depend on what themes happen to emerge. Usually 8 to 12 themes we have found.

Having done this process many times, there tends to be a theme on senior management, on structure, on inter-departmental cooperation, on communication, for example. There may also be enough weight of comment to create a page or so, and therefore constitute a theme, on the way women are treated or the role of IT or… whatever comes up. It is critical not to pre-empt what these themes may be, but be led by the weight of opinion that exists.

If many comments are very similar then at times we would produce an amalgam sentence in bold, and put 'x 6 or 7' at the end. It is important to keep all the colloquial and street language intact, often the most repeated and poignant points can be emboldened to produce sub-theme headings within each main theme.

The text should be put on a page with the margins as narrow as possible in something like 10-point font so that, overall, a theme is not much longer than one page of A4 or maybe two pages maximum, best displayed opposite each other, so each theme can be seen all at once.

Some themes are unexpected – this is the power of the process

These themes then need to be ordered in terms of weight. With one organisation we worked with recently, one of the strongest themes was that of identity. The organisation had been merged from a combination of three companies over the previous five years. Two of the three names still appeared in the title of the organisation which was, in turn, owned by a large corporate conglomerate.

Via the interview process, there emerged a huge range of feelings from many who weren't clear *who* they worked for. Were they part of this company, or that part, or the holding company? Their sense of identity was unclear and so they tended to align themselves either with their discipline or their department. This issue of identity wasn't one that was foreseen in the initial vision that the MD discussed with me, but it did emerge as a critical consequence of poor leadership and an incomplete merger. This is an example of how the **sponsor's 'change-vision' is often incomplete** and the in-depth snapshot survey process being described here can often throw up objectives to work on that are critical, yet were not initially apparent.

Back to the process. Once the individual comments have been categorised into themes, and there are no more random thoughts left in the original 'stream of consciousness' document on screen, then it is important to read and re-read each theme, moving the comments around slightly within each theme category, so that the text starts to flow, as it usually does, with a sense of narrative. This part of the process has always fascinated me, as my logic would say "there's no reason why a bunch of random comments when put in similar categories would necessarily flow", but they always seem to. It's as though they start to collectively tell a story when read out loud.

Finally, these themes are bound together in a 'snapshot report', with the most important highly-weighted themes at the front and the less critical ones towards the back. A summary of each theme, no longer than a simple short paragraph, is placed on the page opposite each theme. It is made very obvious that all of the *summaries* are not from the interviews and that this is the only wording in the document that has been penned by anyone other than the people we talked to, apart from one final addition.

We write a context page explaining the whole process of how this 'snapshot of opinion' came to be, while saying that the components should be read or heard within a framework of 'perception being reality' as, for those who had been interviewed, this was *their* reality and so to agree or disagree at this stage is something to be avoided.

So this 'snapshot' is printed and bound and enough copies made for all the senior management. In all the times we've done this process, we've ended up with between eight and twelve main themes as mentioned, but if there were more or less it wouldn't matter; it is what it is. **The amount of detail described so far as to how to achieve such a snapshot report is intentional, as this document becomes the 'holy book' of change, from this point on.**

The truth, the whole truth and nothing but the *perceived* truth

The next part of the process is critical. This is what we did with OMD UK and many other clients over the years.

We gathered all the senior management together offsite for half a day. All they knew was that they would be given the outcome of the feedback from the interviews we'd been conducting over the previous couple of months. What they weren't warned of, apart from the MD, was the process that was about to take place.

As the senior and top middle management of OMD UK sat round a large table, the 25 people were each given a copy of the snapshot but were asked, under no circumstances, to open it. I explained that the process of understanding what was contained in the document needed to be somewhat visceral and collective, for it to have the desired impact and to this end **I would read each theme, out loud, whilst they followed the words I was reading.** This I did.

Each time I read through such a document, I do so with high energy as though I were reading a script, allowing the colloquial language to come to life. This has the effect, in many ways, of the 50 or so individuals I interviewed **actually being in the room and talking from the heart to their managers.** The themes have not been ordered by what was negative or positive, both are all mixed in, including possible solutions where they arose. At the end of

"How much of this theme do you recognise. Does this feel like your company?"

each theme I would pause and look up and simply say to the gathered assembly words along the lines of, *"How much of this theme do you recognise. Does this feel like your company?"*

Often at the beginning of the first or second theme, there is stunned silence, a few red faces; a couple may voice mild embarrassment, others acknowledge the courage of the MD or sponsor who agreed to the process but, overall, what tends to emerge is that 90 to 100% of heads start to nod in broad agreement.

Letting the level of agreement emerge

As I repeat that process of reading each theme, stopping at the end of it, asking for what degree of recognition of their company is true for them, the dialogue and discussion always becomes more animated and more passionate.

What's remarkable is that I have never conducted this process without achieving a rough average of 80% agreement to each and every theme by 80% or more of the people in the room. Often I'll hear comments such as, "I was kind of aware of this stuff, I mean we do know that we have these strengths and we have these weaknesses, it's just that it has never been said quite so clearly or as boldly as this before."

I had another comment once, "In all the strategy meetings and planning sessions I have orchestrated, I've never had the truth about this company said with such candid directness as is contained in this document."

It is worth mentioning again, at this point, what happened when we did this process with Sun Valley Foods. After Theme Two or Three a colleague pointed out to me that the language they were using had started to shift, the words started to include 'we' rather than 'the management' or 'the board' or 'the factory staff'. Rather than these disparate groups being at fault, the varying labels of the differing components of the organisation were simply being replaced with the phrase, '*We* have got some issues and *we* need to fix them." It was as though the mindful awareness of individuals had been merged into a collective mindfulness. This was true consciousness raising.

It's this use of the word 'we' that is one of the first indications that true **engagement** and, therefore, real responsibility has started to take place. At this stage, it is critical to be clear about what is the *dual* purpose for this document and the way it has been produced.

The themes and desire to act become driven by *personal* commitment

One purpose of the snapshot document is to clearly identify **what is '*true*' about its current status**, i.e. 'so says a representative cross-section of the company.'

It is the *second* purpose that is as powerful, if not more so: to create broad consensus, endorsed by 80% or more of those who read it, so that the themes plus actions to resolve them acquire almost universal agreement.

This consensus will tend to drive change from the bottom up and from the inside out. **When this happens, the mindful engagement and personal responsibility to act, become irrefutable.**

Back to OMD: having read all the themes out loud, we had a coffee break and the OMD UK managers felt a mix of being shell-shocked, excited and slightly overwhelmed. The consensus was that the issues were real and had covered everything that made up the organisation. Themes touched on management structure and strategy, on culture, attitudes and behaviours; they covered processes and systems, even the layout of the building. It was comprehensive and, because of that, somewhat daunting; where would they start?

'Right, let's get out the flipcharts, brainstorm and fix it all'

An important thing to acknowledge at this point was that all of the issues raised had been there for quite a while and, as they admitted, several were even in the process of being addressed in some way. However, the fact that the status of the company had just been revealed in such *detail* didn't mean that it could or should be addressed all at once, although a sense of urgency was acknowledged.

The knee-jerk reaction to get out the flipcharts and move into 'break out groups' and spend an afternoon, or a couple more away days, coming up with solutions would constitute a *massive* mistake!

We've discussed in this book how change needs to be approached in mindful, bite-sized chunks, and that each chunk needs to be learned and absorbed into muscle memory for it to be integrated as the new norm. As with the driving analogy, you don't just teach somebody to drive, you teach them spatial awareness, plus how to find the biting point of the clutch, plus hand/eye coordination. They are a separate set of skills that if taught too quickly will be overwhelming; it's only when each skill is broken down, ingrained and then slowly put together, that you get the collective effect of driving.

This needs to be explained many, many times for real understanding to sink in. This is particularly true to this initial group of recipients. There is a danger that the managers have suddenly 'got the point' and then want to rush off and evangelise the rest of the company. **Another big mistake!**

Live in the question. Don't rush to the answers

In the event, the OMD UK management were guided to their conclusions *slowly*, they were allowed and encouraged to absorb the snapshot over time and come to their own conclusion. They agreed to read the snapshot every day for a week. This also gave them enough time for the rest of the company to be afforded the same courtesy, for the process of **engagement** to *really* take hold.

This reminds me of an important piece of wisdom a friend offered, many years ago. It was encapsulated in this phrase, 'Afford yourself the time to live *in* the question; this will allow the answers to come to you, rather than you trying to rush towards them.' This is so important to remind people about at this stage in the change process.

Democracy, anarchy or common sense (that's not always *common*)

For some, the next part of what I'm about to say may sound daunting and yet we've done it many times, and it works. Simply, the process with the group of senior managers needs to be repeated to the whole company, in small groups of 20-25 people, onsite as opposed to off, over the ensuing weeks. Each group should have the process explained to them of how the snapshot was arrived at. By definition, each group will have several people who have been interviewed and they should not be identified unless they choose to be.

> "Afford yourself the time to live in the question; this will allow the answers to come to you, rather then you trying to rush towards them."

From a confidentiality standpoint, in most situations I advise that the snapshot report in full should not be given to each person who attends a read-through to keep, but that they have a copy and return it at the end of the session. They can also have access to it to read in their own time by borrowing a copy from one of the managers. And, in some companies, each person having a copy of the snapshot to re-read and keep has been a powerful tool for deeper trust being built.

I have usually read a snapshot report out loud, 20 times or so, to 20 different groups within a project. With some companies it can take six weeks or so to get all the groups coming through. They work best by mixing up groups from different departments. This is because some departments may have a collective view that the company is slightly better or slightly worse than the overall snapshot and therefore it is good for them to sit in with members of other departments, as the snapshot will reflect an overall average opinion.

Again, after reading out each theme it is important that the reader stops and engages the members of the group with questions such as, *"How much of this do you recognise?"* Some will be more shy than others and, for the ones who do talk, it's important that you get those that are quiet to at least nod or shake their head in agreement or not with recognition of the themes. Again, this 80% broad agreement with all of the themes, by 80% or so of those in the room, is what tends to happen if the process has worked; so far we've never found it not to work.

Conducting the series of read-throughs for the whole company over a period of weeks is another act of bravery that some managers have baulked at, when the process has initially been explained. However, this is where the need for a strong sponsor who has the clear sense of vision and the power to drive it through is evident. It can be scary, but holding one's nerve and going through the read-throughs has always produced profound results.

Ain't no stoppin' *us* now!

The effect of the read-throughs starts to be experienced outside of the read-throughs themselves. Those who have attended start to seek out other attendees from previous sessions; they also talk to people who haven't attended, even if asked not to do so. Yet from a whole range of corridor conversations, chats in the loo and chats in the pub, a buzz and a range of emotions starts to emerge.

These emotions usually encompass more excitement than danger. It is usually an excitement that things have been said and listened to that most felt were previously unsayable.

There is fear sometimes, but it is usually overtaken by a greater fear of the upshot if nothing was done. Collectively, by the end of the last read-through there is a sense of gritty **engagement** with the issues by the majority of people, who feel that they are like a 'dog who has got hold of a bone' and there ain't nothing that's going to separate them!

There is a groundswell of **mindful and *engaged* awareness**; a commitment and determination from the bottom up, to ***act*** on the issues identified, almost regardless of management; it's a steam train that's coming, and the challenge now is how to direct it.

CHAPTER 13

The fourth golden rule: Involvement

Marmite has a lot to answer for: it's one of those foods that has become part of the British psyche, as Vegemite has in Australia. The advertising tag-line of 'You love it or you hate it' is so clever because not only does it sum up the prominent two reactions to the product, but I feel it started to rehabilitate an acceptance for extreme views, after a period where political correctness suggested that to 'hate' anything was somehow not healthy.

Now we're hardly discussing political revolution; it is just a spread after all. So to have a strong passionate opinion, be it love or hate, is no bad thing. I happen to love Marmite and as I ate my toast this morning I realised that my mind was searching for other things I held extreme views on. For some reason, musicals popped into my mind and I found myself in the opposite camp. Each to their own!

I'm not going to bother to analyse why; generally, I have an adverse reaction to musicals. However, I think that one of the things that irritates me about them is, of the few I have watched, it's so hard to get them out of your head; the catchiness of the songs, the ridiculousness of the simplistic morals and yet they can strike a chord, be it *The Sound of Music, Phantom of the Opera* or for me the first one I watched with my mum, *Seven Brides for Seven Brothers*.

Perhaps my irritation lies with the fact that I secretly admire the simplicity of some of the values and clean-cut morals that many of the musicals - particularly the ones in the 1950s and 1960s - convey; perhaps I wish life was that simple.

Over the years I have had my fair share of struggle and luck in equal proportions in most areas of life, and especially when it comes to buying houses and making them into homes. At times, the initial pressures, plus the emotional pull of trying to create a home while managing a young family and starting my own business as well, felt overwhelming.

There have been several times on such occasions when I found myself thinking of a scene in *Seven Brides for Seven Brothers;* it's the part where the extended families and friends, on a beautiful sunny day, wearing clean gingham shirts, all pull together and build a house from scratch. The house is timber-framed, it all goes together like a big jigsaw and they do it without anyone getting dirty or sweaty *and* they sing and dance at the same time, for goodness' sake! If only real life could be like that!

"Well my, oh my, we can all do anything, if we just pull together!"

Well, the gingham shirts and the songs are optional; however, the process of *engagement,* described in the previous chapter, has produced on many occasions a similar sense of excitement and *collective* 'can do, will do' fervour.

It may be hard to believe, but it *was* achieved – but only by following the detail of the process outlined (this is why *so much* detail was written down).

In the OMD UK case, as with many other similar projects, by the end of the snapshot reading process most employees were **mindfully engaged by choice** with what needed to be improved or changed, as well as what needed to be enshrined or preserved; this had been clearly established. The 80% rule is worth mentioning again. Although 80% of heads tend to nod or verbalise agreement to about 80% of the issues, it is making the best use of this groundswell of opinion that is the next critical stage. How to turn desire into action?

This chapter is about involvement: the fourth golden rule. As with the previous three golden rules, this one is dependent on the previous three. To recap: a leader or sponsor within the organisation has had a VISION of what a changed organisation needs to be like and has exercised enough personal POWER to at least start the process and hopefully follow it through. The snapshot process of interviews,

> "How to turn desire into action?"

198

the themed report and read-throughs, firstly to management and then with the entire company, will have mindfully raised **awareness** to what the organisation feels needs changing. It will also have **ENGAGED** and galvanised a critical mass of people into wanting to be **INVOLVED in, and personally responsible for,** *fixing and changing* **what has been identified.**

People rolling their sleeves up, getting involved in doing the do!

Involvement in delivering or implementing change is also a delicate part of the overall process. A balance needs to be achieved between leadership and direction, and continuing that sense of **engagement** being followed through so that those who want to be involved in bringing about the changes are given the opportunity and mindful **choice** to do so.

INVOLVEMENT needs to take two distinct paths: one is *directive*, the other is *partially democratic.*

The time between the initial read-through to senior management and the final read-through to the last group of company members will probably be six to eight weeks, for many practical reasons. This has an additional benefit in allowing for the information to be absorbed, as it allows crucial time for some of the more **directive decisions** to be thought through and implemented.

Getting as many people as *volunteer* **involved** in *bringing about* change is important if **awareness** is to morph into **personal responsibility**. However, in most cases the snapshot report will raise themes or aspects within some of the themes that can only be addressed by senior management or the board, making directive, leadership decisions.

For example, with another media company we worked with, as was mentioned earlier, some of the strongest themes to emerge were those to do with identity and also the lack of interdepartmental cooperation. I organised several one-to-one coaching and mentoring sessions offsite with the MD and a couple of the other directors. In those sessions I encouraged them to explore ideas on alternative structures of the company and departments as going some way to address the identity and cooperation issues.

The conclusion was to keep the organisation as one profit centre, but to 'de-merge' the two agencies that had been poorly brought together five years previously. The two names that had been conjoined still had brand value as separate entities and so it was agreed that the names would be separated. This meant two new operational boards under two new separate MDs would be created. The exiting CEO would retain the management team that met weekly but its function would change to become more medium-term and strategic, meeting monthly rather than every week.

The creation of these new governance structures for the separated agencies, while still under one company, also addressed another issue that the snapshot themes had thrown up: 'disenfranchised middle management'. Many of the up and coming 'starts' had no broader management function to perform under the existing structure, so creating this new one enabled promotion to real positions of authority and a less narrow progression funnel. This would not have been a sufficient primary reason, but it was a useful by-product of addressing aspects of the identity issue.

Unilateral decisions or democracy?

All of these issues could *only* be addressed by management decisions. It wasn't appropriate to involve the rest of the company in these kinds of decisions; they required a degree of unilateral leadership but, crucially, it was leadership motivated by a collective and mindful *mandate* formulated by the majority of the company, through the snapshot report process. This meant that even unilateral decisions tended to be embraced by the majority, rather than feeling as though they had been handed down from on high, or imposed from outside of the organisation.

Parallel to some aspects of implementation being dealt with via management decisions, the main form of company **involvement** is to guide people within the organisation, inspired by the snapshot process, to take part in fixing stuff and bringing about the changes.

How do you identify such excited volunteers? This is best achieved by an additional subtle stage within the read-through process.

As I read through each theme and looked up between themes to ask for reactions, there would often be the more vocal members of the group expressing opinions about how they recognised the issues and saying words along the lines of, "Yep, our appraisal system is rubbish, it should have been overhauled years ago" or "I agree, X department don't understand what we do, nor the relevance of what we're trying to achieve for them. They're stuck in a silo mentality and we need to change this."

My response would always be, *"Who here would like to volunteer to be part of a working group to come up with the answers for… (this or that particular area)?"* This invitation would be repeated by me, and by somebody else from the client company who would be there to make note of who had attended so we could track how many people had been to the read-throughs.

Inviting the volunteers to take part

Towards the end of the read-through process, an email is sent to the whole company reminding those who haven't yet volunteered during the read-through sessions that they are still welcome to get involved. By the end of the read-throughs, a list of volunteer names has been amassed and it usually encompasses a broad cross-section of experience, gender and managerial level from the bottom to senior management; most importantly, they are all people who *want* to get involved in coming up with the answers.

There is one more part of the process that needs to take place during the six- to eight-week read-through stage: draft solutions will need to be sketched out in response to the themes.

This process is one that I have done many times with colleagues and I believe it is easier and more accurate if done by specialists working on the project who aren't employees of the company. This is primarily to do with the ability to be objective but also the ability to voice politically sensitive or difficult suggestions.

We have found that the best way to approach this is to make a series of notes when the read-through process is taking place, recording suggestions people have made, plus teasing out implicit as well as explicit suggestions, remedies that the comments within the snapshot often record. Overall, it is examining the text of each theme to look for clues and suggestions as to what may need to be addressed in order to improve what's good and change what is deficient.

"If the snapshot is the source of the solutions, then the continued thread of a 'mandate from the staff' is maintained."

Using the snapshot as the source of clues to answers is critical, rather than relying on what, to many seasoned managers, may appear obvious. If the snapshot is the source of the solutions, each one drawn from the themes, then the continued thread of a 'mandate from the staff' is maintained. Thus it is more likely to retain the buy-in or engagement achieved so far.

Identifying solutions to the themes

It may also be that for each theme there are three or four possible solutions that become apparent. In addition, it's important to ensure that thinking isn't restricted to a particular *type* of solution; at this point we're looking for what might be the solution, not how to action it or whether to implement it.

For example, lack of understanding between differing disciplines and departments is an issue that comes up with many companies. How to address this may be multi-faceted and varied. The initial thought when considering possible solutions to this issue might be along the lines of improving process (the set of relay baton-type actions that need to be handed over, one to another).

This may well be a valid solution and, in addition, thinking laterally may also be a powerful idea. In response to such a theme, on two occasions we suggested that two of the departments that had been previously kept on separate floors were physically moved on to one big floor. To counter the issue of preserving departmental learnings and sense of team identity, this was suggested as being achievable by keeping small clusters of one department next to a small cluster of the rival department, next to a cluster of the other department and so on.

This meant that people of their own discipline sat in groups of six or eight, but the people of the 'rival' department were in a group of six or eight next to them and beyond them another cluster of the same department. The idea was that in order for individuals to get to their desks, they would have to walk past the desks of people from other departments and, in the process, given curiosity, over time, would cause them to chat and allow them to get to know each other and what they did.

This created a sense of relationship between individuals, regardless of departmental allegiance and, in turn, when one department had a problem with the other, the person who could fix the problem was someone they had got to know and therefore cooperation would be more likely.

All the solutions will collectively make the difference

Taking time, preferably with an external objective eye, to go through each theme and come up with as many possible solutions as are required, will produce a whole *range* of draft solutions. No single one in particular will necessarily make a big difference (remember the 'no one silver bullet' theory) but collectively they are likely to cover most aspects of organisational change.

Fifteen to twenty solutions may well be identified; they may cover process and systems, strategy and structure, HR issues, management behaviours, cultural norms, strategic direction, clarity of communication and defined objectives.

The set of solutions – no matter how many there are – are at this point purposely called 'draft' because with the **three key principles** in mind, the solutions mustn't feel imposed any more than the identification of the themes in the first place. The draft solutions should be put into a document; each set of solutions pertaining to a particular theme are best put under the heading of the theme summary paragraph (from the snapshot report) so that in each case the document reads 'summary theme' followed by 'the four or five proposed solutions' for that theme, then the next theme, then the proposed solutions for that theme, and so on.

This draft solutions document needs to be circulated to the board and a decision meeting called to discuss whether the draft solutions *en masse* will, in all probability, affect the themes collectively enough to deliver the desired overall change vision.

The overall purpose of this meeting, which can often take a morning, is to agree which of these draft solutions become the *adopted* solutions. In most cases, the majority of solutions put forward tend to be adopted. This is primarily because the route for choosing solutions has been grounded in the studying of the themes. If the perception of those interviewed is taken as being a snapshot of 'reality', interrogating the themes will, in turn, have given rise to solutions that will be appropriate to the themes being addressed. Once senior management has agreed the thirty to forty solutions, one task remains before action on the solutions can begin.

> "Fully engaging the 'leading' third through involvement in implementation is critical to delivering mindful change by choice."

Dovetailing the sponsors change vision with that of the company

This stage is another critical turning point. In the golden rule about **vision** we discussed the importance of a sponsor having clarity of what he wants to achieve, yet the majority of the process, explained in the **engagement** chapter and thus far in this one on **involvement**, has talked about the snapshot themes being the driving force for solutions. I've also said that in some instances, where the vision is very clear, be it to change the company for a merger or an acquisition or to prepare for a new market, etc., then that can be stated upfront. In other instances, it may not be as visceral a vision and is therefore best not stated, but the snapshot process contextualised to the workforce as being a routine 'service check'.

In either of these two scenarios, the sponsor may understandably feel as though his vision is being subsumed by some grand democratic process, that is defining change through a series of random unstructured interviews, rather than a strategic process!

After or around this solution decision meeting, it is important to meet with the CEO and have a conversation about his vision for change. Once this vision has been rekindled and articulated, something along these lines is generally asked, *"If all of the solutions agreed to in the draft solutions document, which emanated from the snapshot themes, were delivered in a coordinated way over the next say six to nine months, do you feel that your vision is likely to be a reality?"* This, in truth, is more of a discussion than a single question; however, I have never known the answer to this be anything other than a resounding 'yes'!

Vision brought about by momentum; a third, a third and a third

I know of several CEOs and MDs who have been concerned about losing control to such a process. They had fears about not being as demonstrative in expressing how *they* wanted to bring about *their* vision as their instincts would have normally guided them to do.

In nearly every case, however, the power of the process thus far has shown them that their people not only know *how* to identify what doesn't work, as well as highlight what does, but they also have many of the *solutions* as well as the enthusiasm to bring them about. Establishing the synergy in the eyes of the sponsor, between the sponsor's vision and what the snapshot process has delivered so far, is a final important step, before a wider implementation of solutions begins in earnest.

The route to achieving this lies in a variation of the 80% rule, or perhaps it should be called the '66.6% rule'!

What to do with senior people who no longer 'fit'?

Observation of the dynamics within organisations has revealed a curious thing that most will instinctively recognise. If you get a 'critical mass' of people actively engaged and involved in something, around a third of the total seems to be a rough guide, then you also tend to get approximately another third empathetic to the first; the remaining third may contain some cynics who will jump up and down for a while, will either tag along, eventually get involved or, in extreme cases, leave.

I mentioned earlier that there are often a small number of decisions to do with structure that can only be taken by senior management and in some cases only by the MD or CEO. This is only right and proper. There have been some instances where the snapshot confirmed that one or two directors were 'wrong' for the organisation and were part of this latter third.

In some instances, I have seen directors in question who are completely oblivious to this mismatch. In other instances, it became clear that they had realised this, but hadn't the courage to do anything about it. Part of the coaching and mentoring role of the change expert is to become a confidante of the sponsor, often the CEO, and guide them in some of these difficult decisions. This can result in exiting or moving one or two key individuals if the snapshot has confirmed that they are wrong for the new changed organisation.

Management decisions or working groups

To summarise: we have covered the formulation of the 'actual' solutions from draft ones drawn from the snapshot themes. We have also talked about leadership decisions that may need to be implemented during the six weeks or so period of the read-throughs, especially if to do with restructuring of governance.

However, beyond these top level sensitive decisions, the adopted solutions need to be gone through by the management team and divided into the two broad categories of intervention, as mentioned earlier in this chapter: solutions actioned over the weeks and months to come by **management decisions** or those delivered by the formulation of **working groups.**

Which solutions can be addressed by assembling various **small working groups** of four to eight from the volunteer pool? Which solutions really need to be taken and followed through as **decisions by senior management?**

Where possible, the more solutions that are addressed by working groups made up of volunteers, the more there will be a sense of personal ownership and **INVOLVEMENT in the fixing or implementation process.**

The general rule is only to keep those solutions for management decisions where you believe democratic involvement is unrealistic or inappropriate. For example, it may be that one of the themes talks about the lack of clarity with the direction of the organisation. One of the solutions to this may be to write or re-write a three-year strategic plan and communicate it well to the organisation. The communication of this plan could be worked on via input from a working group but the strategy document, at least in its initial form, will need to be written by the directors. This would put this solution into the management decision pile, rather than that of the working groups.

As a general rule of thumb, when all the adopted solutions have been talked through, roughly a third of them will tend to be management decisions that will need to be worked upon and concluded over the coming months.

The remaining two thirds of solutions will need to be addressed and resolved via working groups over the following months. This one third/two third split is a rough guide, but one born out of a psychological dynamic rather than pure maths.

This fourth golden rule of 'involvement' is 'the involvement to fix stuff that needs changing', and so 'involvement' refers to the *manifestation* of the second key principle of 'responsibility' or ownership.

People will only feel as though they *want* to be personally responsible for something they are involved in or can at least influence. **If the larger proportion of the solutions to themes they've co-authored is ultimately addressed by senior management, there's a danger it will come across as 'being done to', thinly disguised as involvement.**

It's all to do with the critical mass I mentioned earlier; there is a herding instinct amongst us humans, and the 'third, third, third 'rule, tends to work if the first two thirds are going in the 'right' direction! Fully engaging the 'leading' third and keeping them **engaged** through **involvement** in implementation and follow through is critical to delivering mindful **change by choice.**

This dynamic needs to be mirrored at each step of the process. Getting the balance between management decisions and solutions driven by the volunteer pool organised into working groups is critical: two thirds to one third in favour of the working groups tends to be about right.

An 'electrifying' case history

The power transmission and distribution infrastructure of the UK was built over forty years ago. Much of the work necessary to refurbish, replace or add to the networks is undertaken by specialist engineering contractors, of which there are several. One of the major players in this field was Eve Transmission, now owned by Babcock. EVE was originally a family business that had a long history in the design and construction of power transmission lines.

An acquaintance who had become a strategy consultant contacted me out of the blue several years back and asked if we'd be interested in helping a 'specialist engineering company' through a period of growth and change. I remember my first reaction was to be tentative, as our experience of change processes had worked across a broad spectrum of industries, but how relevant would they be with an engineering company?

I remember first meeting the director who had a firm handshake and a broad Northern Irish brogue with an engaging grin. Pretty much from that point on, I realised that bringing about change has principles that are common whether you are working with an investment bank, a pharmaceutical company, a youth club, a family or, in this case, an engineering company. **The common** denominators are the way people as individuals and in groups resist or respond to things being different.

In EVE's case, the MD's vision was crystal clear. The national transmission networks with their miles of pylons had been built due to mass expansion of electricity needs, fifty or sixty years ago, and the pylons and wires were all starting to reach the end of their 'shelf life'. Therefore, there was a vast opportunity over the coming years to build a business capable of meeting a surge in demand for transmission network replacement programmes.

However, nothing in this world is a given and the MD realised that establishing a differentiation point between EVE and its main competitors should be a constant goal, if increasing volumes of work were to be awarded to EVE. The key point in the mind of the MD was innovation. This is a much-used and, in my opinion, over-used word of late but in this case it was literal and completely appropriate. For example, if they could design electricity cables that hung from pylons that were lighter than their predecessors and more conductive, then the amount of steel used in the pylon construction could be decreased, cutting the cost of raw materials and possibly the cost of construction.

Innovation, for real

The company was abuzz with many clever, practical ideas that would save materials, time and cost and so collectively give the company a competitive edge. The problem was the mentality of some of the managers was a bit 'old school' and the way the company was structured appeared old fashioned to my eyes. In other words, there were many aspects of the way the company was being run that were antithetical to the notion of being inventive and being able to think differently.

So the process that has been described so far in this book was slowly followed, step-by-step. A number of one-to-one coaching days were delivered between myself and the MD, as well as separate days with some of the other senior directors. Out of these sessions emerged personal realisations about them and their management style and, most importantly, there evolved a clear **vision**. These sessions also established an ability and determination in those individuals to make things happen. They had the **personal power**, especially the MD, which would be needed, in some ways despite their corporate bosses, to make the vision real.

At the same time as these one-to-one sessions were taking place, a good proportionate cross-section of the company had one-to-one confidential chats with me and my colleagues. The stream of consciousness from these conversations was moulded into a themed snapshot report which was read out to the MD and his Board. This process was very similar to the OMD UK example.

The response from the EVE management was a typical mix of discomfort, recognition and yet, overall, a galvanising agreement that most of it was true and importantly *they* needed to act.

Implementation needs to start with the changes to the day-to-day

At this stage in the process I became a 'non-executive director' on the board and attended all their meetings. Part of this role was to point out the mechanics of how they ran their meetings, to help them become more structured, more aware of their personal or collective '**impact gaps**' and, particularly, more action-orientated. This was an important part of them changing and the rest of the company would see the benefits of these shifts in senior management behaviour over time.

It's easy to talk about being more innovative and yet not realise that the way meetings are conducted and other simple day-to-day management behaviours can be at odds with the grand notion of 'innovation'. For instance, I got them to bring discussions to a close with phrases like 'so what does someone propose?' and 'what's the action and who's prepared to do it and by when?' We worked through their irritation to these simplistic questions which initially occurred and, rather than detailed minutes, they recorded, often in a simple line, what was discussed, what was agreed, or what would be actioned (by whom and by when) at each meeting.

These output notes were then gone through at the start of each subsequent meeting and actions were revisited. This process had a subtle but critical difference between that of recording minutes and agreeing them at the next meeting, which can often be a laborious process. The act of recording what was agreed or decided upon, plus recording actions with names and completion dates, sowed the seeds of the third key principle: **accountability.**

"How is innovation linked to the way we run meetings?"

This simple practice became a powerful device. The directors were seasoned engineers who between them had been involved in business for many years. Having their suggestions at board meetings challenged with 'so what will you do about it and by when?' felt a bit patronising to some. However, at each point I'd remind them of the contents of the snapshot and how they'd accepted those truths, so they realised pretty quickly that the solutions had to start, to a great extent, with them changing *their* behaviour. They became more mindful of their impact in the change equation.

They understood that this begins with small steps, like agreeing specific actions to be done by specific times. The constant questioning of 'who will do this and by when?' also served another purpose. Initially, most of the directors would say, "Oh I'll do that by next week or by next board meeting" and when, by the following meeting, fifty percent of the tasks were incomplete, the excuses would flow.

In most cases, the excuses or reasons were very real: business pressures, emergencies to 'firefight', etc. My challenge would be, "If your son or daughter had been ill and you *had* to go to them, what would you have changed to make that possible?" This, as you may imagine, sparked some lively debate but in the end they started to realise that they either became victims of circumstance or they become much more in control. (Masters, practising; finding the mindful 'choices' in apparent no-choice situations.)

In practical terms, when an action was agreed, rather than saying, "I'll do it by next week," they would more mindfully pause and think, mull over what workload and pressures they had, then would come up with a realistic completion date, maybe two or three weeks hence. This had massive consequences to start with; over a period of a month or so the actions completed by the agreed deadlines rose from 50% to more than 95% and, in the remaining 5% of cases, they'd often send a quick email ahead of the board meeting to warn colleagues that the deadline would be shifted to a new one, but never left hanging. This also started to positively affect their very human relationships with each other.

> "If your son or daughter had been ill and you *had* to go to them, what would you have changed to make that possible?"

Involvement by the many starts with the actions of those at the top

Another consequence was that because people started to think about what they could do, or were *prepared* to do, *within* realistic deadlines, a lot of their goals had to be re-thought. Agreeing to do this meant them reviewing agreements to things that were impossible to deliver. There is a limit to stretching goals and levels of stress; sometimes being truly innovative has as much to do with acting and managing more rigorously as it does with coming up with a new lightweight electricity cable!

The board started to question their own impact, to hold each other accountable for actions agreed to, challenging each other personally but within an increasing environment of reinforced trust and relationship-based team than existed previously. These shifts were as critical as discussing the draft solutions and turning them into an agreed solutions document. Their ability to challenge each other mindfully, supportively and be more open and honest with each other also helped in their ability to decide which of the solutions needed to be management decisions, who on the board would carry them out and which of the solutions they would entrust to the volunteer pool acquired through the read-throughs, to form working groups.

How to get the working groups started?

The next step of EVE's journey is an example of the general process that I have observed and carried out with many clients including OMD UK, Pfizer and Starcom MediaVest.

It involved me sitting down with the MD and some of the other directors to sketch out a 'brief' for each of the working groups, based on the agreed solution to address, as a part of the solutions addressing each theme.

An individual solution from the solutions document may have described 'reviewing the internal communications within the organisation to address poor communication issues raised within the snapshot'. The task was to write a simple one or two paragraph brief as to what was expected from a working group in order to sort this solution by coming back to the board with a set of recommendations.

Once all the briefs for the various working groups were written, the next task was to look through the volunteer list and assign four to six people to each group. Sometimes volunteers will have expressed a preference to work on a particular solution or a particular theme; those requests should be honoured where possible.

A leader for each working group should also be *suggested* within the spirit of taking **responsibility**, rather than being given the role; working group leaders as well as the volunteers must be given choice. Armed with a written brief, the leader of each working group would convene his group to discuss the brief and how they would go about solving it. The groups may need to meet for several one to two hour sessions over a period of weeks or months before they can formulate a set of recommendations to be presented to the board for sign-off and, crucially, implementation!

How to guide the working groups

At this stage in writing the chapter, I am again aware of giving quite a lot of detail. This is a conscious decision and it plays to one of the points I made earlier in the book about there being no one silver bullet. It is only in the range of subtlety and detail of each stage of the process that I have found the collective answer to sustainable change.

For instance, the working groups need to be a balance of experience, but not dominated by a senior manager as it may feel as though it's just an extension of the management structure. Each working group also needs to be allowed a couple of meetings, at least, to come up with its *own* timescale for delivering its recommendations as time to interrogate the brief, and their approach to solving it, will be important.

It's critical to recognise – if you are the sponsor, a senior director or, with the family analogy, the parent – not to fall into the trap of 'I could have done this better and quicker myself'. Not really so because the job of a good manager is to hire people to do what s/he hasn't the time or skill to do and do it better, i.e. recruit experts in their field. As we discussed earlier, **empowering** others is inviting *them* to take the authority and the accountability to do what you've asked them to do, within a certain brief, but *their* way and, within certain stated boundaries, *their* timescale.

When I'm working with an organisation, a colleague or I will attend *all* the working group meetings in the role of a guide or mentor. I have helped organisations reengineer processes, design new systems, restructure departments, adopt values and accompanying behaviours. However, the key to all these activities is to guide the principles of awareness of those I'm working with, so *they* come up with answers they can own, so *they* can be prepared to be accountable for the results, out of **mindful choice.**

Bringing all the pieces together

When the working groups at EVE Transmission had been established and had met at least once or twice, the next crucial part of the communication process within the project of change needed to take place. Up until this point, most of our client organisations had become aware of the change vision, either stated before the snapshot took place, as with EVE Transmission, or stated after the snapshot and all the read-throughs, as with OMD UK.

At this stage, both EVE and OMD, as a whole, had been made aware of the 30-40 solutions that had been adopted and which ones were going to be addressed by **management decisions** and which ones tackled by **working groups.**

However, it is unrealistic to expect the vast proportion of employees within an organisation to hold all of this information without it being communicated in a simple and connective way. The solution to this problem was pioneered several years back and has since been used in all change projects with, predominantly, great success.

The idea is to create a 'mindmap' that conveys the **theme headings** from the snapshot in the centre of the map then, from the themes, the next layer of **agreed solutions** in the next 'circle of information'. Finally, the outer circle contains all the **actions** being delivered, both by management **decisions or working groups.**

You will see in the diagram opposite that each action box in the outer circle has the initials of those in working groups for decisions who have offered to be accountable for the delivery of this piece. This mindmap should have several reiterations and, as progress is made, dates for the delivery of each action box should be inserted into these later versions as deadlines are declared.

The critical importance of role-modelling *behavioural* change

There is one further type of intervention that is critical and in addition to those covered by 'decisions' and 'working groups': some form of management workshop.

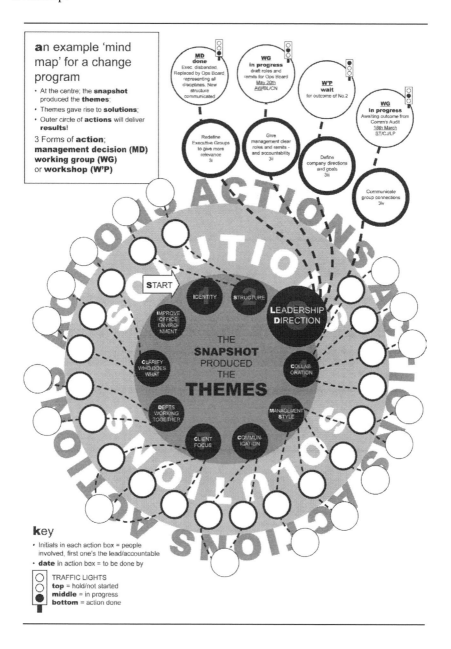

We have discussed the importance of defining management behaviours, drawn from values, which when role-modelled will reflect the new culture. The question of how to establish these behaviours is best achieved through a series of workshops, in my experience. Now I realise that the word 'workshop', or 'seminar' or 'training' for that matter, will bring up different things for different people. I am talking about an offsite setting where managers can, through professional facilitation, **start to make their relationships more gritty and real; not role play and theory, but gloves off and robust!**

It is in this setting that differences in *behaviours* as opposed to *values* that managers *believe* they stand for, can be shown.

Here is an analogy to illustrate how surface differences in behaviour can occur despite similarities in values, below the surface.

As a parent, it's often difficult to strike a balance between the enthusiasm for hobbies/activities that *we've* done and trying to enthuse our children about similar activities without coming across as trying to straitjacket our offspring into their parents' mould!

My love of the outdoors is something I've shared with my children as best I can over the years. The excitement when I was about 12 of planning my first expedition for the Bronze Duke of Edinburgh's Award with my Boys' Brigade Company is something I still feel when I think back all those years. There were about thirty boys in the 43rd Birmingham Company of Boys' Brigade; my father was a captain of the Life Boys; I started there aged seven. This was the equivalent of the Cubs in the Scouting Movement. My two older brothers, being eight and ten years ahead, had also joined at seven and continued right through until they became role models, through their long involvement in the BB. So to me, the Boys' Brigade was *the* way to run a youth organisation.

"Defining management behaviours which when role modelled will reflect the new culture."

How we act is initially how we are judged

Fast forward thirty years to my son at 12. We'd been on a few walking trips to places like the Brecon Mountains where we'd camped and practised a little with map and compass and I had told him about some of my boyish antics in the Boys' Brigade. I can't remember whether it was my enthusiasm or his interest, but somewhere between the two I investigated what youth groups were available close to Henley-on-Thames where we live. The Boys' Brigade no longer had a presence but there were several Scout Groups and so we went along one evening to see what it was like.

To my surprise, the troop only had about 15 members and I remember thinking 'how will this work?' comparing this number to my Boys' Brigade experience of 30 plus. The bigger surprise lay in the fact that the scout leader was reluctant to accept my son as they were short of leaders and so an 'ultimatum' was offered; a place would be given to my son if I was prepared to help out. So I found myself going through the statutory process of being vetted to work with young people (that never happened with my Boys' Brigade leaders!) and donning neck scarf, woggle and accompanying paraphernalia of 'the enemy'! Why *the enemy*?

There was a culture within The Boys' Brigade, or at least in my Company, which thought the Boys' Brigade were 'hard' and the Scouts were 'soft'; they sang 'polite campfire songs' and we were more raucous. On annual camps it became a tradition to 'play commandos' and in the dead of night to steal our way into a neighbouring camp and nick something for a laugh. It was always in good fun and always returned. The delight of such pranks was amplified if the neighbouring camp happened to be one belonging to the Scouts!

On one jaunt, I remember being part of a night-time raiding party that removed the Scout camp flagpole and hid it in our marquee. The scout leader came looking for it the following day and our captain denied all knowledge, as he didn't know at that stage what we had done. When eventually we came clean, his reaction was two-fold, as you'd expect from a man nick-named 'Feisty Jack'. His reply was along the lines of 'You bloody idiots…well done!'

Form over essence?

Thirty years on, here I was with a 'girly' scarf round my neck, thinking I'll have to sing 'dib dib dib' with my trousers rolled up, or whatever it is Scouts do!

In those first two months as a probationary scout leader I found myself on many occasions wanting to say 'we shouldn't be doing it this way', or 'why don't we do it like this?' Bottom line was I couldn't get the cultural expectations that I'd grown up with, of how the Boys' Brigade did things, out of my mind, and

I was constantly comparing my experiences of the past to what I was seeing around me.

Of course, sometimes I could bring some constructive criticism or observation born out of the objectivity that somebody fresh to the organisation could offer, yet often I was just uncomfortable with the unfamiliar and 'them' doing things the 'wrong' way. After those initial few weeks, things had settled down in my mind and, more importantly, I looked at my son enjoying himself and getting what *he wanted* to get from the experience of being a Scout. It was different from my Boys' Brigade days – of course it would be – but in truth it wasn't better or worse. The 'form' of it may have been different but in *'essence'* my son got many of the experiences I wished him to have but on his own terms and in his own way.

What was critical for me in those early weeks was to identify the *values* of the Scouting Movement and in particular those of the leaders I was working with. I reflected on how they dovetailed, or not, with my own set of values. In truth, the overlap was enormous and once I got past the difference of uniform, the difference in routines, the structure of some events – in other words surface differences – the *behaviours* of the leaders, for the most part, reflected their *values*.

Acting on solutions: decisions, working groups and workshops

Within any change programme, the question of behaviours and how they are lived, particularly by senior management, always needs to be explored. An American CEO of an investment bank we worked with once described culture as 'the way we do things around here'. As with the Boys' Brigade or the Scouts or one company to another, 'the way we do things around here' is rarely written down and, even if it is as with some organisations, I've never seen a company handbook that really reflects the truth on the ground.

"An American CEO of an investment bank we worked with once described culture as, 'The way we do things around here.'"

Whenever I go into an organisation, particularly on the first few occasions, I'll often make a point of getting there early. I'll sit in reception or outside the MD's office, often in an open-plan area, and simply observe. Do people wear ties or jackets and if so do they keep their jackets on or hang them up on their chairs? Do they eat food at their desk? How many times does the telephone ring before it is answered, how do people greet each other when they arrive, do I get seen on time or am I kept waiting? All of these and a hundred and one other simple minute-by-minute behaviours are, in truth, the culture of the organisation, the ways in which 'we do things around here'.

The themes of any snapshot report will produce a range of solutions that are likely to cover every aspect of the organisation. 'Leadership and management style' or words close to these have been part of one prominent theme in every report I have ever compiled. This is to be expected as the leadership and people management within any organisation will always play a critical role.

Management decisions are likely to cover solutions such as strategy, structure and direction; the working groups may cover areas such an interdepartmental co-operation, process alignment, reconfigured systems, appraisals, communication, etc., etc. In addition to all of this, establishing a set of **agreed managerial behaviours** is another goal that a snapshot theme is likely to highlight. This will therefore need to be addressed and, in my experience, this is best done by a series of workshops.

Establishing management behaviours

In previous parts of the book I have touched on the importance of a 'relationship-based team' as opposed to one purely focused around task. I've also talked about establishing the 'values' supporting a statement of vision. Within the cycle of the change project, I'd suggest that two or three months into the project, when working groups are starting to come to conclusions and a good proportion of management decisions have been made or implemented, the timing will be right to organise a series of workshops with the senior management.

These workshops will typically be a mixture of mindfulness, personal development, communication and leadership skills. I have tended to run programmes that are emotionally challenging but help people create further trust between each other so that they can even talk about aspects of their childhood and upbringing that have shaped their management and communication style, such as their approval-seeking or control tendencies. In short, help the management team build relation-ships: sturdy vessels, rather than 'relation-skiffs' that sink in a difference of opinion!

This kind of exploration of personal style will be balanced with practising communication and leadership skills, but on 'live' issues between participants so that, as I mentioned, the experience is as real as possible, not just theory.

These workshop experiences can be both challenging and testing, yet reveal to their colleagues aspects of each other's humanity that usually engender empathy, trust and a deepening of the relationships between them. This in turn produces a sense of the relationship-based team I have talked about. The workshops would typically be in blocks of two days, maybe two or three of these blocks over a couple of months.

Skills and defined behaviours to role-model change

The outcome should be at least two-fold. In addition to furnishing some of the communication, management and mindfulness skills needed to increase the sense of relationship-based team, the second goal is to identify and agree a set of management behaviours.

To a certain extent, we have already explored ways to 'uncover' management behaviours as expressions of sets of values. In my experience, a tailor-made workshop setting is the best way to do this. As mentioned, at some point in the workshop process, the senior managers would be encouraged to think about what they stand for in life, what items in the news or in their life spur them into action; it may be injustice or inequality. They may demonstrate this through charities they are involved with. Asking people to define their values isn't easy as we discussed earlier. More important than values is how they show up so, as part of the workshop programme, I would help individual managers identify ten or twelve 'black and white' behaviours that they and their colleagues are prepared to sign up to.

The guidelines around meetings explored in Part One is one possible behaviour. Other behaviours may include 'give a piece of constructive feedback to each in your care at least once a week'; 'ensure you complete all your appraisals inside the agreed deadline'; 'always return a client's telephone call or email within a maximum of 24 hours'. These examples, and there are many others, shouldn't be intended to fully reflect the individuals' or company's set of values. The question to be asked of the set of behaviours before they are

> "More important than values is how they show up."

finally adopted is this: 'If these behaviours were adhered to by, say, 80% of the managers, about 80% of the time, would they on the whole convey to most people our value set as a company?'

As it is the *managers* that mindfully define their *own* set of behaviours, through raising their **awareness**, then *they* should be given time to live them, day-to-day. If the overall process of change and their sense of **personal responsibility** is strong, then, at some point, the management will want their behaviours to be measured so they, through some sense of mindful choice, offer themselves to be accountable for these behaviours to their colleagues.

Overall, this whole involvement stage of the process is usually the longest of the entire change programme as implementation takes time if done thoroughly. The mind map should plot the *progress* of the **decisions** carried out, **working group recommendations** implemented and behaviours defined in **workshops**, and a measure of how they are displayed.

The final stage is to start **measuring** the results!

CHAPTER 14

The fifth golden rule: Measurement

'How long is a piece of string? Twice the length from the centre to the ends.' This was one of my daughter's favourite 'jokes' when she was young.

At the beginning of the book, I mentioned that one of the paradoxes of being human is, on the one hand, our ability to adapt to our environment, living as we do in all kinds of extremes on this planet of ours and yet we can often be incredibly resistant to any form of change, unless we happen to think of it first. Another paradox I would suggest seems to be with our relationship to **measurement: the fifth golden rule.**

We have managed to measure so much of our world, from knowing the number and type of genes in DNA, through to dissecting time into nano-seconds, measuring wealth through money that in most cases doesn't physically exist (just figures on a computer screen), yet we are prepared in some contexts not to measure outcomes and we occasionally argue against doing so.

Art and, to an extent, architecture, is an area of human endeavour that has had a curious relationship with measurement. There have been instances where wealthy patrons in previous centuries have commissioned a piece of art to be done in a certain way, in a certain time, so to that extent they imposed a form of measurement. However, the quality of the end product would only be measured by a subjective liking or disliking. Monetary value only became a form of measurement, often years after the artist had died.

There is time and there is money and then there is art

A couple of years ago, I visited Barcelona for the first time and had the opportunity to visit the Gaudi-inspired cathedral. Like many, I was struck by the extraordinary organic shapes that seemed to mirror nature, throughout the exterior and interior of this still unfinished monument. The attention to detail and unwavering obsession, as it appeared to me, with still attempting to follow Gaudi's principles of shape and form, seemed astounding. This really did seem a supreme example of organic change (in more than one sense of the word) as opposed to 'planned' change.

To my surprise I had the opportunity to speak to one of the project managers on the site. My Spanish is virtually non-existent and his English was sparse so this made for a stripped-down conversation. After complimenting him and his colleagues on what I saw around me, I then asked a question which left him perplexed. It was simply, "When will it be finished?" He pulled back his head and threw up his arms in a way that seemed to convey not just surprise but also a sense of impudence.

It started to dawn on me that this was a project clearly committed to a sense of purpose, in delivering a sense of style and form that would be achieved with no feeling of compromise. Therefore, in this instance the only measurement criterion was integrity of delivery, which outweighed time and cost. This is a rare example in our outcome-driven world.

If you asked most people, up until a couple of years ago maybe, what they thought of the O2 arena in London, or Millennium Dome as it was originally dubbed, the knee-jerk response from most would probably be, 'What a fiasco!' What's behind such a response? A few months ago, I listened to a programme on architecture and in particular exploring iconic buildings in recent years. To my surprise, I heard two architects talking about the Millennium Dome as an 'iconic' building. "As time washes away the context out of which this building was first born, history will prove," they argued, "that it has a rightful place amongst Britain's most iconic buildings." So what led to the initial poor reputation for the Dome in the minds of the media and many people?

> "I heard two architects talking about the Millennium Dome as an 'iconic' building."

Again, I suggest it boils down to how we measure success. When it comes to a building or most civil engineering achievements, three of the main measurement criteria will tend to be budget, agreed timescale and purpose or function. Unfortunately, in the case of the Dome, it came in way over budget, it also came in late which was particularly unfortunate given that it was called The *Millennium* Dome, as it wasn't finished by 31 December 1999. Thirdly, its purpose was felt by many to be weak and ambiguous, as the volumes of visitors for the installed exhibition were way down on those projected and people started to ask, "What is this expensive and late 'white elephant' for?"

Building for the future

Overall, the fact that the building failed to hit all three of these measurement criteria managed to overshadow the perception held by some, that the '*aesthetic* box' had been ticked. In other words, its 'beauty' as a building was being removed from the discussion, even as a topic worth discussing, because time, budget and purpose were all so wide of the mark. Interestingly, now that the debts have been written off or absorbed, the timing issue relating to its completion has faded from memory and it has been renamed with a clear purpose and a set of functions that seem to deliver; the building's status has largely been restored, and its aesthetic achievements more widely recognised.

Measuring anything in human endeavour has to be understood within the context of the third key principle, **ACCOUNTABILITY.** Offering yourself to be held to account for what you have agreed to do is often critical when it comes to really achieving what you set out to deliver. A friend of mine was talking to me recently about how she is going to employ a personal trainer in her quest to do well in a marathon she has entered next year. I was surprised, as this is a person who is a personal trainer *herself* and so I didn't quite understand what she hoped to gain by employing the services of somebody who did what she also does.

Others holding us to account can help take *off* the pressure

Her reply was simple, "If I pay him to crack the whip over me, then I won't be prepared to let my money go to waste. I also know he will be tougher on me when I think I can't do any more than I will necessarily be on myself."

Her reply sounded somewhat obvious when she said it out loud, yet it was a great reminder of how important it is to get friends and colleagues to hold us to account for what *we* say *we* *want* to achieve. This point was reinforced when she retorted with, "Besides, he's helped me take my mind off running the marathon by designing a training schedule over the next nine months; all I have to do is forget about the marathon and do each session day-by-day."

This approach to breaking activities into bite-sized chunks is important with any period of change.

As I mentioned near the beginning of this book, developing mindfulness through my Vipassana meditation seemed too daunting when I thought of the years of practice at up to two hours a day! It was only when I broke it down to a manageable chunk of 20 minutes as a minimum per day, and then took each day one at a time, did I have a chance of sticking to what I'd set out to achieve. I also shared my daily commitment with a couple of close friends, which helped me be accountable to them and ultimately myself for staying on the course I'd set myself. Once the results became more obvious, then the discipline became easier to maintain, as with most newly adopted habits.

Within a company change setting, cynicism and fatigue is bound to happen at various stages. They can only be combated by helping people to concentrate on the *next* stage of their **working group,** or the *next* bit of the **management decision** to be implemented, as well as constantly referring them back to the solution, then the theme of the snapshot behind their action, i.e. reminding them of the '**mindful mandate**' for doing anything in the first place. It's the ability to keep going, chunk-by-chunk, that delivers results. Reinforcing the mentality of doing lots of little things, but importantly **measuring the progress** of all these little tasks will collectively indicate progress, while measurement also reinforces a sense of reward for people who have decided to get involved in this mindful **change by choice.**

Timed goals for each small chunk of the change process will need to be established, but it's imperative to encourage the working group *leaders* to establish timeframes for the delivery of their actions. These may be influenced by the overall change objective but they have to believe it is do-able, given their day jobs. If they are given timescales that are too tight, or if it is attempted to force too much change at a pace or a volume that becomes overwhelming, then the sense of personal ownership and individual **responsibility** will be replaced with a top-down pressure that is likely to lead to resentment.

Remember the speeding analogy in the second example, the **accountability** of the fine for a speeding offence that wasn't **owned** because the driver wasn't **aware** that the speed limit had been changed; this creates resentment. These principles in reverse never work.

So **measurement** has to be done but done around goals that those delivering the outcome can, as far as possible, set themselves. This principle will ensure that the goals are not only achievable, but are actually *achieved* and will also ensure that any resentful sense of 'not invented here' is mostly overcome. This approach may mean that the overall change progress is slower than the sponsor and other directors may wish for, but speed by itself may undermine the sustainability of change if it is pressed for at the expense of individuals' ability to deliver.

Pulling the strands of a change project together

Offering ourselves to be held to account, be it a pact with ourselves or an agreement with others, is for most people the way of defining the difference between success and failure.

When it comes to a change project, striking the balance between imposed measurement and targets that have an element of **mindful choice-led** agreement by those delivering them is critical if change is to be embraced.

In Chapter 6, during the section headed, 'If it's worth defining, it's worth measuring,' I wrote that the way to measure behaviours would be covered in more detail later in the book.

Within the senior management workshop setting, when the behaviours are agreed, the managers are encouraged to explore what form of measurement or accountability mechanism *they* would be prepared to put in place. This can only be done once they are all fired up and mindful about the behaviours they have adopted. Sometimes it works best to let them 'try out' the behaviours day-to-day for a while before re-convening to help them agree measurement.

Within the change project at Sun Valley Foods, the management team developed something they called MAMA, Management and Measurement Accountability. The senior managers who had been through the workshop process decided of their own volition to introduce an intranet voting mechanism which operated once a month. It turned out to be quite a radical and bold move.

MAMA meant that anybody in the company could vote electronically, monthly, on any of the senior managers who had been through the programme, scoring each manager. These scores were against the twelve adopted behaviours, on a sliding scale of one to five, one being poor, five being excellent. The fours and fives were grouped together, (although in some settings it is better not to do so), and percentile favourability scores for the whole of the management group, per behaviour, were calculated a week after voting every month and communicated to the company. Only the managers had access to individual scores, which were discussed amongst themselves.

All for one and one for all

The behaviours 'quotient' formed a part of a version of a 'balanced scorecard' (a way of measuring a range of indicators) that we'd been asked to produce for the company. After three months of scoring we could see which behaviours were strong and which were weak. At that point the managers agreed realistic targets for each behaviour and they set about mindfully supporting and coaching each other to ensure behavioural improvement in all areas, especially where there was weakness.

What became fascinating to us was the degree of **choice-led accountability** the managers started to show by 'exposing' themselves in this way. Nine months before, their **awareness** of there even being a *problem* in the company was limited and, where it did exist, it was restricted to inter-departmental blame, not joint managerial **responsibility**. The snapshot raised collective awareness to the point where they all started to feel personally responsible for doing something about it, and MAMA was a culmination of their willingness to be mindfully **accountable** to each other for making day-to-day behavioural changes.

Another point to note is that, as with the whole change process, these individual behaviours by themselves weren't mind-blowing shifts; even the behavioural changes of the managers collectively would have made little difference on the culture if it was the *only* change brought about. **Again, change is only achieved by breaking down the whole into many bite-sized chunks, be it processes, systems, structure or behaviour. It's the collective effect of all of these that will have the desired result.**

The bravery of the managers at Sun Valley was further confirmed when they agreed that their behavioural scores through MAMA would become part of their personal annual review. This meant that they could hit their financial targets and departmental goals, but if they hadn't achieved their behavioural targets it would affect their salary and, ultimately, their progression in the company.

A radical approach but fine if they thought of it!

This may sound a radical and even draconian approach and to some, when I have relayed the story, it has sounded punitive. If this kind of mechanism had been imposed, it could well have *been* punitive and it's certainly not something I would have wanted to suggest.

The critical point was that when you get a group of people sufficiently mindfully **aware** of what they need to do differently, such that they are prepared to take **personal ownership** or **responsibility** for making those changes, then they'll *want* to be held to **account, to be measured** – sometimes, as with Sun Valley, in radical ways!

Engaging senior managers in the workshop process as a whole, serves as a micro-form of engagement that is critical if the macro change in the organisation is to be sustained.

Troubleshooting fruit

One of the first change projects we were involved with was in the now defunct Apricot Computers. The company was featured in one of the programmes in the Sir John Harvey Jones *Troubleshooting* series in the early 1990s. The Birmingham-based entrepreneur Roger Foster who founded Apricot was still at the helm. At the end of this episode, Sir John concluded that the only way Apricot could survive was for it to sell out, to merge with a bigger player. It would need to be a company big enough to afford the investment and economy of scale

> "They could hit their financial targets and departmental goals, but if they hadn't achieved their behavioural targets it would affect their salary."

needed for Apricot's sustained growth in an increasingly globalised and competitive market.

Foster was resistant to the selling idea on screen and yet, in the tradition of good television, whilst declaring he wouldn't sell, right up to the end of the programme, his indignant stand was superseded by a voice-over during the credits, which announced, "Subsequent to the making of this programme Roger Foster sold Apricot to Mitsubishi Electric."

We became involved when Peter Horne, the then MD of the newly acquired Apricot, became aware of the need to change the culture dramatically if they were to move from an autocratically-led Birmingham-based computer company to the European arm of a Japanese owned multi-national. Initially there was one Japanese addition to the long-established board and, other than that, the same players, with their well-established attitudes and behaviours from many years with Apricot were still round the same boardroom table. After the initial period of establishing a range of themes that needed to be addressed, and working groups set up to address most of them, management workshops to establish new behaviours started to be organised.

Talking of 'buy-in', would you pay for this change out of your own pocket?

As with every workshop I have ever taken, I do my best to apply the three key principles with all participants, at every stage. In the case of Apricot, I started this process by having a series of one-to-one chats with each board director, in confidence. We talked about the change programme and to what extent they had understood and bought into the changes identified at that stage.

We also talked about what changes to their *own* managerial style may be needed if the new processes and culture were to take root. I then, as with all clients, prepared a pre-workshop questionnaire that would help them establish their strengths and areas for improvement as managers and communicators, as well as identify a personal objective for taking part. An objective, not only for the change programme as a whole but a personal objective that *they* would be able to make significant progress towards, as a result of taking part in the workshops.

After these one-to-one interviews had taken place and I had received the completed questionnaires from the participants, I would get them all together a couple of weeks before the workshop. This was to give them a chance to collectively discuss their personal objectives and air any remaining considerations.

When it came to doing this with the group of Apricot directors, I raised the subject of personal objectives again. I asked them to reconsider their objectives, but within a context, that for some, sounded a little quirky, if not shocking. The question I posed was, "If you were going to be asked to give up days from your annual leave in lieu of attending these workshops, plus pay for the cost of them out of your own salary, what objectives would you have to achieve for you to want to take part, out of choice?"

'Do you want the truth...?'

I then went round the room to each director, who restated his objective as being enough of a motivator, even within this hypothetical context, until I got to one of the directors. He was a no-nonsense kind of bloke. He had been with the company for many years and had made a great deal of money in the process, as was evident from his well-cut suits and his general good lifestyle.

When I turned to him and asked him what personal objectives he had for taking part in the workshop, as part of the change programme that would be worth giving up time and holiday for, his reply was initially daunting. "Do you want the bullshit answer or the truth?" I said that I preferred to hear the truth and so he proceeded to reply with this:

"I've been a part of this company, almost as man and boy, for many years. It has done well and I have done well and things are now changing. I wish the company all the best and I'll try and change where I can to help it into its next phase. However, I wouldn't give up any of my pay, or my precious holidays, for a workshop to further the company." He paused and I thought about what my reply might be to such a straightforward answer. However, before I could say anything, he came back with this "...however, you did say I could choose an objective about a personal change issue, rather than one relating to the company. Is that still OK?"

How badly do you want change?

I indicated that would be fine and he continued. "Well I've got a daughter. She's now 18, has become a vegetarian, and has painted her bedroom black. She dresses as a Goth and goes to art college. We used to be really close and now all we seem to do is argue. If there's anything I could learn from these workshops that could help me recreate my relationship with my daughter, then I would gladly pay for it and give up some of my holiday to do so."

For somebody so apparently self-confident, he looked at his colleagues rather sheepishly. A couple went red and there was definitely a feeling of tension in the room. I replied by assuring him that what we would explore on the workshops would indeed have benefit in this aspect of his personal life and I was sure the changes we would look at may well help him achieve this personal outcome.

The workshops went ahead. They were quite emotionally draining, from excitement through to anger, from upset through to optimism; 'par for the course' in my experience, when helping a **relationship-based team** to grow.

Through these workshops and over time, putting what they had learned into practice over the following weeks, relationships between those guys became deeper, more mindful and as a result, more real. I also wondered how this particular director would take what he had gained and apply it to the relationship with his daughter.

Several months later I heard some startling news; he had decided to become a vegetarian for a month, quite an achievement for a steak-eating Scot from the rough part of Glasgow! Also, people who knew him said that he was still the same guy but somehow he'd become more mindfully aware of other people, of his impact on them, and had gained more tolerance in general for people being just different from him. He also told me later that he did regain the relationship with his daughter and, for a number of years, Apricot did well within the Mitsubishi Empire.

> "If there's anything I could learn from these workshops that could help me recreate my relationship with my daughter, then I would gladly pay for it."

Implementation is key

Another example of accountability within the change project is that of the working groups delivering their proposed outcomes.

It's important that *they* are given some time to explore the brief they've been assigned so they can assess how long they will realistically need to meet, over the coming weeks and months, in order to formulate proposals.

Likewise, when they have proposed deadlines and they've been negotiated in conjunction with the timelines of the overall project, they need to be given the freedom to come up with their own proposals within any specified limitations and maximum allotted time. Once agreed, these individuals need to be firmly **held to account** for delivering their proposed actions, within the time agreed.

I've also witnessed many working groups delivering their proposals to the board of directors.

In most cases I would encourage the individual within the working group who has the most enthusiasm to be the leader, to take this role rather than it going to the most senior person within the group. This can have additional benefits when it comes to presenting their ideas to the board. The leader chosen can, in many cases, present with such enthusiasm that their *potential* future as a manager and leader becomes more obvious to many than was previously realised. The presentation can become a showcase for new talent, as well as delivering recommendations on how to fix this particular part of the change puzzle.

Once proposed recommendations have been negotiated and accepted, post-presentation decisions need to be made on how the change ideas from each working group are to be implemented.

The more the involvement in change implementation the more the 'ownership'

In some organisations, as many as sixty to several hundred people may be involved in working groups, and they may have put many hours into formulating recommendations. It's pretty obvious in the cold light of day to realise that change doesn't happen via a bunch of recommendations; it only occurs via the collective effort of many.

It is also important to work out *who* will be **responsible,** and ultimately **accountable,** for implementation. In many cases, the working groups are best placed to carry out the implementation of their recommendations with one possible addition of the relevant director, be it Operations, HR or Marketing, depending on what is proposed to be changed.

However, in the spirit of *inviting* personal responsibility before holding anyone accountable, it's more effective to re-*invite* working groups to see their recommendations through to implementation rather than assume they will do it. Workloads may prevent some from wanting to continue, others may just have change fatigue. However, in our experience, most choose to stay on and implement what they have helped formulate.

An answer in some instances is to help those who have helped formulate the recommendations to implement them by 'farming out' aspects of their day job, just for the time it may take to see implementation through. However, if they want a break let them pass on implementation to others who are willing.

Overall, be they 'management decisions' or solutions defined by 'working groups' or management behaviours defined through 'leadership workshops', it's implementation that matters and agreeing deadlines, criteria, performance indicators that are *key* (Key Performance Indicators, or KPIs) is critical in this final stage of the change cycle.

The collective effect of change actions

Coordinating all of these measured change activities over the six to nine months it usually takes for the collective effect to start showing up, is another critical element.

As an objective external change agent, although usually cast in a non-executive role, it has been my job to ensure that all of the management workshops, working groups and management decisions are implemented over agreed timescales, whilst maintaining a balance.

The balance is between guiding individuals to come up with the right ideas regarding their particular brief, while avoiding being too directive.

The balance comes between helping those who have chosen responsibility for an outcome to come up with their *own* measurements of accountability, be it timescale or budget, etc., with the constraints of the business and the market environment.

There is also the balance to be sought between the speed of outcome that the sponsor and the senior directors want, offset against what is truly realistic.

Targets, goals, timescales: all points of **measurement** and accountability are, at the end of the day, critical in registering success and yet integrating all these activities can take a lot of skill and in many ways require the attributes of a world class 'conductor'.

The role of the change 'conductor'

My children have grown up on a wide-ranging musical diet but, like many of their generation, the classical music component has been akin to their fruit and vegetable intake, before the 'five a day' rule started to hit home. Recently my son was struggling with a piece of music homework for his GCSE curriculum. When I sat down and listened to his confusion, the world through his eyes became clearer to me. He was asked to describe over a couple of paragraphs the function of a conductor; he was struggling to expand much beyond a couple of sentences.

For someone who had grown up in the digital age where singers are fine-tuned via a computer and the final sound is, in many ways, the product of the sound engineer and the record producer, it was hard for my son to fully grasp the importance of a person waving a stick!

So as the change programme goes through its implementation phase, it will need a change 'conductor': someone who has the objectivity yet intimate understanding of the snapshot, its themes, the solutions and all the actions to be implemented, as well as an intimate understanding of the organisation or business and the constrictions that will be there as a consequence.

The person who occupies this change-directing role will need to have created an intimate relationship with the sponsor and, like a conductor, be able to bring on certain groups to 'fortissimo' and hold other groups back with a sense of 'piano', thus ensuring that some decisions are implemented with particular timings to enable the process from one working group to combine with a department change proffered by another.

As the changes start to deliver, the mindmap will need to be updated on a regular basis and an agreed form of **engaging** communication undertaken. This is to ensure that all of the company has every opportunity to understand and interact with the whole change process, so this sense of personal **involvement** is continued throughout the implementation phase, towards the **measurement** of outcomes.

Communication is also a vital part of the change conductor's role in ensuring that everything is guided and integrated so the final 'orchestral change crescendo' occurs in ways that create a sense of unified positive effect, rather than splintered, ad hoc, discordant change, as so often can be the case.

Measuring the overall output

As the various solutions start to be implemented, the effect of each action will begin to be noticed. Some changes, like moving departments to sit in different places, will be quite tangible; agreeing a set of managerial behaviours and voting on their implementation over a period of months will have a more subtle impact. Reengineering a set of processes will make a difference to varying degrees in an obvious sense, dependent on who within the organisation is involved in which aspect. Deploying new systems can notoriously take time to get right before benefits start to become apparent.

Unlike organic change, where continuous improvement and the ability to be agile is, for many organisations, a constant pursuit, a **planned piece of change** as we've discussed needs to be defined and so measured. However, it isn't always obvious from examples such as a merger or a move into another market what the change outcome would be. For instance, if two companies are to merge, when is it deemed that this has taken place? Well, from a legal standpoint it's fairly simple: when due diligence has been accomplished, contracts negotiated and signed, then they are merged. Not for most of the people in the merged companies; *merged* in the literal sense can take a lot more time than a physical joining and the point in time of its eventual full achievement isn't usually that obvious.

In nearly all cases, a merger never feels like one on the outside, it always feels like an acquisition. One company or culture feels dominant over the other. There is almost certainly duplication in certain aspects of both businesses to be addressed which, in most cases, will result in redundancies. So has the merger or acquisition been completed when offices and workforces are consolidated? Again the answer is probably 'no'. In one way, defining when such an objective has been achieved is very difficult because it is arguable that it's a never-ending journey.

Avoiding the 'groundhog day' of change

However, this brings me to a further point which has to do with another aspect of basic psychology. Few of us cope well with a sense of never-ending monotony; it's part of the human need to punctuate work with play, activity with sleep, talking with silence. If a group of people is subjected to change consistently then, no matter how engaged and involved they are, initiative and change fatigue will kick in at some point.

So another critical reason to **measure** the overall effect of a **planned piece of change** is to do so to create a sense of progression and achievement for those within the organisation. In some way, it is to draw a line under that phase of the organisation's development, fully in the knowledge that nothing stands still, but recognising that people have the need to have progress acknowledged, from one phase to another.

Many change initiatives *fail* for two main reasons: firstly, there is insufficient follow-through and lack of engagement, combined with poor measurement, so what was started was allowed to fizzle out. This leaves people with the experience of raised expectations dashed by poor results.

The second reason, which is often a consequence of the first, is that poor follow-through often results in another initiative being launched, in most cases to address the failed outcomes of the previous one. This can result in a syndrome I would describe as 'initiative fatigue', resulting in cynicism and the sense of a relentless treadmill of change activity that appears to deliver little.

> "A merger never feels like one on the outside, it always feels like an acquisition. One company or culture feels dominant over the other."

The psychology and practical processes outlined in this book have attempted to work around these two pitfalls by understanding what and how to measure when it comes to the collective outcome. This is a final and crucial aspect of ensuring that progress has been achieved, recognised and, in turn, made solid.

What to measure and how

Generally speaking, experience has shown that in the change process outlined here in Part Two, **six broad areas of measurement are important.**

Three are subjective and three objective

When many people think about business success they may do so in terms of market share, profit, i.e. hard measurements. And yet, if we think of the computer analogy, the notion of 'hardware' and 'software' being separate and anything other than completely interdependent is by now an outdated one. So too when it comes to measuring the effects of change, the 'perception' or organisational 'software', i.e. feel, flavour and culture, is as important as the 'hardware' of process, product or profit.

If you are ever in any doubt about this, just think of the events of 2008. The financial crisis had many complex elements to it and yet at its core lay two intertwined factors: one was the objective fact of debt or credit generated against the questionable value of their secured assets. The other component was the purely subjective notion of confidence and trust.

The collapse of many companies was triggered purely by *perceived* weakness against a backdrop of their hard assets having not changed at all! Yet the phrase 'perception is reality' took on an almost cruel unswerving truth.

So it is with any organisation. Its success generally, and specifically when it comes to assessing a period of planned change, needs to be measured in both subjective and objective terms.

Three subjective measures

The five golden rules started with raising the awareness, through the process of **engagement** within an organisation, as to what needed to be changed or kept the same. This was based on the views of a wide range of people who worked there. Likewise, it is important to measure 'a snapshot of opinion', again after the changes are done, as **one of the subjective forms of measurement**. This should be done between nine and eighteen months into a change project, to gauge comparative perceptions pre- and post-change implementation.

On average, over the past 20 years of developing this process, we have found that the first snapshot may have typically revealed comments that are two-thirds to three-quarters negative, with the rest positive. The comparative snapshot after most of the change work has been implemented and its effects registered usually reveals a reversal, i.e. two-thirds to three-quarters positive comments, the rest either negative or 'still to work on'.

The second area of subjective measurement will come from other stakeholders. In most cases it's rarely a good idea to announce to your partners, suppliers or customers that you are about to embark upon a change project. Even if it becomes public knowledge that you are merging or entering a new market, such a publicly-known general objective, along with the announcement of a more detailed change programme, will in most cases raise more cynicism or false expectations than anything else.

We've found that the most effective approach is to follow the change process in all its stages in ways that are 'quietly concealed' from all but the employees. However, people within the organisation who have any contact with customers, partners, or suppliers should, after six months or so of the change project, be encouraged to keep their eyes and ears open! Look and listen for unsolicited anecdotal feedback from these stakeholders. Generally, it is after six months or so that this sort of stuff starts being said.

Go to the MD's office ASAP!

I was at a client's offices about five months into a change project; most management decisions had been carried out and about half the working groups were starting to implement recommendations. A proportion of these were starting to have an effect – or so we thought. I got a text from the MD which simply said 'get to my office as soon as you can!' This immediately put me back into the class at junior school when I braced myself for something I must have done wrong!

However, when I got to his office I was greeted with an excited smile and an email thrust into my hand. I quickly scanned the top and realised it was from one of their major clients. It simply read 'Hi Ron, just thought I'd let you know, the service we've got from you in the last month or so has been outstanding. I'm getting the feeling that you guys are up to something. I don't know if this is true, but whatever it is, keep it up. From our standpoint, it's working!' Signed, the CEO.

At the beginning of the project, I had explained all six forms of measurement and this one was greeted with the greatest degree of scepticism. The thought of clients in a hard-nosed business environment noticing and being bothered to praise a company, prompted by no other reason than good stuff seemed to be happening, struck this MD as somewhat fanciful. And he wasn't alone over the years! However, this email was the first of several. Other comments were made verbally in presentations or in the lift when clients were shown out of the building after a successful meeting. The key was to collect all this anecdotal 'evidence' and communicate it internally within the organisation as one of the measuring points that all their hard 'change work' was starting to bear fruit.

The third area for subjective measurement is managerial behaviour. I've talked about this earlier and gave the example of MAMA at Sun Valley Foods.

Experience has taught me that defining behaviours that reflect values and then critically measuring them, particularly the senior managers' ability to role model these behaviours, is a crucial part of bringing about overall change.

Having some form of measurement to monitor behaviours, like turning up to meetings on time, giving regular feedback, even answering the telephone in a particular way, may initially sound simplistic, even petty. However, ensuring that some key day-to-day behaviours from the leadership are roughly in line with the overall thrust of how the company needs to change is an important reality check. It ensures that change cannot be subsumed by the big 'process-change', or 'the restructuring', or the building move, important as they may be. Measuring management behaviours will ensure that individuals walk the talk and,

> "The key was to collect all this anecdotal 'evidence' and communicate it internally within the organisation as one of the measuring points that all their hard 'change work' was starting to bear fruit."

through their actions, demonstrate that change starts with individuals doing some targeted things, differently.

The three areas of objective measurement

In addition to the three areas of subjective measurement, here are the three areas of objective measurement of the overall change process, to see how well it has worked: 1) improvement in staff turnover; 2) increase in retention of existing business; and 3) a rise in the winning of new business.

Staff turnover is an important objective measuring point. We recently completed a project for a company that was experiencing a 53% staff turnover rate in the year prior to us getting involved. To many ears this would sound extremely alarming until you hear that this particular industry has an average staff turnover rate of 40%. I tend to hold the view that any form of benchmarking against other companies or other organisations has a part to play and, in this instance, the company was wise to find out the industry norm, to put their turnover rate into perspective.

However, there is a danger for some: if they *only* benchmark themselves against the norms of others, their own sense of vision can be diminished. Encouraging a sponsor or leader to come up with their own benchmark, their *own* goals, is an important step in conjunction with understanding the status of their peers.

The snapshot process will, through its wide-ranging themes and all-encompassing solutions, have highlighted a whole range of factors that will be influencing 'customer satisfaction'. I use that phrase in its broadest context; staff, partners, suppliers, clients are all 'customers' in that, to an extent, they have a choice to be with that organisation, or not, and if they are not getting what they want, they will ultimately disengage or leave.

So it's right to accept that changing an organisation through a holistic and integrated process should result in people wanting to work for and stay with such an organisation. This principle, like the others we have explored, tends to relate to most groupings of people, be it a huge organisation, a smaller company, a salsa dance group or a golf club! In each instance, if there's a high turnover of people there'll be reasons for it. Understanding what those reasons are and bringing about holistic change should result in higher retention.

The more subjective anecdotal evidence, from clients and suppliers, telling you that something is different and it's 'good' is usually the prelude to that sentiment showing up in hard figures. If an organisation has changed for the better, customers are more likely to want to stay. Likewise, if there is a buzz in energy backed up with practical efficiency in an organisation, people will want to do business with it. And so, **measuring year on year figures regarding retained** and **new business are the final two, very important, objective measuring points.**

Measuring 'software' and 'hardware'

These six areas of measurement again represent a holistic approach, covering the 'software' and 'hardware' of an organisation, i.e. ultimately, sentiment and money. There may be other indicators or measuring points that companies wish to adopt; a kind of league table appeals to some cultures. I have worked with organisations that, during the change process, aspired to be included in *The Times 100*. This is a league table compiled by *The Times* newspaper, charting companies who are deemed by their employees to be the best places to work.

At this point I feel there needs to be a flashing neon sign in the book with the word 'WARNING!'

In 1997 a new political change occurred in Britain as New Labour swept to power. Old Labour had attracted many criticisms: being poor at managing the economy was one, spouting generalised promises about health and education was another. Looking back on those early years of the Labour government, while bearing in mind the three key principles of change we've explored, becomes quite an interesting exercise.

The awareness or mood of the nation, as with most changes in government, was particularly high, especially after a period of one party being in power for a long time, as with the previous Conservative administration. The emphasis was on the economy, health and education.

With the economy, there had been Black Wednesday and interest rates at 15% so, unusually for a Labour government, many felt reassured when Gordon Brown introduced his two fiscal rules. Suddenly there was a responsibility that was measured with guidelines as to what the government could borrow as a percentage of earnings. This was further enhanced for many when the Bank of England was made independent regarding the setting of interest rates.

Targets and waiting list times: good or bad?

With the National Health Service, the **awareness** of waiting times, poor service and crumbling hospitals was also high in the country's consciousness. So for a government to take ownership, to say they would be **responsible** but in ways that offered tangible **accountability** in the form of operation waiting list targets, number of hospitals to be rebuilt or replaced, this was something relatively new - or so the government's PR office would have us believe. I'm not going to argue the pros and cons of one political party over another; my only point is to draw attention to the relationship between a government's use of goals and targets in the context of accountability or **measurement.**

There's a phrase I've already mentioned, 'If something's worth doing it's worth measuring' and I'd suggest that in the early years of New Labour, the idea of a government offering itself to be accountable through measuring points like fiscal rules and NHS waiting time targets, initially struck a positive chord with many.

So what, over time, caused 'targets' to become almost a dirty word in the press and for many in the general population? There were two main reasons.

Firstly, the key with any target or measuring point is that it should be accompanied with a phrase that should almost become a mantra to those involved in delivering it: 'All targets should be achievable and achieved'. There is little more de-motivating than being set a target or a goal which feels completely unachievable. Now, there is a range between a target being so easy that it almost becomes de-motivating, through to a goal being a stretch – something that requires a lot of effort but which, in most people's minds, is at the level that inspires and motivates. The other extreme of a simple target, and one that is beyond a stretch goal, is a goal that is clearly *unachievable.*

The second de-motivator around targets is when those involved slowly lose sight of what the target is there to achieve. If the emphasis becomes all about the target, i.e. the measuring point, and the awareness becomes slowly glossed over or confused as to why the target was agreed in the first place, then you can end up with a set of measuring criteria that can feel like a stick that's being used to hit those delivering over the head!

Don't let the targets become the goals

The Labour government fell victim to these two points. Many doctors and other health workers within the NHS felt the goals were simply un-realistic, due to insufficient resources. They also started to feel as though reaching targets had *become* the goal, rather than improving service which most agreed would be a great thing, *then* having *progress* towards this improved service measured by a target.

Likewise, with teachers: targets through exams, SATS, key stages, i.e. procedures that could be measured became, to many, about the target rather than what the target was initially supposed to measure, i.e. improved education.

These two examples highlight very graphically how the three key principles became reversed. Many started to experience targets as the instrument of **accountability** being used to drive personal ownership or **responsibility** in the hope that it would **raise awareness** for improvement. As we discussed in the early parts of the book, this will almost always trigger resentment and disenfranchisement.

So, although this chapter has explored the importance of measurement, I can't emphasis enough that *all* aspects of accountability have to be driven by the degree to which those bringing about the changes are **engaged with the mindful awareness of why they are doing it.** Then, involved with a level of personal **responsibility in fixing or changing things, with a degree of involvement** that ensures *they* decide they would *like* to be **measured and held accountable.**

"Changing things, with a degree of involvement that ensures they decide *they* would *like* to be measured and held accountable."

Although this chapter is ending with looking at measurement of the whole and the big, sometimes many of the small individual changes that go to make up the overall effect are subtle. They are often to do with individuals and the changes *they* have made and are, therefore, often very personal in their contribution, even difficult to measure.

Yet, as we know, and at the risk of appearing contradictory to all I have said in this last chapter, not all that is important to the human condition is always *measurable.*

Small changes can be beautiful, yet very significant…

Nine months into a change project, I met for a review meeting with the MD and his board. We were reviewing the varying stages of implementation; most **management decisions** had been carried out and the effect of many of them was starting to be recognised. All of the **working groups** had presented and formulated the solutions and two-thirds of them had been implemented. There was a buzz in the air and change started to feel palpable. I asked the board for individual examples of change within the context of the overall objective that individual directors had noticed. Some examples were day-to-day behavioural changes in senior management resulting from the **leadership workshops.**

All the examples given were, in most cases, fairly gritty and far-reaching; they were to do with increases in efficiency or a decrease in staff turnover or tangible examples of clients registering greater satisfaction.

When I came to the MD he paused and said, "Throughout this project I have been constantly amazed at the changes to the company, its culture and, most importantly, the increase in business we have achieved."

"However, I've been most astounded by the changes that have slowly occurred within *me.*" He paused, looked at me and smiled.

I had spent several days offsite over a period of months coaching and mentoring him. I had written and delivered leadership and mindfulness workshops for his team. I had watched changes taking place in his leadership and management style, building on the success he had already achieved. I had spent nine months attending his management meetings and helping to guide and shape more honest and mindful communication, and more disciplined meeting delivery and yet I was intrigued to hear an example of what he meant by the comment he had just made.

He continued, "After the last 'mindfulness and management' workshop we did, I arrived for work one morning and noticed there was a beautiful display of flowers in reception. I felt warmed by this little gesture, as it felt another small part of the new energy that seemed to be pulsing throughout the company." He paused and then concluded, "However, when I praised the receptionist for the flowers she somewhat awkwardly said, 'Thank you', but then added, 'I've been doing this for the last two years.'"

The MD looked at me and said, "It's my own personal shift in mindful awareness and changes, both in my impact and what I experience around me, that has probably been the biggest change overall."

CHAPTER 15

Conclusions: summarising *Mindfulness and the Art of Change by Choice*

The Highway Code was never intended to be a manual on how to drive. As has been alluded to within this book, no amount of text can take the place of experience.

So what this book has attempted to do is to provide a mixture of thought-provoking stories, analogies and philosophical and psychological 'truths' to ponder regarding a mindful approach to change and choice, plus some examples of practicalities that have tended to work in various settings and organisations.

The book hasn't been written with the expectation of anyone being able to remember all its points, or replicate them; from my own book-reading experiences and observations of the way people learn over the years, I know that is not a realistic possibility.

What the book may have done is to cause you to reflect on what *you* do and what you know, both consciously and instinctively.

It has also put forward some pointers that may hopefully act as reminders of what you have previously realised tends to work and, in some cases, put forward ideas that may make sense to you that you may not have previously considered.

Final thoughts

All of the ideas within the whole book have been born out of observation, rather than theoretical 'points to prove'.

The central thought throughout is the notion that if change is to work it has to have an element of choice within it, and choice starts with a more mindful approach. Finding that mindful choice, on a personal level, is often the starting place.

Although some of the analogies and examples have been about family life or change outside of the workplace, the majority, especially in Part Two, have focused on examples and case histories of change implemented within business.

This was a conscious decision, as change tends to be planned and executed as a conscious pursuit, within a work context. However, one of my passions throughout my life has been to understand the human condition, both in the observation of myself, as best I can, and of others.

So I offer the thoughts within this book as applicable to *all* aspects of change in which we humans may engage, be it turning around a corporation, improving your local youth organisation or changing aspects of your personal life.

Living through 'change' from a standpoint of 'mindful choice', whether that choice is offered from others or internally acquired, is in many cases the difference between a smoother road through life, or a very bumpy ride.

A final word on mindfulness

As I mentioned in the introduction, I decided not to spend time in the book explaining the various routes or mechanics of how to become more mindful. This was partly due to me feeling that although the basic *form* of what you might do to become more mindful could be written down, I feel that conveying the true *essence* of how to achieve mindfulness in a book is not something that can be done.

Mindfulness has to be *experienced*, and in the way that best suits each individual's life journey. I chose the Vipassana meditation route as Vipassana is the source of mindfulness; there are many other routes that a good search on the internet will reveal.

What I *have* attempted to do in the book is to highlight many different aspects of being more mindful, especially when it comes to finding choices where there may not initially appear to be any: choices rooted in the now, not the past or the future. This is at the heart of mindful change: change by choice.

Appendix: A summary of the main points of the book

In Part One: the psychology of change we started with exploring the concept of **mindfulness and choice** and how to find meaningful choices in situations where there appeared to be **no choice.**

This can only be achieved by strengthening the internal 'muscles' of the three key principles. The speeding analogy, particularly the second part where the speed limit has been reduced without warning, demonstrates the importance of **raising awareness** *before* any sense of **personal ownership or responsibility** can be expected. Only when this second principle starts to occur can the third principle of **accountability** be offered by the individual, rather than demanded against their will.

Chapter 3: the notion of insisting on mindful choice and then applying these three principles of awareness, responsibility and accountability was explored against the backdrop of **change** that is constantly happening to us **organically** as well as **change** we might **prescribe or plan.**

It's often difficult, even within a piece of planned change, to spot in advance all that may need to be done differently. This took us into the next chapter.

Chapter 4: the notion of change being a **contact sport**, a visceral experience. Absorbing the new into **'muscle memory'** and learning various techniques that may, separately, appear disconnected from the overall outcome are aspects of the nitty-gritty relating to the change process that are often forgotten. It's so easy to focus on the outcome, rather than realise without being reminded that it is techniques and learning many new disciplines, across a range of areas, that will finally allow **'technique to free the artistry'.**

This all takes time. Change in general, if it is to be sustained, especially following the notions of choice, will take longer than expected in most cases. This is compounded when, as with many aspects of change, it will need to be fulfilled through managing other people.

While managing others, the skills of **context setting, effective delegation** and **troubleshooting problems** without acquiring others' tasks are all-important yet time-consuming. Allowing the time to become more mindful, for 'your soul to catch up with your body' is a truth most of us know intellectually yet in our busy lives, especially at times of change, one which seems so easy to overlook. Acquiring the discipline of mindfulness on a daily basis can assist greatly with managing time and stress.

Then there is **empowerment,** key for mindful and choice-led change to take place. Empowerment can't happen as a dictate, but only as a set of circumstances you can help create so that people feel trusting enough to take the **authority** and be **accountable** for the tasks they have chosen to undertake.

In Chapters 6 and 7 things got personal as we started to talk about **being the change** you want to see, mindfully walking your talk and also **what stops us.** The principles of mindful self-awareness and personal responsibility kick in to a new level when looking at issues such as the personal **gap between intention and behaviour**, between declared values and your day-to-day actions.

We are all kids at heart and the vulnerability of a child that is still there within us can't be underestimated. All we do as adults is often 'fake it till we make it'. We adopt defence mechanisms such as **approval seeking, controlling** our emotions or those of people around us, or finally **withdrawing** by just refusing to engage. These may offer a temporary sense of 'not being found out' but as we are far more transparent to those around us than we'd like to believe, covering up how we really feel, what we really think, is far less successful or useful within the meaningful **relationships of family or team** than learning to be more straightforward and honest. We looked at being mindful of our underlying negative emotions, learning not to react to them, allowing emotions to come, and letting them go so they no longer cause knee-jerk reactions.

In Part Two: the practicalities of bringing about change, a desire to make things simple and have neatly prescribed solutions was explored, through the notion of there being **no one 'silver bullet'**, be it for change or most other endeavours of importance in life.

A holistic approach is key and the 'wholeness' of an organisation needs to include the many 'organisms' within the whole. Process, systems, attitude, skill set, building architecture, structure, behaviour, strategy, goals and objectives: they are all important. Affecting change on just some of them is more likely to 'warp' an organisation than bring about sustainable change to the whole interconnected organism, be that a company, family or any other group of 'organised' people.

In Chapter 9 and beyond, the five golden rules were explored in some detail. Firstly, there is no point in changing anything for change's sake, unless you are following the old adage of 'a change is as good as a rest'.

Change for a reason is kind of obvious and yet that reason has to be 'seen' and be 'see-able'. Therefore, the importance of a **'change vision'** is the first golden rule but, critically, it goes hand in hand with the **power** to follow it through; one without the other is not very useful.

Next we have engagement. This is where mindful self-awareness gets turned into a 'collective sea of engaged minds'. We explored the process that we have carried out in many organisations, of interviews condensed into themes, then bound into a snapshot report, then read out loud to the whole organisation. This challenging and, at times, uncomfortable process has the powerful effect of creating an irrefutable mandate: a 'change manifesto' by the people that in nearly every case will also dovetail with the sponsor's vision.

The next golden rule, involvement: how to galvanise the level of engagement acquired into action. This was explored, initially, through **leadership decisions**, showing staff that leaders have the ability to lead where needed.

However it's the range of actions mulled over by **working groups** during many months, and the recommendations they come up with that gives the sense of **involvement** required to ultimately get change delivered.

Lastly, the golden rule of measurement, both subjectively and objectively, was explored within the context of accountability. This should only be sought as acknowledgement or reward in the minds of those who have mindfully 'chosen' to be involved. 'Reward' for a job well done and a set of goals achieved, rather than measurement as a stick to be beaten with.

About the author

Born in Birmingham, into a Methodist household, Philip led a diverse life, from joining the Moonies at 16, to working in retail for two years, to training and consequently working as a professional actor for 10 years. He then switched from acting to facilitating and went on to spend five years leading large scale personal development seminars for the public, before being invited to take his brand of development into the business arena in 1989.

Since then, Philip has strived to understand, through the many corporate change programmes he has designed and delivered, what makes change stick. This striving has been greatly illuminated by his practice of Vipassana meditation, the Buddhist mind discipline that gave rise to Mindfulness, which Philip teaches as a key part of his work.

A fundamental belief from boyhood has run through all of Philip's endeavours: that there is good in all human beings and that, on some level, people want to make a positive difference to their lives and to the lives of those around them.

26892395R00142

Printed in Great Britain
by Amazon